The Real
American Cowboy

☆ JACK WESTON ☆

The Real
American Cowboy

NEW AMSTERDAM
New York

First paperback edition published 1988 by
NEW AMSTERDAM BOOKS
171 Madison Avenue
New York, N.Y. 10016

Library of Congress Cataloging-in-Publication Data

Weston, Jack, 1924-
    The real American cowboy.

    Bibliography: p. 253
    1. Cowboys—West (U.S.)—History.   2. West (U.S.)—
Social life and customs.   I. Title.
F596.W52   1988   305.9636'0978   87-35005
ISBN 0-941533-27-1 (pbk.)

Designed by Lynn Braswell

Manufactured in the United States of America

Grateful acknowledgment is made to the following for supplying illustrations from its collection:

Academy of Motion Picture Arts and Sciences (pp. 67, 136, 169, 198, 201, 203, 213, 216, 222, 226, 235, 236, 238).

Grateful acknowledgment is made to the following for permission to use illustrations from their collections:

Adams Memorial Hall Museum, Deadwood, South Dakota (p. 183)
Amon Carter Museum, Fort Worth, Texas (p. 30)
Denver Public Library, Western History Department (pp. 5, 8, 21, 36, 87, 170, 178, 180, 192, 197)
Houghton Library, Harvard University (pp. 23, 198)
The Huntington Library, San Marino, California (p. 230)
Library of Congress, Erwin E. Smith Collection of Range Life Photographs (p. 156)
Montana Historical Society, Helena, Montana (p. 12)
San Antonio Museum Association, San Antonio, Texas (p. 85)
Dr. M. W. Sharp (Castroville, Texas); copy from University of Texas, Institute of Texan Cultures at San Antonio (p. 40)
University of Oklahoma Library, Western History Collections (pp. 36, 166–67)
University of Texas (Austin), Barker Texas History Center (p. 39)
University of Wyoming, American Heritage Center, Laramie (pp. 118, 120, 122)
Watriss/Baldwin, Woodfine Camp Assocs. (p. 157)

Grateful acknowledgment is made to the following for permission to use previously published textual matter:

Excerpt from Américo Paredes, *With His Pistol in His Hand*, copyright © 1958 by University of Texas Press
Excerpt from Eugene Manlove Rhodes, "The Cowboy: His Cause and Cure," by W. H. Hutchinson, Executor

This book is dedicated to Nathan D. Champion (1857–1892), nester ranchman and hero of the Johnson County War; to Thomas B. Harris (dates unknown), LS wagon boss and ranchman, leader of the Texas Panhandle cowboy strike of March 1883; and to John H. Sullivan (dates unknown), "a cowboy since he was twelve years old," and in 1886 a Knights of Labor organizer on the Great Plains.

Contents

Illustrations

Preface

When I was about twelve years old I used to lasso chickens in the pen behind our garage. It was difficult even when I looped one, because the flighty creatures didn't offer enough resistance to slip the noose tight. I learned to throw a knife as well as a Mexican outlaw by hitting a mark on the garage door. I loved the plunk of the point and the quiver of the handle when the knife hit hard and just right. For years I used to wear a throwing knife in a sheath strapped on my back, handy between and above my shoulder blades. I went regularly with two or three buddies to watch Westerns at a movie house called the Hitching Post, just east of Vine on Hollywood Boulevard. Only Westerns screened there—indeed, *all* Westerns premiered there. And in those days, the double features generally changed three times a week. We'd take the La Brea bus and walk a long way east on Sunset. We would pass "Gower Gulch," where the cowboys used to hang out in front of the Columbia Drug Store, waiting for calls from Central Casting to the phone booth inside. I later learned that Nathaniel West's sinister cowboy Earle Shoop in *The Day of the Locust* was modeled on one of them. I also learned later that we used to pass the Water Hole on Cahuenga Boulevard, the saloon where all the cowboys coming to Hollywood from the early twenties on would meet. But we were then just interested in the fantasy on the silver screen. At the movie, we'd smuggle in our cap-shooting six-guns, wait in the darkness for a quiet and expectant moment, fire them off in unison as we let out rebel yells, and then scatter to separate corners as the ushers ran down the aisles to capture us. The tense moment might have been when a Mexican bandit (Charles Whitaker) was sneaking up on Hopalong Cassidy (William Boyd). A dozen times a year we'd rent horses from a stable just east of Griffith Park in the partly wooded plain between the Los Angeles River bed and San Fernando Road. There we'd divide into posses and chase each other and shoot our six-guns until our horses were lathered and excited. Then cold reality would set in: knowing the stable would bar us in the future if we returned our animals in such a condition, we'd walk and gentle and towel them down with their saddle blankets until they looked less wild-eyed and wet. We didn't know then that close by were the stock contractors' barns, like Fat Jones's, where studios could rent horses and wagons for making Westerns, nor that if we followed the road nearby beyond San Fernando a few miles we'd come to Newhall, where William S. Hart had retired on his Horseshoe Ranch. But, for that matter, none of us knew about Hart, although our parents doubtless did.

One summer I was sent to live with my grandmother in Blackfoot, Idaho. She rented a horse for my exclusive use. I kept it in a small pasture behind her house. I remember the saddle she borrowed for me, a California-style one with a single center-fire latigo rig. All alone I rode those grassy hills and roped chickens and fence posts and pursued phantom rustlers down dusty roads and under cottonwoods along streams in a summer world more than half transformed by images from the Hitching Post. And by that time I had plenty more images from pulp Westerns in my head too. I read them avidly, although I couldn't afford to buy them from newsstands but got them from secondhand stores for a nickel each and then traded them with my friends. Before I was thirteen I began reading Zane Grey, Luke Short, and Max Brand from the branch library. And I listened to the Lone Ranger on the radio and never missed Fred Harman's great strip *Red Ryder*. After the war, I contributed to the revival of feature Western movies by seeing *Shane* and *High Noon* and *The Gunfighter* and all the rest several times each. And it is no accident that of all country-western music I came to like best the Texas redneck variety of Willie Nelson, Waylon Jennings, and Tompall Glaser, probably because they sing about cowboys, and when they don't, their songs are full of the spirit of cowboys. I married a Chicago woman who was if anything even more of a popular Western fan than I was—although she was not much inclined to have throwdowns on deserted streets with capguns, she had done lots of Western riding and had read Western stories in *Colliers* and the *Saturday Evening Post*, while

I was reading the pulp *Western Story*. And we'd read, one after each other, all the paperback Max Brands, Van Tilberg Clarks, Ernest Haycoxes, Luke Shorts, Clay Fishers (or Will Henrys), Alan LeMays, Jack Schaefers, Elmer Keltons (to mention just a few) that came our way. We didn't live in a TV area during the height of the television Western series, but by the late sixties we caught up with our kids, who knew every one.

This account may create the false impression that cowboys have dominated my life and determined my tastes and values. I didn't marry my wife *because* she liked Westerns, but I'm sure that interest contributed to her attractiveness. I'm not trying to establish my credentials as a Western buff and cowboy lover but as being fairly normal in this regard. Although the cowboy of popular culture is my oldest and most abiding love, it has not been a consuming or even the most important one except for brief periods during my boyhood and early teens. But I'm sure that the cowboy as I received and partially created him from our culture has contributed to my way of looking at things. "My heroes have always been cowboys," Waylon Jennings sings. Waylon and I are not the only ones, although the media, the messages, and the images change somewhat with the generations and to a lesser extent with the geography. A San Antonian's image of cowboys is different from a New Yorker's, just as a person from Casper, Wyoming, will perceive cowboys differently than a person from San Francisco. My grandparents saw cowboys perform in Wild West shows and read stories about Buck Taylor in dime novels (except for my father's mother, who hated cowboys), my parents read Wister and B. M. Bower, went to rodeos and to Bronco Billy, William S. Hart, and Tom Mix silents. The number of media through which cowboys entered the consciousness of my own generation increased remarkably (comic books, sound movies, radio drama, pop music on cheap records), but the cowboy culture was about the same, if somewhat more intense and ubiquitous. Our children were in thrall to television Westerns, and our daughter, now a young woman, wears modish jeans and boots and occasionally a cowboy hat.

My point is that the popular cowboy hero has lasted a long time and has pervaded every corner of our culture. I can't think of a rival for the cowboy as the most important of our popular heroes, if by that we mean the generic national types, composed of hundreds of individuals in the media. The cowboy is the most durable, the most influential, and the most varied to accommodate our differences and contradictions. Here is a random list of national heroes during the present century: the frontier explorer or mountain man, the pioneer settler, the rags-to-riches business genius, the tough private eye, the GI, the gangster, the fearless newspaper editor, the movie star or entertainer, the on-the-road poet-philosopher, the world-weary expatriate of the Lost Generation, the misunderstood and brooding teenager, the populist politician or organizer, the major league baseball player, the prizefighter, the selfless nurse. (I can't help remarking in passing that this almost all-male list shows how sexist our culture is.) One might question one or another of the types, but no one would deny that the cowboy, in his changing forms, has entered more deeply into the consciousness of more Americans of different generations and backgrounds than any of the popular types I've listed or any I've forgotten.

I first began to pose questions to myself about my old unconscious hero, whom I later recognized as our Great American Hero, the Cowboy, when seven years ago I began teaching a college film course on the Western. In this book I have set down some answers to the questions I've been pondering and investigating. Who was the historical cowboy when his image was forming in the public mind? What was the industry that paid him for his work? What conduct did the industry try to impose on him? In comparison to other workers on the frontier, what was the nature of his work and his relation to it and to his bosses? How did those relations affect his consciousness and behavior? What were the images of him that the popular media presented and that he responded to? What other work did he turn to when his original work terminated, that is, when the ranges closed and the organization of the cattle industry became more specialized? What was the history of black cowboys, women cowhands, and Mexicano vaqueros in the trail and range industry, and what can we learn about ourselves as a nation from the way the popular media presented them? What can we learn about American popular values by studying the interaction between the various faces of the mythical cowboy of the mass media and the historical cowboy as he existed? Finally, I posed a series of questions to myself about the cowboy as the hero of the popular Western: What are the social meanings of the myth offered in Westerns? Why is the form so popular with the people? Did it undergo any basic changes, and if so, why?

Like most of us, I had learned about frontier history from Westerns. What I learned by reading oral histories, memoirs, and monographs contradicted this popular history of Westerns point by point in ways that only later could I make sense of. Although Westerns people the West with pioneer cattle barons, I found that almost all cattle were owned by Eastern and foreign corporations. Although Westerns show cowboys as loyally sharing their paternalistic bosses' interests, I found that cowboys hated their bosses and fought for good wages and working conditions just like most other workers in industrializing America. Although Westerns are silent about or trivialize blacks, Mexicanos, and women as workers in the open-range cattle industry, I found they contributed a great deal. Although Westerns show that cowboys realized their dream of someday having a little spread of their own, I found that most ex-cowboy nesters, after competing with their old corporate bosses for a few years, lost their homestead ranches when the ranges closed and never became rich enough to become independent producers in the modern specialized cattle industry but had to return to wage labor. I account for the popularity of all these lies in our most important myth by the theory that workers in industrializing America needed a fantasy of a preindustrial, rural society to compensate them for the loss of community and nature in their real lives. So they made heroes of strong cowboys who in stories and plays and movies and comic strips saved threatened communities on the edge of the wilderness. Finally, I discovered that this Western myth flourished until Hollywood and the television networks became strong enough, in the fifties, to change it to celebrate aggressive individualism. These are the main ideas I used to shape my material, here just baldly stated without the amplification, qualification, and illustration they have in the chapters that follow.

Although the image of the historical cowboy offered here differs strikingly from the popular image, my intent is not to debunk a national hero. My intent is to understand our society and history by examining the cowboy and what we all, including cowboys, have made of him. After all, we respond to cowboys and want to be them because they are appealing to us. Otherwise, they would not be heroes—perhaps the most important generic historical-mythical hero we have. We have helped to make them and have, in different degrees, become them.

I am proud of my contributions to Afro-American and Chicano history in this book, but I feel my neglect of two other aspects of the history of the dispossessed. By the time I discovered that there were lots of Native American cowboys, particularly in the Indian Territory (Oklahoma) and on the northern Great Plains, I had neither energy nor time to find material for a section on them. A study of American Indian cowboys north of Mexico is still to be written. The other neglect is more complicated. By treating women cowpunchers, I wanted to contribute to the revision of American history begun by the women's movement; but by tucking women away in a separate chapter, I may not have integrated them fully into the general account. I hope this will not be seen as tokenism. I had trouble with masculine pronouns referring to groups that I knew included women. I struggled over words like "ranchmen" when I knew that some ranch owners were unmarried women or widows and that some ranchmen were married and had wives and daughters who roped steers. My subject is parochially masculine—unmarried male workers living together, and a

sexist popular myth of strong male heroes and simpy heroines—and resisted my often contortionate and finally inadequate attempts to achieve
accuracy of gender.

I wish to thank Byron Price, Director of the Panhandle-Plains Museum
in Canyon, Texas, who read the first four chapters in an early form and,
although he disagreed with my way of writing history, corrected many
errors of omission or commission; Harry Chrisman of Denver, ex-cowboy
historian of the West, who read my manuscript and encouraged me early
on by liking it and offering criticism; my colleague Sidney Kaplan, who
showed me how to understand black riders; my friend Barry Phillips, who
read most of the manuscript carefully, with a sharp eye for fuzzy meanings
and stylistic infelicities; my splendid wife, Joan Sammel, who with her keen
intelligence and unique insight spotted most of my pretentious postures
and lazy constructions as she edited and improved all my chapters; and
my friend Richard Ohmann, who read the entire manuscript and offered
many criticisms, particularly in the last chapter, where I am indebted to
him for several important ideas. Although the late Kenneth Wiggins Porter
cannot now be aware of a public expression of gratitude, I want to testify
to his generously sharing several pages of unpublished work, thoughtfully
annotated for me, on pre–Civil War black riders.

The Real
American Cowboy

☆ 1 ☆

Cowboys and Cowmen

The cow-boys ("cow-punchers") to me a strangely interesting class, bright-eyed as hawks, with their swarthy complexions, and their broad-brimmed hats—apparently always on horseback, with loose arms slightly raised and swinging as they ride.

—Walt Whitman,
from his notebook, Kansas, 1879[1]

The West was rapidly being settled before the Civil War, but the frontier was in California, Nevada, and the Northwest, accessible mainly by sea. The attraction was gold and silver, hides and tallow, fur and lumber and Far Eastern commerce. East of the ridge of the Rockies and west of the Missouri River was the unwanted—because unknown—Great Plains, as it came to be known. If you could get past its Indians and heat and cold and drought, and then past the Rockies, you would get to California. People saw no comfort and livelihood and investors no money in the alien, untimbered land of what was then thought of as the Great Desert. The railroad entrepreneurs had started their tracks to California to bridge this barrier, but before the war they only went as far as the Mississippi River at Rock Island, Illinois, in the north and the Missouri River at St. Joseph, Missouri. And then all of a sudden, in two decades after the war, they repeatedly spanned the continent, first by the meeting of the Union Pacific and the Central Pacific railroads only four years after the war, and then four more times with the Northern Pacific, Southern Pacific, Santa Fe, and Great Northern. Events moved fast. After the war laissez-faire capitalism was the uncontested law of the land, Congress was eager to encourage it, native and European financiers were enthusiastic about the possibilities offered by the new frontier for accumulating capital, and the industrial revolution and immigration were providing cheap day labor to create this wealth. The sudden rush to make money and the jobs and land this investment provided caused the Great Plains to be settled in only a quarter of a century. The railroad companies and the land companies that grew up around them realized the untold possibilities of wealth they were being given by their paid congressmen (or legislators, in Texas, where public land was owned by the state)—eventually about one-tenth of the land surface of the Great Plains and the monopoly of transportation over most of the rest besides. And, behold, the land was not desert, but the richest and most extensive grazing area the world had ever known, covered with buffalo grass at times knee high, to say nothing of the future mineral and farming possibilities. All the railroads needed to attract capital was vigorous public relations about free grass for cattle. Railroad promotions lured native and immigrant workers and settlers west with prospects of cheap home- steads or town lots and jobs. The U.S. Cavalry would protect them (except for Texas, where the cattleman's frontier preceded settlement by ten years or so). Thus were born the cattle industry and the cowboys who worked it for a brief two or three decades until the ranges were fenced and the drives ended. There were cowboys afterward to feed and work cattle on smaller fenced ranges growing hay, more specialized ranches, and feeding pens, but these cowboys led different, more routine lives. The cowboy era plays itself out on the open ranges of the Great Plains and coincides with the Gilded Age, the age of the robber barons, the intense labor struggles of the industrial revolution, the rapid settling of the West, and the first stage of the cattle industry.

The cowboy, who worked the cows, and the cowman, who owned and sometimes managed them, created the cattle industry in south and south- west Texas after the Civil War. The raising and marketing of cattle existed before that, of course, in North America, but never was it an industry in which fortunes were made and lost by individuals, by partners, and a little later by stockholders in cattle corporations. Industry, as distinct from busi- ness or trade, signifies a specialized production process for accumulating capital, each part of which is financed by separate entrepreneurs. If the entrepreneurs did own ranches, they did not work them personally, and each dealt with one phase of a regular specialized procedure—raising, collecting, trailing, feeding, transporting, slaughtering, and marketing— many of them on a commission basis. This specialized, entrepreneurial economic activity, the cattle industry, first arose as part of the acceleration of the industrial-agricultural revolution, which took off after the war because of the availability of protected and encouraged capital and a new frontier to invest it in. There were other contributing conditions, of course, like a supply of cattle, skilled cowboy labor, and established procedures of trade; but capital and free ranges accessible by railroad were the new ingredients that determined the rise of the industry.

In California the cattle business never had a big enough market to take off into an industry. The markets for the few attempts at driving cattle to the Pacific Northwest proved insufficient to compensate for the hazards of the trail. And the considerable commerce in hides, tallow, and horns from California ports and the local demand for beef created by the Gold Rush had reached their peak and were on the decline when the cattle industry arose in Texas. Thousands of cattle were driven from ranches in Los Angeles County to San Francisco Bay between 1849 and about 1875, but the traffic was insular, ruined the southern ranges, and nothing came of it. Illinois bought lots of Texas cattle after 1854, and during the war it produced more cattle in the Union than anywhere else, but eventually its prairies proved to make better feeding farms than grazing ranches for breeding. New Spain and Mexico, of course, introduced cattle and a way of handling it onto the North American continent, particularly the southern end of the Great Plains on both sides of the Rio Grande to the east and between the Sierra Madre ranges to the south. But the Spanish feudal relation of *hacendados* (cattlemen) and *vaqueros* (cowboys), which continued after independence, existed more for social control in the interest of the pampered luxury and proud life-style of the *patrón* class than for accumulating capital by finding and exploiting markets. (Later, in Texas, King colonialized this feudal relation and used it for capital accumulation on his ranch run by Anglo Texan managers and wagon bosses and worked by vaqueros conditioned for more than a century into subservience and acceptance of extreme exploitation.) Mexico was at too early a stage of capitalism in the late sixties to develop a cattle industry. And because the Mexicans collected cattle by trapping them in pens around a few watering places or in the brush by tying them to stalking oxen, and because they drove no herds regularly to distant markets, they did not provide all the range and trail methods and skills that Texans later were required to invent to meet new circumstances.

Most Anglo cattle raising and marketing north of the Rio Grande before the Civil War was on the pine barren belt of the southeast coast, beginning in colonial South Carolina. From Carolina, cattle raising moved first south to north Florida, where it was influenced by Spanish-American ranching; then along the Gulf Coast prairies to Mississippi and Louisiana, where there were some French herding outposts; and thence into east Texas and Stephen Austin's colony there. Some of these Anglo cattle raisers spread into glades and prairie barrens in Tennessee and Kentucky and the Midwest, and the more southern of these sent immigrants into the northeast Texas prairies in the early nineteenth century. This Anglo-American cattle business differed strikingly from what later developed on the Great Plains, although in its first stages it also was on open ranges and used brands and mounted herdsmen: herds were mixed with hogs and were wintered on lower slopes, cattle were controlled with dogs, bullwhips, and salt; and in the South perhaps half the herdsmen were slaves, many using ancient African herding practices. But by the time the Anglo cattle business had reached southeast Texas, it had learned roping from the Mexicans and no longer controlled cattle with dogs or salt.[2] The herds of these Anglo settlers along the southeast coastal prairies began to mix with the Mexican herds when in the fifties settlers began to move west of the Guadalupe River into the southern coastal prairies. This meeting of Anglo and Mexican cattle, Anglo cowmen and Mexican rancheros and hacendados, Anglo and Afro cowboys and vaqueros created the conditions for the later rise of the American cattle industry and the distinctive work of the Great Plains cowboy.

In the plains west of a timberline stretching north and southeast from San Antonio, the Texas cattle business began with Spanish longhorns in the eighteenth century, in small herds near a few missions and presidios but mainly running wild because of fierce and successful Comanche and Apache raids on all Spanish attempts at conquest. During the next century, attempts by the growing number of Anglo settlers to catch and sell or otherwise market wild cattle and to move their own herds westward were also hampered in the less settled regions by Comanche raids and after the Texas Revolution by the resistance of Tejanos to appropriation of their land and cattle. But besides the market in hides, tallow, and salted meat, and even live cattle shipped from Gulf ports, there were an increasing number of small herds (by later standards) trailed north and northeast to Midwestern markets after the late forties and from even earlier times east to Louisiana and then along the coast or by riverboat on the Red River and the Mississippi to New Orleans. In the early 1850s, Texas capitalists risked all to make fortunes with a few dangerous and epic trail drives to California for a temporary market of gold seekers. After Texas was annexed

A DROVE OF TEXAS CATTLE, 1867

*A woodcut from a drawing made in southwestern Louisiana, said to be the first representation of a cattle drive in an American magazine (*Harper's Weekly, *October 19, 1867).* (COURTESY OF THE DENVER PUBLIC LIBRARY, WESTERN HISTORY DEPARTMENT.)

in 1845 and most of the herds and lands of the Mexican ranchers between the Nueces River and the Rio Grande were expropriated, the cattle business flourished, until by the beginning of the war there were more cattle in Texas than any state in the Union.

Thus by 1860 and the beginning of the Civil War, Texas had all the elements except ready markets for the later cattle industry. It had lots of cattle. It had Afro and Anglo cowboys and vaqueros with Texanized and greatly augmented Mexican skills in hunting, raising, taming, and training horses, and in using them to hunt and capture open-range cattle and to mark, castrate, and otherwise tame them and separate them into private herds to drive them on wild trails to market. Texas also had the century-old Anglo-Afro methods of stock raising on open ranges and the conventions and procedures, supported by the county governments, of security, ownership, and transfer and exchange necessary for a complicated business. The war interrupted this developing business by cutting off trail drives (Union troops soon controlled the Mississippi so beeves could not be trailed to Rebel forces) and by taking younger men away from range work; but, partially balancing the losses of the terrible drought of 1863–64, the war also provided several years of virtually untapped increase of cattle. After its conclusion an economic-political environment developed of abundant capital for gigantic markets on the Plains frontier and for dependable rail freighting to huge and growing markets in the Midwest and the East. New markets created by Yankee and European money invested in the Great Plains catalyzed these elements of the cattle business formed by almost half a century of Anglo Texas practice built on centuries of Spanish and Mexican experience with horses and longhorns on untimbered, unfenced ranges. And the original worker in this industry was the Texas cowboy, who emerged from the "Cradle of Cowboys," the grazing lands of Texas below San Antonio. Across the Rio Grande onto this undulating, almost tropical plain of thorny mottes and grass came the Mexican longhorns and ponies and some important range practices. From the east, out of the woods along the Colorado River, came the Anglo and Afro cowboys with ways of handling cattle developed in the savannahs and pine barrens of the southern coasts. From this blend there emerged a distinctive Texas craft of cowboying which soon spread to all the cattle ranges on the Plains.

Here is a patriotic defense of the originality of Texas methods of handling cattle told by an Arizona cowboy who spent twenty or thirty years in Sonora, Mexico. With all its partiality, it is convincing and tells a lot about how Texas cowboys learned the skills of their work.

> There are some very good Mexican cowboys, but they are all some that learned from the Americans. Take the crude *hombres* that came out of Old Mexico with a *zarape* wrapped around them—they could not keep up with the chuck-wagon for a week. Then they began to get on to our ways and a lot of them made good hands, but they dam sure had to learn it from us, as they did not have wild cattle to handle in their country. They would have a number of ranches and one old Don would own them all and have peons milking the cows and keeping them gentle. There was seldom a wild one and if there was one they would run it down and butcher it.
>
> Now our cowboys had to be bred and raised with wild cattle and when the cattle business came into Texas and Colorado and the cows got into the brush or out on the plains with the buffaloes, then it was that the real cowboy work commenced. Men had to learn the dispositions and other characteristics of the cow, and the wilder she got the more they had to ride and rope. The real cowboy was first made in the New Country. The way of rounding up big countries, and roping calves and branding cattle out in the open, was done there.

There were no corrals and the Indians were so bad that people just got their cattle branded up and left them to increase until next branding time. When I came into the picture it was a little late, but the American ways of handling cattle had been learned, and the Mexicans had to learn from the Gringo how to work cattle. The Mexicans have always built traps to catch any cattle that got a little wild. Mexican branding was always done in a corral, both in Chihuahua and Sonora.

The round-up system is all American. Branding up calves out of a round-up is Texan. And until today a Mexican cannot drive a big herd of cattle—say fifteen hundred and up. They do not know how to string out a herd. I worked with them all my life and never saw one, old or young, that could handle big bunches. American saddles and outfits are superior in every way, just as our ways of handling horses and cattle are superior.[3]

Charles Siringo, a tough, expert cowboy who emerged from this Texas cradle and who wrote the original firsthand, book-length account of cowboy life, said there were three stages of cowboys: (1) the "trail cowboys," mostly Texans, but many from other Southern states; (2) the cowboys of the new cattle ranges on the northern Plains, mostly Yankees, who were taught by Texas trail cowboys who stayed north; and (3) the cowboys of the Wild West shows and the movies.[4] There are many overlaps in this division, and it doesn't account for the significant influence on some parts of the northern Plains of California vaquero culture by way of the Pacific Northwest; but what is apparent is that the Texas origin influenced the life and work and consciousness of most subsequent cowboys and the national myth they provided the materials for. In one important way, cowboys were united by their Texas origin: they were unique among frontier workers in being almost completely native-born (Anglo, black, and Mexicano), compared to the other industries in the West—the railroads (Italian, Irish, Mexican, Chinese), mines (Irish, Polish, Bohemian, Swedish, Mexican, Chinese), and timber (Irish, Polish, Swedish). One of the reasons the cowboy became a national hero is that he and usually his parents were born on this continent north of the Rio Grande. Indeed, even strong racists could make heroes of cowboys, like Owen Wister and his friend Frederic Remington and their admirer Theodore Roosevelt, all of whom believed in the superiority and manifest destiny of what they called the "Saxon race." Of course, they had to close their eyes to African- and Mexican-American cowboys—not an uncommon accomplishment—but what remained were gratifyingly blue-eyed, light-haired, and light-complexioned

FRONTISPIECE IN SIRINGO'S *A TEXAS COW BOY* (1886)

J. Frank Dobie called Charles Siringo, "the first authentic cowboy to publish an autobiography." The caption of this colored lithograph is "Representation of Life in a Cow Camp." (COURTESY OF THE DENVER PUBLIC LIBRARY, WESTERN HISTORY DEPARTMENT.)

native Anglos who spoke English without a foreign accent. Our national hero had to be acceptable to racists and xenophobes, always a majority among us, by coming from native, Anglo stock.

What was the trail and range cowboy like? (We'll put aside for now the separate questions of what black cowboys and vaqueros were like.) We can make general statements about him because he self-consciously identified with all other cowboys and thought of himself as a member of a class or social unit. News about individual cowboys would spread from Montana, said Teddy Blue, "clear down to Texas." "The reps [of smaller ranches] would ride around to the roundups and carry [the news] along, and in the winter time the grub line riders would carry it."[5] Those who have read Charlie Siringo's books on cowboy life and the two volumes of 1920s reminiscences by hundreds of old trail drivers will know with what minute attention friends and comrades were noted and remembered and gossiped about in this kind of trade fraternity, which was informal but very real nevertheless. "Sullivan was an old cowboy," said an unfriendly boss helping a detective catch a suspected rustler, "and he was in that charmed circle of freemasonry which is part of the calling. It is an unwritten law

among the punchers never to give away a pal."[6] Old cowboys could see
more unity than there probably was through a nostalgic haze of forty years,
but on the other hand a perspective of years could give them some clarity.
Teddy Blue reasonably generalized in the 1930s about his comrades of
the eighties: they were "medium-sized men, as a heavy man was hard on
horses, quick and wiry, and as a rule good-natured; in fact it didn't pay
to be anything else. . . . wild and brave . . . two things the old time cow-
puncher was afraid of, a decent woman and being set afoot."[7] Or Siringo's
striking declaration: "Cowboys took great pride in small feet" (he is ex-
plaining how during a two-week wet spell he left number five boots constantly on his size-six feet).[8]

But contemporaries also thought of themselves as a social unit without
the oversimplifying vision of hindsight. The songs sung around chuck
wagons or to herds at night repeatedly assert or imply the fraternity of
occupation. A cowboy wanders into town and, finding it is Sunday and
thinking of his boyhood, enters a church, where the congregation thinks
he is disreputable because he wears leggings. But he, like the parson in
the pulpit, is dressed in the "trappings of his trade." Cowboys are forced
together and separated from society by being stereotyped:

> Though the congregation doubtless thought
> That cowboys as a race
> Were a kind of moral outlaw
> With no good claim to grace.
>
> Is it very strange that cowboys are
> A rough and reckless crew
> When their garb forbids their doing right
> As Christian people do?[9]

Even after death, cowboys will all be together:

> They say there will be a great round-up
> And cowboys, like dogies, will stand,
> To be marked by the Riders of Judgment
> Who are posted and know every brand.[10]

The only common distinction is the elitist one between Texas cowboys
and all the rest, or, what comes to the same thing, old-timers and tenderfeet.
"The Texas Cowboy" sings:

> But the Bad Lands of Montana
> Are the worst I ever seen,
> The cowboys are all tenderfeet
> And the dogies are too lean.[11]

There was considerable variation in ways of working cattle and horses and in equipment and style between ranges—for instance, the Texas double-cinched saddle in contrast to the center-fired California saddle; tying the reata fast to the horn after throwing it, as opposed to the Mexican method of making a nonbinding snub or "dolly welter"; the contempt of Texas Panhandle cowboys for the "taps" (*tapaderas*, pointed stirrup coverings) of the cowboys of the brush country along the Nueces. But in spite of such differences, they thought of themselves as a proud fraternity.

They were a unit because of their self-respect and pride in their craft. They were, they thought, better than other workers, let alone all the flotsam of drifters on the frontier, a true worker elite, not based on income but on character, style, way of life. Teddy Blue said that "while cowpunchers were common men without education, they set themselves away above people who chances are were no more common or uneducated than themselves." In Miles City in the eighties there was a park, he says, where people without four bits for a hotel could sleep out, although "not cowpunchers, but buffalo hunters and bullwhackers and that class of people. . . . A cowpuncher would never hang around town after he ran out of money" but would go back to the ranch or the trail camp. Cowboys were "a totally different class from the other fellows on the frontier. We was the salt of the earth, anyway in our estimation, and we had the pride that went with it."[12] Cowboys started fights in trail towns to show they were better than anybody else, as happened when Siringo's "cowboy chum" in 1877 in Dodge City started a saloon brawl "to show the long-hated buffalo hunters that they were not in the cowboys class."[13] Even the very late cowboys-turned-riders in Hollywood Westerns, according to a daughter of one of them, scorned "streetwalkers," that is, unmounted extras on Western sets, and "never lost sense of their own dignity that made them as proud to be called picture cowboys as they once had been called top hands."[14]

They wore their pride in their craft in their clothes and the way they handled themselves. When Siringo lost his Mexican red silk sash, which he couldn't replace as far north as Caldwell, Kansas, he had to wear suspenders to keep his pants up for the first time in his life, which "almost broke my heart."[15] Teddy Blue sums up the colorful style and its changes: "The drovers of the seventies were a wild and reckless bunch . . . mostly Southerners," each of whom wore a "wide brimmed beaver hat, black or brown with a low crown, fancy shirts, high heeled boots, and sometimes a vest." His shirts and saddles were often homemade, and he wore an Army coat with a cape, instead of the later slicker and blanket, and bullhide chaps or "leggins." In the eighties changes were introduced: "high-crowned white Stetson hat, fancy shirts with pockets, and striped or checkered

California pants made in Oregon City. . . . In winter we had nice cloth overcoats with beaver collars and cuffs. The old twelve-inch barrel Colt pistol was cut down to a six- and seven-and-a-half inch barrel, with black rubber, ivory, or pearl handle. The old big roweled spurs with bells give place to hand-forged silver inlaid spurs with droop shanks and small rowels, and with that you had the cowpuncher of the eighties when he was in his glory." Of course, not everybody thought such clothes and gear were classy—the costume and manner were garish and swaggering, even noisy; and precisely because it meant "cowboy" in the eyes of farmers to the east it was disreputable. When Blue first returned from a trail drive to his farm home, he bought in preparation for the visit "a white Stetson, new pants, good shirt and fancy boots. They had colored tops, red and blue, with a half-moon and star on them. Lord I was proud of those clothes. . . . the kind of clothes top hands wore." On seeing him, his sister said, "Take your pants out of your boots and put your coat on. You look like an outlaw."[16]

The cowboys' style was partly a deliberate imitation of how the public saw them; as we shall see, by the early seventies cowboys developed a bad image from newspaper accounts of them, and cowboys would defiantly and defensively justify that image by exaggeration, live up to the reputation, even go beyond what the public expected. They would take advantage of their wild public image to scare hell out of people. They would stage mock holdups and shootouts timed to shock passengers on a train stopped in the station and travelers gaping out coach windows. They would devise events involving stereotype lawless cowboy behavior to encourage rich Eastern or English dudes to shorten their visits to ranches they or their fathers owned shares in. They very early exaggerated their tough-man image by costume and poses in commercial photographer studios in trail and range towns, often with props on hand at the studio: Colts, Winchesters, and Bowie knives, always prominently displayed; cartridge belts, chaps with fringe or rows of silver conches, fancy shirts and bandanas, saddles slung over papier-mâché rocks, rawhide reatas and quirts held menacingly as if they were weapons. Along with other frontier types who were not cowboys, they would look particularly tough, occasionally with a cigarette or cigar slanting down from the corner of their mouths. This kind of exaggerated personal style, reinforcing and responding to a public image of a wild class of society, bordered on parody, often encouraged by photographers and most readily complied with by the cowboys. When the traveling photographers would ask them to pose for a picture (they would have to hold still for several seconds), they would often pretend to drink whiskey from a bottle or freeze a wave of a bottle to exaggerate their

SOME XIT COWBOYS

In the photographic studio of Wiley Bros. these cowboys typically pose to look tough, displaying their boots, spurs, guns, holsters, and cigars. (COURTESY OF THE MONTANA HISTORICAL SOCIETY.)

POSING AS COWBOYS

These men in L. A. Huffman's studio in 1889 could be either the real thing or dressed up in clothes and props provided by the photographer. (COURTESY OF THE MONTANA HISTORICAL SOCIETY.)

reputation of being he-man hard drinkers. An early mass media market grew up for cheap prints of these photographs, and as we shall see, commercial photographers sold postcards, scrapbook pictures, and stereoscope cards in series to satisfy the public's strong interest in the West. This happened long before photographic reproduction in half-tone and photogravure in the nineties and in movies during the next decade. The popularity of these commercial photos of Western drama in the eighties and nineties shows the growing mass market that both caused and supported movie Westerns only a little later.

The culture of real cowboys was more like that of current stereotypes of Appalachian farmers than like the colorful frontier image the public made for them and that they partly grew into. We think of cowboys as unique products of the rocks and plains, Mexicanized to a degree, with big hats and guitars, tough and silent. But the Texas cowboy came from Southern farms in timbered valleys—at least their parents did—and this traditional farm culture clung for a while. For example, accounts of camp activities on the trail seem to us now more suited to farmers than cowboys. They would have wrestling contests while they waited for supper. They would listen to the music of fiddle, mouth organ, or banjo (seldom guitar, which was Mexican), music played by one of their number or the cook. The tunes would be things like "Billy in the Low Ground," "Dinah Had a Wooden Leg," "The Devil's Dream," "Sally Gooden," "Arkansas Traveler," and "Give the Fiddler a Dram." They would take the endgate off the chuck wagon, lay it on the ground, and one cowboy would noisily dance a jig on it with his high-heeled boots while the rest would clap in time.[17] Doesn't sound much like cowboys.

That these Southern-bred Anglo cowboys—that is, two-thirds of all early cowboys—were terrible racists ought not to surprise us much. Most Anglos were racists in the 1870s, so it is a matter of degree and comparison. Cowboys were no better than they should have been, perhaps a little worse. Since in the beginning they came from the farms and plantations of Austin's colony along the Colorado River, we wouldn't expect them to be otherwise. Intensely patriotic to Texas and the Confederacy, they reacted to the Confederate defeat and Reconstruction the way most other Anglo Texans did. Their bosses, pursuing their own profit by using the best workers available at the lowest wages, integrated their outfits and, again for their own profit, because blacks were good cowboys, even put blacks in front or in charge of herds. Siringo once rode left point with "negro Gabe."[18] Dobie tells of one black who went up the trail thirteen times, four times as a trail boss.[19] His name was Al Jones, and he is mentioned as bossing a herd in 1885 by one of the old-timers in the monumental collection *The Trail Drivers of Texas.*[20] This is the only mention of a black trail boss in these two huge volumes, and Al Jones didn't get a separate biography because the organization was Jim Crow. Blacks get the silent treatment; Anglos pretend they weren't there.

Most blacks in these volumes of firsthand accounts have no names at all: one old cowboy typically lists seven full names of the boys of his crew when he first went up the trail as a wrangler in 1877 and then adds, "two negro cowhands and a negro cook." This is one step this side of invisibility into anonymity. A black isn't a person: Jack Potter, the "fighting parson" of southwest Texas fame, "when he had overcome an assailant in a fist fight or otherwise, *if he chanced to be a white man,* he always gave him fatherly counsel and offered him his hand" (emphasis added). If old-timers give names, they are only first names, like Siringo's "negro Gabe." If very occasionally we get a full name, he is always identified in parentheses: a cowboy and one mate were cut off from the rest of the outfit and they alone had to put the herd across the river; the fellow worker's name was "John Walker (a negro)."[21] The editor might have added these parentheses in the twenties, and evidence from these reminiscences may tell more about Texas racism of the twenties than of the 1870s and 1880s. But they tell us something.

All the later cowboys' praise of and expressions of affection for black fellow workers are dreadfully patronizing and strain to use respectable language, the way Lyndon Johnson would struggle to say "Negro" instead of "Nigra." A black's occasionally superior skill in range or corral work is often noticed with unqualified admiration, but then, typically, the black's loyalty and subservience to whites is added defensively. The attitude is, "I admired this Negro cowboy, but that's okay because he was one of the good ones." Or, "Forgive me for admiring that Negro a long time ago when I was forced to be in the same outfit with him—I'm not a nigger-lover ordinarily." Working and living together did inevitably make Anglo cowboys forget their deep racism for a time, but it would return, and, like Huckleberry Finn, they were ashamed of their lapse. We get faithful-old-darkie stereotypes, the obvious lie very comforting to the ears of oppressors: "cold rainy nights when negro hands stood double guard rather than call the white folks." And assertions of "good Negroes": "These [cowboy] negroes knew their place, and were careful to stay in it."[22] And non-sequitur, defensive concluding tags: "We have had some real cowboys of the darker race here in Wyoming. Their ability . . . was outstanding and they were true to their employers."[23] There was mixed camaraderie in camp, which lasted into the generally integrated cattle towns of the North, but the friendships were shallow and tenuous, and there might always be trouble in town that would expose their shallowness. Most outfits would fight for the rights of their blacks in town but only so long as the blacks kept their places. A black couldn't ever get drunk and swagger around and run whores like all his Anglo mates. If he did, he would get shot or otherwise taught his place, like the black cook in an outfit in the New Mexico Territory who got branded on the thigh with a red-hot shovel for shooting off his mouth about Rebels.[24]

Andy Adams, in *The Outlet*, his second novel about the trail driving he knew firsthand, presents an episode that sums up Texas attitudes to black cowboys. The hero is in charge of a herd in 1884. At a river crossing they come on an outfit ahead of them, a "negro outfit" with a black foreman. The white outfit makes them give way so that they can cross their herd first, because they deem the black outfit "water-bound," that is, unable to make a crossing. There is no violence offered, even of language, but there is obvious disdain toward "darkies," "niggers." A cowboy summarizes the merits and limits of black cowboys: "Under a white foreman, I'll bet that's a good lot of darkies. . . . As good cowhands as ever I saw were nigs, but they need a white man to blow and brag on them. But it always ruins one to give him any authority."[25] The hatred of blacks by Anglo cowboys seems to have increased with time, but seldom to have come to a range or wagon boss's refusing to work with blacks. Ike Blasingame records an exception on the Matador range in Dakota in 1905, when the range and roundup boss Con McMurry—like Ike, a Texan—refuses to let a black rep of a half-breed rancher, Benoist, use the outfit's wagon. Ike's puzzlement and surprise show the occurrence as exceptional:

> Benoist sent his cowboy, a colored man named Bunk White, to rep with us. White was to represent the W B Bar brand, and Bill intended him to stay right with the Matador wagon. . . . White was a very good cowboy and rider. There could have been no real aversion toward him among the men. I know I did not dislike or refuse to work with him, but for some reason, Con would not allow Bunk to work with the wagon. One morning, he told him to get his horses out of the *remuda* and go home, which Bunk did.[26]

Elmer Kelton's *Wagontongue* (1972), an excellent Western novel and one of the very few with a black hero, treats racism on the southwest Texas ranges quite accurately, although the author's race prevents him from getting into the consciousness of his hero with much accuracy. The Anglo outfit's attachment to the hero has limits and qualifications, and he eats alone on the tongue of the chuck wagon.

The general Anglo cowboy conviction that Mexicans are inferior comes from deep Texas feelings conditioned by war and raids in both directions across the Rio Grande and competition for land and jobs and business. We always tend to hate or despise our victims in order to justify our victimization, in this case the Tejanos who refused to leave their native land or submit agreeably to expropriation or colonializing. Before the war, they were regarded, wrote a distinguished Yankee traveler, Frederick Law Olmsted, "with a great contempt and suspicion, for their intimacy with slaves, and their competition with plantation labor."[27] Rangers still beat up, sometimes murder, Tejanos, although presumably they don't extract names of compatriots by torture before summary execution as they regularly used to do.

Frank Dobie, the great old cowman turned professor, folklorist, and writer, not surprisingly had typical Texas prejudices. In his chapter "The Bloody Border," about events during the same time as McNelly's raids, when Rangers and other vigilante posses were cleaning out Mexican raiders and the small Tejano ranchers of the Nueces Strip, he actually distinguishes between "good" and "bad" Mexicans, the latter being ones who are not content to be subservient, compliant workers.[28] The prejudice runs so deep that it crosses classes. Texas cowboys admired the generally accepted superior skills of the vaqueros at roping, riding, tracking, and bronco busting. They noted and admired individual acts of bravery and endurance. They marveled, like Andy Adams, "how a Mexican or Indian knows so much more about a horse than any of us."[29] But they never became close in their friendships, even in passing contacts on a drive or during a roundup, as sometimes happened between themselves and blacks. Mexican women were another matter—there are lots of references to love affairs with them. With dark-skinned women (and with white dance hall ladies) they could have relations without giving up their feeling of superiority. And the language barrier need not interfere because with women (other than decent Anglo women) a cowboy need not communicate verbally except on a word and phrase level. Besides, white males in the U.S. have always indulgently put their racial feelings aside in relations with dusky *women*, be they black, Indian, or Mexican.

Cowboys would reaffirm the racial feelings inherited from their society by experience with the Mexicans they worked and lived with, that is, the one or two vaqueros with most wagon crews of eight to twelve men. This was their social unit, and they had by comparison little relations with the

Tejano small ranchers of the brush country, who tended to be more assertive of their rights and dignity than vaqueros working for Anglo outfits. These vaqueros helped the cowboys reaffirm their superior feeling toward them by in fact being or pretending to be the inferiors in the feudal class system of peonage they had always been a part of. But the cowboys didn't see them as a people suffering from long oppression by the Spanish and then Mexican and finally Texan *patrón* class but as members of, as Andy Adams says with the shocking but typical racism of Texas cowboys, an "inferior race" with "Aztec blood"—lacking in "courage and leadership, but never in cunning and craftiness."[30] His hero at this point is commenting on a Mexican outfit threatening to leave the herd of their Anglo, tenderfoot Wyoming boss. Our Texas hero, familiar with Mexicans, soon puts an end to this threat by some threats of his own, proving that vaqueros need white bosses who rule with the secure strength that comes from natural superiority.

Another old cowboy expresses the fact of the relationship without the racist explanation. He went up the trail for "Old Captain King of Nueces in 1880" with an Anglo trail boss but otherwise all Mexicans in the outfit: "all the old-timers know how King handled the Mexicans—he had them do the work and let the white men do the bossing."[31] Examples of cowboys' condescension toward and patronizing of Mexicans and Tejanos, of their cruel indifference to Mexican life, even their apparent pleasure and pride in torturing and killing them could be multiplied with painful amplitude, but the subject is distasteful and the point is probably already made. There were a few exceptions: Siringo, on an undercover job as a Pinkerton, after living eight months on terms of everyday intimacy with "lower class" Mexican-Americans in 1890 in New Mexico, declared that he liked them;[32] and most of what else he reports of his life confirms the declaration. But Siringo's values are difficult to fathom.

Teddy Blue married the half-Indian daughter of his rancher boss and says that his ability to see the Indians' "side of things" came after a conversion from a former hostile attitude. He implies that his old prejudiced attitude is the common one among cowboys, although he says that cowboys "as a rule had some sympathy with Indians," and that he had heard them say "it was a shame" in regard to the government policy of starving Indians or forcing them onto reservations by killing the buffalo.[33] But such sympathy would not extend to those Territory Indians who would stampede a trail herd at night in retaliation for a refusal of a tribute of a few strays for passage through their land. The loss of sleep, comfort, skin, and often life that would result didn't cause any more friendly feeling toward Indians than toward jayhawkers and rustlers, who also stampeded herds. But sometimes their anger would probably be directed partly to the trail boss too protective of his boss's cattle to give tribute.

Early cowboys, particularly Texans, doubtless associated Indians and Mexicans and blacks together in their minds in a vague way, not only as dark-skinned unlikes and therefore enemies but because of other historical and social connections. Mexicans disliked slavery and encouraged slave revolts and protected thousands of black fugitives as citizens in Mexico immune from extradition or capture. Tejanos "consorted freely with negroes," noted Olmsted in 1855, "making no distinction from pride of race."[34] Tejanos sympathized with abolitionists and most refused to serve the Confederacy during the war. Blacks fled slavery also to Indian nations and became Indians. And the Mexicans whom cowboys saw were not Spanish or Creoles but mestizos. They indeed looked like Indians and had, as Andy Adams said, Aztec blood. These dark associations reinforced the fading memory after the seventies of the Comanche massacres and depredations that their kin a generation back had experienced. The Texas Rangers fought Indians before they harassed and chased Tejanos, and cowboys were eager to volunteer their services because of their taste for this kind of fun. But on the whole, because of their love of nature and freedom and space and their admiration for bravery and horsemanship and sympathy for underdogs, cowboys probably had, as Teddy Blue states, somewhat more sympathy with Indians than did the other classes of people on the frontier, although contact and their skills and job made them more dangerous to Indians than most of the rest. There is lots of evidence that cowboys profited materially from depredations against Indians, and a justifying prejudice likely resulted. For instance, the owner–trail boss of a large herd on the way to California in 1854 gave fourteen of his cowboys moonlighting as Rangers $300 to divide between themselves after they brought back "8 horses, two mules, a jack and a jenny" from a raid on fifty Indians in New Mexico Territory.[35] But there was no need to hate Indians as a threat (as distinct from hatred as a justification for oppression or attempted genocide) after the buffalo were gone and after Indians were pretty nearly all on reservations (except for some Apaches); and this end of the Indian wars came about early, soon after the first decade of the cowboy era. Like Remington, who painted a past he never witnessed, we tend to exaggerate the role of cowboys as Indian fighters.

During the cowboy era on the Great Plains, cowboys were all unmarried and lived alone in a line camp or together around chuck wagons in small groups of other unmarried men. If they married, they would have to give up cowboying for wages, because no provision was made for wives of workers on the range or the trail. Part-time cowboys could have a wife on a homestead ranch, but cattle companies blackballed cowboys with herds of their own. They were like sea-duty sailors in the navy or merchant marine: no wives, but a girl in every port. They had the attitude toward women that one would expect of strictly raised but observant country boys now spending their time, except for brief holidays in town, isolated from female society. As Teddy Blue stated, they had a reverence for respectable women bordering on fear.[36] This reverence came from the values of their traditional, preindustrial communities of small farmers, and undoubtedly in some complex way it related to their reverence for motherhood, particularly on the frontier, where women were scarce and thought by men to be in need of protection. Barred by their occupation from marriage, they consoled themselves with a sour-grapes response—pretending not to want it or the respectable women it involved. This response to their deprivation often approaches misogyny, elevating to an ideal the male bonding of cowboys and denigrating the company of treacherous women:

> *I'll go back to the Western land,*
> *I'll hunt up my old cowboy band,—*
> *Where the girls are few and the boys are true*
> *And a false-hearted love I never knew.*
>
> *Whoo-a-whoo-a-whoo-a-whoo*

and,

> *When you are single*
> *And living at your ease*
> *You can roam this world over*
> *And do as you please;*
> *You can roam this world over*
> *And go where you will*
> *And slyly kiss a pretty girl*
> *And be your own still.*
>
> *But when you are married*
> *And living with your wife,*
> *You've lost all the joys*
> *And comforts of life.*
> *Your wife she will scold you,*
> *Your children will cry,*
> *And that will make papa*
> *Look withered and dry.*

> *You can't step aside, boys,*
> *To speak to a friend*
> *Without your wife at your elbow*
> *Saying, "What does this mean?"*
> *Your wife, she will scold*
> *And there is sad news.*
> *Dear boys, take warning;*
> *'Tis a life to refuse.*

or, a variant of the same song,

> *Come fill up your bottles boys, drink Bourbon around;*
> *Here is luck to the single wherever they are found. . . .*
> *Never place your affection on a charming sweetheart.*
> *She is dancing before you your affections to gain;*
> *Just turn your back on them with scorn and disdain.*[37]

Since their training prevented aggressive sexual behavior toward respectable women, they avoided women in favor of "ladies." Sometimes their Southern "notions of chivalry toward women," as Teddy Blue says of himself, operated with prostitutes, and, he continues, many cowboys married them.[38] As with all small groups of males isolated from women, their talk about them and about sex was frequent and coarse, with lots of dirty stories, songs, and horseplay. But cowboy smut is ephemeral, in spite of the folklorists. At the end of a paper before a folklore society in Texas, John Lomax, more of a symbolic cowboy and cowboy lover than even Teddy Roosevelt, said he had collected some cowboy profanity, some even of the vulgar variety, which he was willing to share "on some future occasion . . . with just the right kind of audience."[39] He was making an appeal to be asked back. If he did share this material, the event went unrecorded, as have all the dirty cowboy songs he also undoubtedly collected to entertain select male groups.

A great deal is to be understood about cowboys if we see them as products of special, small male groups, all the groups together constituting, in their collective mind, an elite class of men. Each group generates its own warm feeling of friendly unity and collective pride at the same time that each of its members competes against all the rest to excel in the manly virtues of strength, bravery, and physical skill. The Dallas Cowboys today probably feel something of this competitive male bonding of the elite group in the locker room. Only men (and indeed most American men) can really understand or feel from experience what is being said here about group competitive macho.

FRANK LESLIE'S ILLUSTRATED NEWSPAPER

No. 1322.—Vol. LI.   NEW YORK, JANUARY 29, 1881.   [PRICE 10 CENTS.

THE PUBLIC IMAGE, 1881: VANDALS

This wood engraving takes up the whole front page of a leading national weekly newspaper. (COURTESY OF THE DENVER PUBLIC LIBRARY, WESTERN HISTORY DEPARTMENT.)

Let's take an example of the cowboys' well-known chivalry toward "decent" women. A cowboy in Andy Adams's first novel included in a letter home a saying that we can find with variations in literally hundreds of frontier sources: "Texas is a good place for men and dogs, but it's hell on women and oxen."[40] The phrase tells us a great deal about cowboy attitudes. Putting aside the more obscure implication of the second pairing (usually it is with horses)—that women are like castrated males—we see that the whole saying means that men, coarse brutes that they are, thrive on the harsh conditions of the frontier because they enjoy having their strength and toughness tried by them; that men not only survive on the frontier but become stronger in their natural element, the wilderness; that women, being weaker, on the other hand hate the frontier, or should by their nature hate it, because it is alien to them and wears them down. So the woman (the decent one), being weaker, has to be protected by the brave, strong cowboy and his friends, particularly on the frontier, where the helpless creature is threatened by everything alien to her—like Indians, panthers, and dust storms. And the cowboy can feel good about his mother and sisters because they need him for survival. Whether or not women are like this is irrelevant to the fact of the cowboy's conception of them as such, which is the point here. But there is growing evidence provided by historians in the women's movement that many women on the frontier liked it and the adventurous life there and were not unhappy martyrs living in a harsh and alien land, which is a stereotype created by men.

When they were letting off steam in town, after long periods of uninterrupted hard, dangerous, often monotonous and lonely work, there is no doubt at all that they really raised hell with their fights and drunkenness. Most of this wild, antisocial behavior in town was not essentially mean or belligerent, just rough, macho, big-boyish play—perhaps expressing repressed sexuality—dangerous, but one of the hazards of the trail, necessary periodic rest and rehabilitation—like U.S. combat soldiers on leave in Japan from Korea. In spite of their frequency, the instances of belligerence seem to occur because of the few but inevitable mean and pugnacious drunks among the cowboys. Such a cowboy would deliberately pick fights, often by Yankee-baiting, and then his mates would back him up out of loyalty to the outfit and their liking to fight as a form of recreation. A drunk cowboy on the prod, although most of his mates weren't, would tell in a crowd of Yankees a story like this about his wartime experience, with predictable results: "I was coming down the road and I met a damn blue-bellied abolitionist, and I paunched him [that is, shot him in the belly]. And he laid there in the brush and belched like a beef for three days, and then he died in fits. The Bastard."[41] Andy Adams in his first novel has an

THE PUBLIC IMAGE, 1874: HOODLUMS

From Joseph G. McCoy's Historical Sketches of the Cattle Trade of the West and Southwest *(1874), the first book about the cattle industry. McCoy called himself "the pioneer Western cattle shipper." His stockyards at Abilene, Kansas, provided the first railhead market for Texas trailing contractors in 1867. The woodcut was made from a sketch by Kansas artist Henry Worrall.* (COURTESY OF THE HOUGHTON LIBRARY, HARVARD UNIVERSITY.)

authentic-sounding account of a fight caused by an argument over the South and patriotism: in a buffalo-hide town on the trail in Montana in 1882 a Texas cowboy and his buddies fight an insulting Yankee gambler.[42] But mostly their behavior was boyish play in deadly games, using guns as toys. They came from a bold people who had left the safety of settled farms to live on the frontier of southwest Texas, where almost every man "had to have his six-shooter always ready, every house kept a shotgun . . . because they were always looking for a raid by Mexicans or Comanche Indians."[43] They were having fun showing off to the world their bravery and their skills with guns and horses. A few were revolted and refused to carry guns, and as a consequence had better chances of avoiding Boot Hill—like the twenty-year-old on his first trail drive who every morning had to shoot with a borrowed gun all the calves born that night and was so "disgusted" with six-shooters that he "never owned much less used one." But he was only a cowboy for about six years; although he represents a larger minority than the cowboy myth depicts of the pacifist cowboy, one who relied on "unpreparedness [to keep] me peacefully inclined," as he put it, he was the exception, not the rule.[44]

Journalists early reported the cowboys' destructive and lawless play in towns. The earliest picture of a cowboy on a tear is in Joseph G. McCoy's pioneer book *Historic Sketches of the Cattle Trade of the West and Southwest*, published in 1874. In a crude woodcut, a man on a running horse at night in a prairie town is shooting off two revolvers in the air while a small group of citizens stands cowed and appalled in the background. The highly stylized crudeness of the picture lends authenticity to the perception—the artist hasn't got much right at all, not the saddle or the clothes (except for the hat) or shooting Colt .45s—but the concept is clear: cowboys (who are identifiable by huge Mexican spurs) are lawless and shocking to honest citizens. The caption spells it out so there can be no mistake: "Drunken cow-boy on the 'war-path.' "

The hyphenated uneasiness of journalists with the new word *cowboy* also appears the year before, 1873:—an account in the local newspaper of the early railroad cattletown of Ellsworth, Kansas, shows how remarkably early cowboys were conceived of as a recognizable social group noted for uncivilized behavior:

> The "Cow-Boys" of Texas are a peculiar breed. They are distinct in their habits and characteristics from the remainder of even the Texan population as if they belonged to another race. The Lipan and Comanche are not more unlike the civilized white man than is the nomadic herdsman to the Texan who dwells in the city or cultivates the plains.

A few years later a correspondent reported from Fort Worth to another Kansas newspaper (the Baxter Springs *Times*) with additional details and even a charitable interpretation for the now stereotyped wildness of the cowboy:

> He comes here from his home on the plains to spend his money at the saloons, swagger in the streets, buy himself a new sombrero . . . , and make merry with the painted syrens of the variety theater. Full of strange oaths, free with his cash and his revolver, boisterous, lawless, but not hard-hearted, the cow-boy is a character *sui generis*. . . . [He] is altogether the most free and independent fellow to be found in this peculiarly free and independent country.

In a national monthly a year later (1880), a journalist praised Texas cowboys for their skill but again reinforced the now firm reputation for wildness, by this time a commonly-believed characteristic:

The Texans are, as far as true cowboyship goes, unrivalled: the best riders, hardy, and born to the business; the only drawback being their wild reputation. The others are less able but more orderly men. The bad name of Texans arises mostly from their excitable tempers, and the fact that they are mostly "on the shoot."[45]

After telling of a bloody fight in Dodge City in 1877 between cowboys and buffalo hunters, begun over a trifle and pursued with irrational fury, Siringo comments that "this little scrape illustrates what fools cowboys were after long drives over the trail."[46]

What fools, indeed, but even in their drunkenness there were social forces and principles involved. Cowboys were eager to fight because they liked it, but particularly if by fighting they demonstrated their loyalty to other individual cowboys or to cowboys as a group. They had a knee-jerk response to cowboys in danger or threatened by loss of dignity and rep-utation—immediate, unquestioned willingness to join a fight. This is a common male-elite-group response of solidarity to threats from outside. It can still be observed among Hell's Angels, sailors from the same ship on shore leave, NHL teams, and frat men. Riding into Dodge City the year after the fight referred to above, Siringo, with a bunch of his cowboys, sees twenty-five mounted cowboys lined up facing a saloon, holding rifles in their hands. He notices one cowboy he has seen before. "Calling me by name he said: 'Fall into line, quick, hell is going to pop in a few minutes.' We jerked our Winchester rifles from their scabbards and fell in line, like most any other fool cowboys would have done."[47] After it was all over, he discovered that they had a fight going with local sheriffs and marshals. Some could have been killed (but were not this time) in a fight the grounds of which they knew nothing about. They responded instantly without question to an appeal from their fellows. This is macho behavior: to respond decisively without thought or introspection with swift, violent action, par-ticularly in defense of one's own male group. A Texas journalist in 1883 called such behavior not macho but "heroic": cowboys "cultivate the heroic rather than the intellectual part of their nature and when they come to town often insist on giving the citizens public exhibitions of their personal bravery and skill in horsemanship and the use of the six-shooter."[48]

This reputation for lawless wildness, earned doubtless by their public behavior during their brief off-duty hours in cowtowns when they were letting off steam and storing up memories for the lonely work days and nights ahead, led respectable citizens of the West to think of cowboys collectively as disreputable. Cowboys were not a respectable class on the frontier. A very proper Southern woman who married a cowboy turned family rancher recalls her unusual views in the early eighties:

> Our bedroom with its huge fireplace, where we burned logs five feet long, was again the living room for all when the day's work was done. I never regretted the arrangement whereby we shared our home with our own nice cowboys, and with every stray rider who came our way. This was Mr. Alderson's [her husband's] idea; he had the highest ideals of the home of any man I have ever known. Few families living in Montana had their cowboys live with them as we did. Nobody then thought of them as romantic. They were regarded as a wild and undesirable lot of citizens, but I always thought there was much injustice in this. Nice people in Miles City would as soon have thought of inviting a rattlesnake into their homes as a cowboy. The *only* places that made them welcome were the house of prostitution and the saloon. The wonder is that they kept their finer qualities intact.[49]

Although cowboys indeed were wild, violent, and addicted to boyish games and displays, there is plenty of evidence that, contrary to their reputation, they were quite socially respectable—in their protectiveness of women, children, and family, in their eagerness to help out in times of community or family distress, and in their touching yearning to be loved, honored, or at least remembered. The fact is that they were not essentially different in social virtues from the other main groups of frontier workers.

Cowboys are remarkably loyal to their outfits—to all the workers in it, including the cook and the wrangler and usually the boss: not the big boss—that is, the manager of the ranch, who worked for and sometimes was one of the capitalists who held shares in the corporation; and not the trail contractor company, which owned the cattle just for the duration of the trip north; but loyal to their fellow workers and their immediate supervisor, the wagon or trail foreman, who was chosen from among the ranks of cowboys partly for his ability to attract such loyalty. It was not loyalty to the *herd*, as Frank Dobie has John Young, his cowboy-turned-cowman informant, say: "no cowboy ever quit while his life was hardest and his duties were most exacting. . . . [No one ever] even expressed the intention of quitting instantly. *A certain sense of loyalty to his herd, an ingrained code of fidelity to his trust*, kept him rubbing tobacco juice in his eyes to stay awake and risking his life after some wild, crazy brute of a gaunt, ten-dollar cow" (emphasis added).[50]

Since Dobie always saw the cattle business through the eyes of his own class of owners, never through the eyes of the workers, he here expresses worker loyalty as devotion to the well-being of the commodity he works, the herd, and implies that the "fidelity of trust" was to the owner who trusted him with this commodity. This is a mighty comforting thought to the owning class: my workers are absolutely loyal to my interests, not out of fear or coercion but willingly as part of their "ingrained" code of behavior (that is, deep conditioning), which works for the benefit of me as a member of the owning class. This view is embodied in the myth of the cowboy, which Dobie has accepted uncritically, but it is palpable nonsense. One of the central points of this book is that cowboys were loyal to the outfit, not the herd, fellow workers, not capitalists or commodity, in spite of the myth that reverses these loyalties and presents cowboys as eager to face death to protect the interests of their employers, who were more often than not absentees.

Teddy Blue, one of the few old cowboys to have expressed this important distinction, explicitly states that cowboys took a pride in their outfits and were not motivated by concern for the owner's money but the reputation of the outfit, although this worked incidentally to the benefit of the owners by nurturing their property. This is the way we are to understand his statement that cowboys "were intensely loyal to the outfit they were work-ing for and would fight to the death for it."[51] Siringo sometimes glimpsed this truth fleetingly and confusedly when he was no longer a cowboy and had come to hate corporate capitalists. Adams never sees it and helped create the myth of the cowboy as loyal worker. Even Dobie, whose interests are served by this myth, says that Adams's main fault is "love of pros-perity," which in context seems to mean love of rich men.[52] During a stampede a cowboy would risk his life to outrace and turn the lead cattle on broken ground in darkness lit up only for moments by lightning—not because he would earn the praise of the owners a thousand miles away whose financial interest was threatened or to protect their property, but because he wanted the silent admiration of his fellow workers for his bravery and skill and their silent thanks for saving them the further dis-comfort and danger that would come from gathering a scattered herd. An outfit would take pride in getting a herd to the railroad fat and glossy and with few losses, not because they thus benefited the owner but because they thus testified to how good they were as cowboys. They would take pride in their collective accomplishment.

Even though they had little loyalty for their distant big bosses or the bosses' managerial agents, they weren't often successful in collective wage disputes (which they attempted more often than is generally recognized) because of their intense individualism and independence. Their individualism fitted perfectly with their group loyalty, but it prevented them or at least discouraged them from acting together to set limits on their exploitation. As we shall see, cowboys developed ways of getting some part of their own back from the capital they created for the owning class, ways more suited to their individualism than organizing craft brotherhoods, although they tried that too. The other workers on the frontier, like miners and lumberjacks and railroad workers, even teamsters—to designate only those who organized against corporations, thus excluding most women workers, such as laundry hands, cooks, prostitutes, farmers, Harvey Girls— responded to their exploitation by organized group struggle. Though cowboys attempted this route, it didn't work out as well as it did with other frontier workers. Even during the Great Depression of the 1930s, when everyone was organizing, the cowboy extras in Hollywood refused to join the Screen Actors Guild ("I wouldn't trust unions as far as I could throw a steer. . . . It's just another way of getting control of a man's life"), and their own organization, the Riding Actors Association, soon fell apart "like a rotten saddle."[53]

Cowboys were "the most independent people on earth," asserted Teddy Blue, and gave this example: a boss would have to ask permission of a wrangler, the bottom dog in the outfit, if he wanted to get his own horse out of the remuda. Cowboys didn't operate well together in military-type operations, like the horseless charge up San Juan Hill. They made shockingly bad soldiers not because they lacked joy in the work but because they couldn't take external discipline and control. Again, let's listen to Teddy Blue: cowboys liked being representatives of their outfits during roundups on neighboring ranges because "you were on your own instead of working for a boss. For months on end you never saw him, and they all liked that. At the worst, there was never very much bossing done around a outfit, but any at all was too much to suit the average cowpuncher."[54] They functioned perfectly together at their work, because everyone knew what to do and could do it and had the motive to do it without instruction. Cowboys wouldn't stand for instructions, bossing, reprimands. By refusing them, they didn't get them; thus they gave their hazardous work some dignity and, in spite of the exploitation most of them knew they were subjected to, preserved, with their individuality, their self-respect. Cowboys alone of all workers of the new industries of the frontier maintained their dignity and individuality in the face of exploitation, although this didn't long survive fences and managed herds. And the unique way they developed of combining group efficiency and individualism, their method of cooperative anarchy in their work, would have been resisted more if it hadn't resulted in advantage for the bosses. In fact, when as a result of changes in the cattle industry their original and unique methods of work and their own work ethic no longer produced profits, the bosses changed their work, restricted it to limited tasks, made it more routinely repetitive, controlled it, and supervised it. Remington's sad picture of two beat-down cowboys, one dismounted to open a gate, shows the beginning of the process.

To understand the old and original methods of cowboys and the work ethic or "cowboy's code" that grew from the work and supported it, we can do no better than to hear from Eugene Manlove Rhodes, a working cowboy from New Mexico Territory:

Humility was not headlined in the cow countries. With the cowboy, the cornerstone of character was pride. He was proud of his skill, swiftness, daring, hardihood, endurance, and loyalty.

Let me set down a few sections of the code, as they come to mind.

Your loyalty was to the job, not to your employer. You might fall out with your employer; you might privately resolve to evidence your dissatisfaction by deleting your employer, in due time. But you were not supposed to quit the job until another man— another good man—was ready to take your place. "To quit a man in a tight" was the unforgivable sin. This, of course, had its origin in the days when herds were trailed a thousand miles to market. . . .

There was another side to this. *Provided the job could spare you,* you were supposed to put up with no harsh talk from foreman or owner. At the first rough word you said: "Who, me? Hell, I done quit twenty minutes ago."

. . . The idea was that you were supposed to know your job and to have done your best in a difficult and ticklish business; when you failed, no reproaches were due. This also worked out beautifully. You did not often quit your job in anger—perhaps never in a lifetime. What happened was that no one used tall talk to you. . . .

Again, you might never have seen your employer. You might work for a stock company, or an absentee. You worked for the job. You stayed with the stampede; you might not know how to swim and might have grave doubts as to your horse—but you crossed the flooded river with the herd; you went sleepless through stormy nights, as you "rode 'round them." . . .

It followed that "the alibi" was unknown. When you came in without what you went after, you made no excuses. At most,

"THE FALL OF THE COWBOY"

This is the title of Frederick Remington's painting for Owen Wister's article "The Evolution of the Cow-Puncher," Harper's Monthly, *September 1895, where it was reproduced by photogravure. In the openly racist article Wister treats cowboys as Saxon descendents of King Arthur's knights, united by the "bottom bond of race," their "admirable Saxon contempt for foreigners," leading them to use but then reject "the small, deceitful alien" Mexican vaquero. Cowboys now are "dispersed, as the elk, as the buffalo" by the end of the frontier, wire fences, and "Mr. Armour of Chicago."* (COURTESY OF THE AMON CARTER MUSEUM, FORT WORTH.)

you jerked a thumb at the pinnacles, with the casual and indolent explanation: "I wasted 'em." No post mortems. . . .

Better still—whatever your misadventure, no matter how painful the experience—*you did not complain.* There was a good reason for this and that reason was not because you were such a fine fellow. It was because your audience knew all about it: exposure, fatigue, hardship, suffering—the bunch had been there. . . .

The blurb was as unknown as the alibi. Men said—without emphasis: "He'll do to take along.". . .

Consider Johnny, the boy who herded the saddle horses through the long nights. "Is Johnny a good night hawk?" "He holds the horses." . . .

In practice, the foreman said, when no other was by to hear: "Charlie, I reckon you might go to represent with the V Cross T, tomorrow." If there were extra horses in the *caballada*, not in your mount, but which he was willing for you to take, he mentioned them. That was all. He didn't suggest that you leave Jug who was lame, Tiger who was thin, or Rebel with a cinch-gall. He didn't tell you what to do or how long to stay. You were supposed to know your business. If the V Cross T work made an early shipment of steers, you were to use your judgment, to ship steers of your brand if you thought best. If you needed an extra man to drive back, you hired him. . . .

"Representing" is given as a sample, only. It was the same with other work. You were told to take seven peelers and work Hueco Hills. Details were left to you. "Hank, you go with the wagon to Cedar Spring." But Hank was not told where to make camp, where to get wood, and so on. That was up to Hank. . . .

I worked on the range twenty-five years, and in that time I did not hear any man told what to do. If it was obvious, a gate had to be opened, bars to lash fast on a pen of cattle, wood to be rustled for a branding fire—the nearest man did it, untold. When the boys came in at night—too tired for any type to tell—if beef was low, the first four men killed a beef. The horse wrangler was supposed to keep the cook in wood and water; sometimes he was prevented; for good reason. In such case, the first men to reach camp rustled that wood and water. No one asked them to do this. Some strange instinct seemed to tell them that the cook would need wood and water. . . .

Whatever was fine in the cowboy was because he was interested in making the best possible job of his work, with an unexplained indifference to the financial rewards of it. As it happens, his pay was at all times laughably inadequate to the "services rendered."[55]

The reader will have perceived that Rhodes's interpretation is somewhat different from the one offered here, because Rhodes, like most former cowboys, looks longingly back on the good old days and sees the cowboys' work-style and ethic as an eternal ideal, practical but ignored in the present day. It was rather a way of work cowboys alone developed, of all the frontier workers during the industrial revolution, to keep for a brief time their dignity and identity. Society soon changed and made that way of life impossible—alas for our nostalgia and present alienation. Most of us long to be cowboys because we feel that their work developed them as individuals the way our work does not, now that almost all of us work for someone (or some*thing*!) else in robotized, specialized, hierarchically supervised, and Taylorized jobs. But Rhodes does describe that work-style and ethic accurately, and he would agree that his "loyalty to the job" is almost the same as "loyalty to the outfit," that is, to the small group of your fellow workers.

One other respectful disagreement, also based on our view of cowboys not as eternal but as products of a changing historical society. We shall see that the cowboy was not "indifferent to the financial rewards" of his work (as Rhodes implies is always the best way for all workers to be), but that—unlike miners and quartz-mill hands, lumberjacks and lumber teamsters, brakemen and switchmen and roadbed workers, and mule skinners and bull-whackers—they contrived for a time, by preserving a degree of freedom in their work, to remain unalienated by it; indeed, if they didn't get killed, to find considerable satisfaction and fulfillment in it and as a result to be less concerned with material rewards. And they made perhaps somewhat fewer efforts than miners and the rest to improve their salaries and work conditions by organized struggle because by the time their work had become mechanical and supervised and specialized they were living in their minds and their life-style the code that they had created.

If we put together all these qualities of cowboys and add a few more, we shall see how it follows that cowboys are generally reactionary and imperialistic. They are racist, macho, competitive in male groups, aggressively individualistic, bellicose and inclined to violent rather than negotiated solutions. They are dominated by a Texas Republic and Confederate tradition of Yankee, Indian, and Mexican fighting. This heritage makes them hostile to U.S. law, free blacks, and non-Anglo foreigners of all kinds. We can add another quality: their occupation of handling cattle in violent ways, as the author of *Hud* has observed, makes them, on the whole, not very gentle. "I had never known a cowboy who was also a truly gentle man. The cowboy's working life is spent in one sort of violent activity or other; and ability to absorb violence and hardship is part of the proving of any cowboy, and it is only to be expected that the violence will extend itself occasionally from animals to humans and particularly to those humans that class would have one regard as animals."[56] Also, we might add, the cowboy's isolation from women reinforced his roughness.

Put these qualities together and it is no surprise that in 1914 a group of Texas cowboys during a roundup on an American-controlled ranch in Sonora, where they worked together with some vaqueros, would see the Mexican Revolution then going on as an opportunity to continue their southward territorial expansion: "We dismounted on the slope of a distant hill and looked off down into Mexico, and if the Texans had their way we would never stop until all that good cow-country was ours. It seemed as if destiny was driving us on and, before the fighting ended, we would take all Mexico as our fathers had taken the Far West."[57] These cowboys wanted the actual physical possession of Mexico, not just the corporate control of almost all the ranches of Sonora, which the U.S. already had before the Revolution. Later that year, Texas cowboys in particular supported the U.S.'s so-called "punitive expedition" against Pancho Villa, as they had other forays in the previous century, not only because it offered revenge for a half century of border raids and a way of putting an end to them completely, but because it was a violent adventure of men on horseback (with a few airplanes and Apache scouts).

Long before our last Mexican incursion, Teddy Roosevelt had recognized and used the warlike, expansionist, super-patriotic tendencies of cowboys. In 1886, on his ranch in the Badlands of Dakota, he participated with his cowboys in a patriotic hanging in effigy of the Haymarket anarchists on the day they were hanged in Chicago.[58] We suspect TR of helping organize the patriotic event and generally encouraging cowboys in their jingoistic and filibustering tendencies, even in a kind of transference, seeing more of the tendencies in cowboys than there really were because of his own emotional needs and political values. He devised the Rough Riders on the basis of what he took to be cowboy methods and ideals; and cowboys, clinging to a vanishing past and looking for a final fling, eagerly volunteered for those regiments to teach the Spanish a lesson. Among the names proposed for the three regiments of cowboys TR recruited (probably only one-third were real cowboys): Teddy's Holy Terrors, Roosevelt's Rough 'Uns, Roosevelt's Wild West, Teddy's Texas Tarantulas, Teddy's Cowboy Contingent, Fighting Cowboys, Cowboy Regiment, Cowboy Volunteers.[59] While campaigning in the West five years after his (horseless) charge up San Juan Hill, he met a group of cowboys and other Western workers "of my former regiment" (the Rough Riders), and he associated them admiringly with imperialism and violence: "death by violence had entered into their scheme of existence in a matter of course way which would doubtless seem alien to the minds of Boston anti-imperialists."[60] Many years before, in response to some blown-up diplomatic troubles with Mexico, he organized his first abortive version of the Rough Riders, which cowboys of the Badlands flocked to join—or so says TR:

In the summer of 1886, at the time of the war-scare over the Cutting incident, we began the organization of a troop of cavalry in our district, notifying the Secretary of War that we were at the service of the Government, and being promised every assistance by our excellent chief executive of the Territory, Governor Pierce. *Of course the cowboys were all eager for war, they did not much care with whom; they were very patriotic, they were fond of adventure, and, to tell the truth, they were by no means adverse to the prospect of plunder* [emphasis added]. News from the outside world came to us irregularly, and often in distorted form, so that we began to think we might get involved in a conflict not only with Mexico, but with England also. One evening at the ranch the men began talking over the English soldiers so I got down "Napier" and read them several extracts from his description of the fighting in the Spanish peninsula, also recounting as well as I could the great deeds of the British cavalry from Waterloo to Balaklava, and finishing up by describing from memory the fine appearance, the magnificent equipment, and the superb horses of the Household cavalry and of a regiment of hussars I had once seen. . . . At the end, one of them, who had been looking into the fire and rubbing his hands together, said with regretful emphasis, "Oh, how I *would* like to kill one of them!"[61]

Well, that cowboy was entrapped by TR's romantic warmongering; and in his enthusiasm for aggression and he-man violence, TR may to a degree have shaped cowboys to his own values; but there is no reason to doubt, because of his shocking admiration for these very American qualities, the essential truth of his observation of them in cowboys:

A cowboy will not submit tamely to an insult, and is ever ready to avenge his own wrongs; nor has he an overwrought fear of shedding blood. He possessed, in fact, few of the emasculated, milk-and-water moralities admired by the pseudo-philanthropists; but he does possess, to a very high degree, the stern, manly qualities that are invaluable to a nation.[62]

Change "pseudo-philanthropists" to "bleeding-heart parlor pinks" and it sounds just like John Wayne. And, indeed, this is one of many instances where the myth of the cowboy expresses his essential reality, even though in simplistic and exaggerated ways. Real cowboy jingoism contributes to the myth (John Wayne), which in turn supports the Green Berets. At the same time, the process, of course, works the other way around: national ideals of Manifest Destiny encourage people to mythologize their hero cowboys into imperialists and militarists, and real cowboys in turn develop these tendencies to conform more closely to their mythical images.

☆ 2 ☆

Cowboys as Workers

As soon as Fall work's over
  We get it in the neck
And we get a Christmas present
  On a neatly written check.

The wages that a cowboy earns
  In Summer go like smoke,
And when the Winter snows have come
  You bet your life he's broke.

—from "A Busted Cowboy's Christmas" (1893)[1]

Most of the old Anglo cowboys and cowmen who joined the Texas Trail Drivers Association in the early twenties and came to their annual meetings in San Antonio, wrote about their early lives fifty or so years before and looked back across the years toward a golden time when men were men. Their visions were colored by what they became: some few had gone into the cattle industry as owners or managers, and many had become small ranchers and merchants, comfortably middle-class, with big families, complacent and sentimental. Quite a few of these autobiographical accounts made it through the editorial process to stand out in contrast to the rest—

IN FRONT OF VERAMENDI GARDEN SALOON, SAN ANTONIO, ABOUT 1885

Such photographs of early working cowboys passing through the first cowtown are rare. This is from one of a series of stereoscope cards made by the photographer Frank Hardesty of the San Antonio View Co. (COURTESY OF THE DENVER PUBLIC LIBRARY, WESTERN HISTORY DEPARTMENT.)

MOUNTED COWBOY, SAN ANTONIO, 1880s

Photograph reproduced commercially for souvenirs, scrapbooks, graphoscopes. The lariat is of rawhide. Between the fingers of his left hand is a cigar. (COURTESY OF THE WESTERN HISTORY COLLECTIONS, UNIVERSITY OF OKLAHOMA LIBRARY.)

unvarnished, even a bit defiant and embittered, like the following laconic story by an old-timer, G. D. Burrows of Del Rio, a self-proclaimed loser. We suspect that such unvarnished accounts are not represented in the Association volumes in the proportion that would represent historical experience because the ordinary sad-sack waddie who did not make it big or even moderate would not be inclined to join the Association, or if he did would not feel inclined to blow about his life.

> I had my share of the ups and downs—principally downs—on the old cattle trail. Some of my experiences were going hungry, getting wet and cold, riding sore-backed horses, going to sleep on herd and losing cattle, getting "cussed" by the boss, scouting for "gray-backs" [body lice], trying the "sick racket" now and then to get a night's sleep, and other things too numerous to mention in this volume. But all of these were forgotten when we delivered our herd and started back to grand old Texas. Have often stopped a few days in Chicago, St. Louis and Kansas City, but always had the "big time" when I arrived in good old Santone rigged out with a pair of high-heeled boots and striped breeches, and about $6.30 worth of other clothes. Along about sundown you could find me at Jack Harris' show occupying a front seat and clamoring for the next performance. This "big time" would last but a few days, however, for I would soon be "busted" and would have to borrow money to get out to the ranch, where I would put in the fall and winter telling about the big things I had seen up North. The next spring I would have the same old trip, the same old things would happen in the same old way, and with the same old wind-up. I put in eighteen or twenty years on the trail, and all I had in the final outcome was the high-heeled boots, the striped pants and about $4.80 worth of other clothes, so there you are.[2]

Cowboys in the Texas brush country between the Nueces and the Rio Grande always have had particularly painful work, especially in the early days of cow hunts before chuck wagons, when you'd eat dry jerked beef and biscuits from a bag carried on your saddle and you'd sleep without a bedroll. Here is a portion of an account by an old trail driver whose family set up one of the first Anglo-Texan ranches in this wild country. The Leona River goes through the southwest corner of Frio County, halfway from San Antonio to Laredo:

> We then moved down to Frio County in the fall of 1858 and located on the Leona River, where we found a fine country, with

wild game and fish galore. We brought with us about four hundred head of cattle, which were allowed to roam at will over the excellent range, there being no fences to keep them confined to the immediate vicinity of our ranch. But they did not get far away from us for some time, or until other ranchers began to locate around us, when the cattle began to mix with other cattle and then began to stray off, some drifting as far as the Rio Grande or the coast. Soon the settlers began to organize cow hunts and work the cattle. I have been on cow hunts when there were as many as one hundred men working together from different counties. Stockmen of today do not know anything about the hard work and the strenuous times we encountered in those days. Sometimes we would be out for weeks at a time, starting every morning at daylight, and probably not getting in before dark, tired and hungry, and having to do without dinner all day. Our fare consisted of cornbread, black coffee and plenty of good beef.[3]

The "brush popper," who runs wild cattle through the thorny thickets of the Nueces valley (the Brasada), was one of the first workers of the industry, and his work was not only the hardest and most painful but, with one exception, the least known of all range work (the exception is the work of black cowboys of the bayous and coastal prairies of southeastern Texas). Here are portions of a striking account of this work by John Young, who as a cowman in the 1920s remembered when he worked the brush forty years before as a cowboy (or "vaquero," as he calls all southwest Texas cowboys of all races). He speaks through Frank Dobie, who doubtless adds something of his own, because he knows the Brasada from family experience and as a ranch manager.

In running in the brush a man rides not so much on the back of his horse as under and alongside. He just hangs on, dodging limbs as if he were dodging bullets, back, forward, over, under, half of the time trusting his horse to course right on this or that side of a brush or a tree. If he shuts his eyes to dodge, he is lost. Whether he shuts them or no, he will, if he runs true to form, get his head rammed or raked. Patches of the brush hand's bandana hanging on thorns and stobs sometimes mark his trail. . . .

Let us draw a picture. Down in a *ramadero* of spined bushes and trees that seem to cover all space except that occupied by prickly pear, a man with scratched face, frazzled ducking jacket, and snagged leggins is sitting on a horse, one leg thrown over

OUTFIT IN DILLEY, FRIO COUNTY, TEXAS

On the back of this old photograph appears one word in pencil, "Dilley," which is a small town just south of the Frio River on the road from San Antonio to Laredo. Everyone but the Mexican cook, even the wrangler, wears chaps for protection against the thorny brush. The cowboy on the far left seems to be Mexican. The tall cowboy in the center wears bib-overalls. (COURTESY OF THE BARKER TEXAS HISTORY CENTER, UNIVERSITY OF TEXAS, AUSTIN.)

the horn of his saddle. He is humped forward and seems almost asleep. The horse has gray hairs in his flanks; his knees are lumped from licks and thorns of past years. He is an old timer and knows the game. He is resting one hip and he seems to be asleep. The man is waiting, for some other vaqueros have entered the *ramadero* above him to start up the wild cattle. Presently he thinks that he catches the high note of a yell far up the brush; he feels a quiver in the muscles of his horse. The horse thinks that he hears too; he no longer appears to be asleep; his ears are cocked. A minute later the sound of the yell is unmistakable. The brush hand takes down his leg; the horse plants down the leg he has been resting and holds his head high, ears working. Again the yell, closer.

Pretty soon the popping of brush made by the running cattle will be heard. There will not be many cattle in the bunch, however—just three or four or a half dozen. Outlaws like company

BLACKSMITH'S BARN IN CASTROVILLE, TEXAS

The cowboy's or ranchman's name is Fritz Folk, the two blacksmiths are John Mechler and Les Schroeder, all part of the prosperous German community which settled just west and north of San Antonio before the Civil War. Folk has brought his saddled horse (hitched to the ground) to be shod along with the one he holds with a hackamore fashioned from his rawhide reata. Except for the oversize horn, the saddle is a Texas model of the 1880s, double rigged with a slick fork. His chaps are hung on a tie across the fork of his saddle and obscure the front latigo and cinch. The taps (tapaderos) are necessary to keep broken branches of south Texas brush from wedging his boot in a stirrup. The old man (Mr. Hartman) is the bookkeeper or owner, and the two young town dudes seem to have just arrived in the buggy, rear right. (COURTESY OF DR. M. W. SHARP, CASTROVILLE, TEXAS; COPY FROM INSTITUTE OF TEXAN CULTURES, UNIVERSITY OF TEXAS, SAN ANTONIO.)

but they are not gregarious. The vaquero's feet are planted deep in the stirrups now. *Pop—scratch*—silence. In what direction was that sound? The old horse's heart is beating like a drum against the legs of his rider. *Pop—scr-r-atch*—rattle and rake of hoofs. Man and horse hit the brush as one. They understand each other. They may get snagged, knocked by limbs that will not break, cut, speared, pierced with black thorns, the poison from which sends cold chills down the back of the man and makes him sick at the stomach. No matter. The horse and rider go like a pair of

mated dogs charging a boar. The brush tears and pops as if a
team of Missouri mules were running through it with a mowing
machine. The brush hand is in his element. . . .[4]

Cowboys collected herds of cows in the Brasada and in the coastal
prairies of the Gulf to send north in drives after the Civil War. The first
drives after the war came from the bayous of southeast Texas and from
the Cross Timbers region west of Dallas and the Heart-of-Texas region
west of Waco. The Texas cowboys, collecting the first herds and trailing
them north, taught all the Southern and Midwestern farm boys who came
west their working methods and skills. Those who had worked with cattle
to the east in the Southern pine and prairie barrens brought their older
working skills with them, to be selectively used and modified. By using
the century-old Southern Anglo experience, modified by the older Spanish-
Mexican experience, they made a new industry. As the industry grew
rapidly, the Texas cowboys were joined by migrations of cowboys new to
the Plains, from the piney woods of east Texas, the grassland prairies of
northeast Texas, the ranges of the Midwest and the Appalachian South
and the pine barrens coastal belt around the coast south from Carolina.
Together they devised and perfected the techniques required by the work
on the Great Plains. These were further modified to deal with barbed wire
and windmills and with fed and sheltered herds. The cattlemen, like Shanghai Pierce, who started as a cow hunter and drover, then became a rancher
and land speculator, then a drover again, and finally an entrepreneur in
all cattle dealings, helped to shape the industry too, but their stories, along
with those of the hired guns who protected their property, have already
been adequately told, often without mention of their hired hands.
   In the broadest view, an open-range cowboy worked with slaughter or
stocker cows, ideally one man for every 700 to 1,000 head on the range,
two or three for that many on the trail. They had to work with cows on
horseback, so they also had to work with horses. Corral and camp work
was on foot, but most of his working time was spent on a succession of
the six or seven horses, changed several times a day, in each cowboy's
mount. As a consequence, he had to know how to ride, gentle, train, and
care for any horse he was given. His horses were just tools owned and
provided by the boss. If a range cowboy owned a saddle horse, he had
to keep it in a special pasture at the headquarters ranch and pay his boss
for its feed. Having his own horse with him in the outfit's remuda would
make him too free and independent—he could quit and ride away. The
cowboy-worker always provided his own bed (tarp and blankets), saddle

blanket, saddle, bridle, and spurs. His work with cows was all concerned with maximizing the profit of the cattle company—the cows' welfare always came before his own, as did the welfare of the horses he rode, which were also capital investments of the owners. The cowboy was not a capital investment (although for a hundred years some black cowboys were); he just sold his work power to the cattleman or cattle company. When there was no work to do, he was let go at the end of the trail or the end of the fall, at which time he was out of work until he returned to his home ranch, if he had one, or until the cows lost their winter coats and brands were readable for the spring roundup. A few were kept on to chop wood and do odd jobs. The cowboy is a seasonal, migrant, agricultural laborer, and you couldn't get much lower than that, outside of casual contract workers with no trades, like hod carriers and ditch diggers, or the unemployed, such as drifters and petty thieves. But unlike the other main classes of workers in the big industries of the West—railroad employees, lumberjacks, miners, teamsters, sheepherders—and unlike service workers in support of the corporate employers, like prostitutes and sheriffs, there was a developing mystique about the cowboy craft which made them voluntary and proud. They had to have more skills than did the other kinds of Western workers hired by or supporting corporations; they had less supervision (until their work was specialized and rationalized); and, with the possible exceptions of miners and railroad brakemen, they worked under conditions of greater hardship and danger. Because they had the most skills for extremely hazardous and arduous work and received in return little security and material reward, they were among the most exploited corporate workers of the West. But they endured their exploitation, though to a lesser extent than has been realized, because they were proud of their skills, their craft, their tough and manly reputation, and their buddies in the outfit. Employers exploited them the more because of the growing myth of the cowboy, which made would-be cowboys plentiful and most employed cowboys willing to be exploited.

Andy Adams, an early range cowboy of southwest Texas, wrote in 1905, "If I have any word to say of these range riders, it is that no harder life is lived by any working man."[5] It is particularly important to realize how hard they worked because we tend to think of cowboys as idlers who break the monotony of lounging in saloons by an occasional fistfight. But during most of their working years, that is, on trail and during the long spring roundup, when steers were cut out and driven to railheads or stockyards, they worked from sunup to dark, besides doing a regular shift of two or three hours of guarding the bedded cattle at night. That is, they put in a

regular eighteen-hour day, although there could be long periods of monotonous watchfulness. During irregular circumstances they would go without any sleep or only catch snatches of sleep for several days on end—
holding milling herds on a dry run, collecting strays after a stampede,
getting a herd across a river before it was due to rise in spate.

We all have a dim knowledge of the old cowboy's working life, sleeping
on the ground on a bedroll, only a slicker to keep the rain off when he's
mounted, a diet of beans and beef and coffee, the dust of the trail and
the branding corral; but the details are vague, and lots of his jobs we don't
know about at all because we don't think of him as a laborer. Texas
cowhunters before the corporate era didn't have bedrolls (use your back
for a tarp and your belly for a blanket) or even beans, because there was
no chuckwagon, usually not even pack animals, on the hunt. But they
probably fared better on beef and game than later cowboys did from food
provided by cattle companies concerned with cutting costs. When Texas
chuckwagons later followed outfits, cooks served just beans, sowbelly,
cornbread, and coffee, and only occasionally beef when a crippled stray
turned up.[6] Some Wyoming chuckwagons provided better by adding some
dried apples, prunes, even canned tomatoes and peaches, because a few
sons of English and Eastern stockholders out West playing cowboy ate
from them. It is difficult to find evidence to prove it, but Texas cowboys
must have suffered from scurvy; there is evidence that they craved vegetables and fruit—they would eat the raw parsley that grew near streams
and wild plums and grapes, and they would bolt down boughten vegetables
when they came to town, often before going to the barber shop or saloon.
One outfit that had no vegetables on a drive from south Texas ate a whole
keg of pickles in Dodge: "the men would eat nothing else until they were
all devoured." One very early observer recognized that chuckwagon food
caused scurvy and that the cowboy particularly craved potatoes and on-
ions, but "any kind of vegetables will disappear in haste when put within
his reach."[7]

To continue our consideration of the rigors of cowboy work, we note
that they fought prairie fires as long as was necessary to protect the grass
on public land used by cattle companies. Siringo reports that in the late
seventies when fires blew southwest from the Staked Plains to threaten
grazing grass on the Canadian River Breaks, near present day Amarillo,
crews of cowboys from potentially affected cattle companies fought them
by dragging split steer carcasses over the advancing fire line and on foot
with wet saddle blankets or pieces of fresh hide for sometimes twenty-four
hours or more without relief.[8] It was the same grueling work required of

cowboys employed by the corporations leasing the Cherokee Strip to the north ten years later:

> I have seen a prairie fire break out from the reflection of the sun on a tin can. . . . The first men to arrive would begin back or counter firing as it was called, . . . with saddle blankets, beating out their own fire on the leeward before it could gain headway. . . . Within two or three hours after a prairie fire had thus started, there might arrive fifty to one hundred men. . . . Frequently several light cow brutes were killed, beheaded, and split down the spine, leaving only the hide to hold the body together. The carcass of the animal was then turned flesh down, ropes were fastened from a fore and hind foot to pommels of saddles; and riding astride the burning grass, the body was dragged over the fire, virtually rubbing it out. Other men followed on horseback, to beat out any remaining flames and relieve the mounts by pulling on the ropes; . . . Such a fire might last three hours or three days, at the termination of which, the men would ride for the nearest camp for rest and refreshment.[9]

Cowboys would have to control drifting herds of cattle during a dust storm, sometimes for so long that they would temporarily go blind from inflamed eyes. Cowboys riding drag, or on the leeward side of the herd, sometimes came "off herd with dust half an inch thick . . . on their hats and thick as fur on their eyebrows and mustaches." They would go to the water barrel and rinse their mouths and cough and spit up "black stuff."[10] If the remuda got tick-infested ears, they had to throw and hogtie each horse to swab out their ears with ointment. Regularly they had to work overtime to groom the horses in their mount: remove "witches' bridles" from manes, thin long tails, trim hooves.[11] If a steer became thoroughly mired, it was not just a matter of roping the critter and hauling it out by the horn of your saddle but first wading into the mess and tying back each of the hooves to prevent further miring by their thrashing. This was tedious and exhausting. During hailstorms, when there was no shelter or when cowboys couldn't leave cattle to seek shelter, they would hold their saddles over their heads. Cowboys drank *after* the wagon horses, the remuda, and the herd: "I had to chew that water before I could swallow it."[12]

There were the hardships of deep frosts and freezing winds on the northern ranges, caught here by Wallace Stegner in his story of Rusty, a young T-Down cowboy during a late fall roundup in southern Saskatchewan along the Frenchman River:

Sometime during that roundup they may have had a day of decent weather, but it seemed to Rusty it was a procession of trials: icy nights, days when a bitter wind lashed and stung the face with a dry sand of snow, mornings when the crust flashed up a glare so blinding that they rode with eyes closed to slits and looked at the world through their eyelashes. There was one afternoon when the whole world was overwhelmed under a white freezing fog, when horses, cattle, clothes, wagon, grew a fur of hoar frost and the herd they had gathered had to be held together in spooky white darkness mainly by ear.

On bright days they were all nearly blind, in spite of painting their cheekbones with charcoal and riding with hats pulled clear down; if they could see to work at all, they worked with tears leaking through swollen and smarting lids. Their faces grew black with sun and glare, their skin and lips cracked as crisp as the skin of a fried fish, and yet they froze. Every night the thermometer dropped near zero, and there was an almost continuous snake-tongue of wind licking out of the north or west.[13]

Their work was not only hard but extremely dangerous. One old Texas cattleman who started as a cowboy in the late seventies testifies that "no insurance company would in those days insure the life of a cowboy; nor is insurance for cowboys obtainable even now [late 1920s] except on payment of a very high premium, about three times that required of miners." (One wonders how many cowboys in the eighties tried to buy insurance.) He then gives a partial list of the main hazards that threatened the cowboy's life and limb: prairie fires, swollen rivers, stampedes, storms, freezing blizzards, man-killing horses, fighting cattle, holes for horses to step into, trees to run against, desperate outlaws and savage Indians, and ropes to betray him if used wrong.[14]

The least of the threats to his health were Indians, although we tend to think it the greatest. But cowboys *were* killed by Indians in the performance of their work during the first decade of the era. An old trail boss tells this story with cold, businesslike casualness as if it were all in the day's work, and he doesn't even give the names of the two cowboys who were victims. On the trail in 1871 in north Texas near Victoria Peak the day after a night stampede, two cowboys go off tracing two hundred strays. When they hadn't returned by the following morning, the boss and several more cowboys followed their trail about eight miles "and found the two men had been murdered by Indians, scalped and their bodies mutilated. We buried them and returned to our herd" to move it on to Red River Station.

Two workers died for two hundred cows purchased on speculation by a trailing company.[15]

The greatest of the deadly hazards was swollen rivers. Cowboys were not only drowned in putting herds across rivers under ordinary circumstances, which were dangerous enough, but trail bosses often ordered especially perilous crossings in order to maintain schedules imposed by owners or contractors concerned only with profits. Siringo tells of another common hazard—the serious maiming of a cowboy by an angry steer: the cowboy's spur had caught in the flank cinch of his saddle when the wild steer he had just roped jerked his horse over backwards on top of him; unable to free himself, he was badly gored and trampled. If he had not tied his rope fast to the saddle horn, he could have lessened the shock of the sudden jerk by slipping the rope and thus prevented a spill. But all Texas cowboys were trained to tie fast, instead of loose snubbing, to avoid the other danger of severing fingers or a thumb caught between rope and horn when the rope jerks tight with tremendous force. Either way has its dangers—losing fingers or getting gored. Siringo also tells of the dangers of corralling wild steers in the brush country of Texas. You couldn't get some "old fighting steers" into the corral because they'd break for timber nearby. You had to "tie the mad brute down till morning . . . a dangerous job for a lone cowboy if the night were dark." (If you ran out of bits of hobble rope or "piggin string," usually tied to your saddle for such occasion, you had to hogtie the steer with its own tail, although this was "against the rules" because he'd be lame for a few days.) If you were detailed at the railhead to accompany the cattle to market, there were still more dangers: on a trail taking a herd to Chicago, cowboys are in the caboose during a sleet storm. When the train stops, they all run forward along the tracks, dutifully punching up the cows in the cars that are not on their feet and could be injured by trampling. Just as they get to the front of the train, it takes off and they have to jump aboard and make their way back to the safety of the caboose along the icy walk on top, slipping in their high-heeled boots as they jump between cars.[16]

Another cowboy wrote about the same experience:

> The boys had to get what accommodation they could in the caboose, which was often jam-packed with railway officials; . . . at every halt the men had to jump out, one with a lantern and others with goads, walk along the rough ballast and peer into each car to discover beasts which required stirring up.
>
> "Having found an offender," wrote Tex [Bender], "you poke her, prod her, twist her tail and do your utmost to make her rise.

In the middle of your efforts the bell rings, the train starts; you clamber up the side of the car onto the roof, and when there make the best of your way back on top of the train to the rear car. . . . If you do not climb onto the roof you must take your chance of jumping onto the step of the last car as it goes by; this would be the reasonable way if you were allowed to do it; but as the engineer does not care to look back, you must consider whether you are sufficiently an acrobat to rejoin. Having reached Chicago there is an end of the business; the cattle are turned into the big stockyard, and sold by commission.[17]

All to protect corporate investment of probably not even the contract trailing company they worked for in Texas but some faceless cattle commission company with headquarters in Kansas City.

After windmills came to the plains, cowboys even had to fight snakes in wells to water the company's cattle:

The windmills and pumps of a ranch were in constant need of repair. In advance, in working in a well in the far South, we always lowered a man with a lantern and hatchet on the lookout for live snakes. Not a desirable task by any means, but with a pump out of order and a thousand suffering cattle lowing in their thirst, there was no alternative but to go down, kill the reptiles, hoist the piping, and repair the machinery. In an arid country, moisture attracts snakes, and many a fine well has been taken possession of by them, requiring a strenuous fight to recover it from its creeping possessors.[18]

Here's how one old cowboy explained his forced retirement after fifteen years of abuse to his body in grueling range work:

I have done as most cowpunchers do after they have got too stove up to ride. For a man to be stove up at thirty may sound strange to some people, but many a cowboy has been so bunged up that he has to quit riding that early in life. . . . My advice to any young man or boy is to stay at home and not to be a rambler, as it won't buy you anything. And above everything stay away from a cow ranch, as not many cowpunchers ever save any money and 'tis a dangerous life to live.[19]

As an example of the ordinary hazards of the roundup that brought him to this pass, we can cite this lively account the stove-up cowboy gives when he was a rep for the St. Louis Cattle Company:

> I was going to tell how near I come to getting my neck broke.
> We had all split up and started back. I was all alone on the drive.
> I struck a bunch of about seventy-five head and was trying to
> drive them. But they was very contrary and would not go the
> way I wanted them to go. I was riding like a drunk Indian trying
> to put them in the right direction. All at once my horse fell and
> rolled over me—turned a complete summerset. He mashed me
> some. When he fell he kindly knocked me senseless, as my head
> hit the ground first. The horse broke a front leg, as he stepped
> in a prairie dog hole and fell. He could not get up and I could
> not get my leg out from under him as it 'twas still fast in the
> stirrup. I could not see anybody as they had all gone on with the
> drive. I was dropped off soon and we had split to make the drive.
> All the boys had all left me. There I lay until about twelve o'clock
> [they had left the wagon "very early" that morning], as I was
> not missed until the roundup was all made and they all had
> changed horses.
>
> I was in a low place. They come to where I was dropped off
> and started the way I was to have went. I heard them hollow,
> which was good news for me. My pistol was still in my belt. I
> took it out and fired in the air. 'Twas not long till they found me,
> as I would fire a shot every little while. I had no bones broke but
> was mashed and skinned up to beat the band. My leg the horse
> lay on was nearly paralized. Poor old horse! His day was over.
> We turned him over and he could not get up. I hated to kill the
> poor fellow but it had to be done. A forty-five ball went through
> his brain. One of the boys took my saddle, another my blankets
> and bridle. I got up behind the other and we put off for the
> wagon. The St. Louis Cattle Co. was out a good horse and like
> to have been out a cowboy.[20]

To complete this picture of the occupational hazards of the trade, the
following summarizes a random collection of contemporary newspaper
and magazine accounts of injuries to cowboys in the eighties and nineties.
A cowboy with the Shoesole outfit in Idaho, when his horse stumbled in
trying to turn a stampede of 2,000 cattle, fell and was "mangled to sausage
meat"; the cowboy just behind him escaped with a broken leg because
he fell between the first cowboy's body and horse. In another stampede
in Idaho, two cowboys were killed in a fall off a cliff when their efforts
failed to turn the herd just on the brink. After tending herds in a Montana

winter, "with the snow belly-deep and the mercury often frozen in the bulb . . . lots of boys are in the hospital," and those still at work are in bad shape. "One chap that I saw out there had his fingers all off, but when I asked him to take something, he said, 'I will, pard' if you hold the bottle.' " About four in the morning in November an unexpected blizzard hit a herd of 1,800 beeves in New Mexico, which some cowboys were holding to load on railroad cars; the outfit became separated in attempting to hold the drifting herd, and three cowboys froze to death. A cowboy returning to his ranch after a roundup in Wyoming drowned in an attempt to swim his horse across a swollen creek. A cowboy on night herd near Pueblo, Colorado, was dragged to death on the prairie when "he became sleepy and tied himself on his horse with his lariat." Another Colorado cowboy seriously injured his leg when his horse stumbled and pinned him to the ground while he was "chasing some cattle." A 4-J cowboy near Newcastle, Wyoming, was trampled to death by a "bunch of horses" into which he was thrown by his pitching horse. A cowboy was knocked to the ground by a wild steer and "his nose . . . torn completely from his face. That he was not killed was owing to the fact that the long horns, wide apart, touched the ground on either side of the poor fellow's head as he lay prostrate." Another cowboy near Ogallala was repeatedly gored in the chest by a wild Texas steer as he lay with his legs pinned beneath the body of his horse, fallen in pursuit of the enraged steer.[21]

Most cowboys on ranches worked for very rich capitalists. In the seventies they typically worked for a partnership of a Western owner-manager and an Eastern financier or two. In the next two decades, with the need for increased capitalization, they worked for a joint stock corporation, with controlling shares owned by Eastern and European investors who as a board received reports from a Western manager. If he were a stockholder, the manager usually didn't have a controlling interest in the corporation. The stockholders made the big decisions; the manager gave the orders to the wagon bosses, who in turn controlled the cowboys. Cowboys were required to do what the changing economics of the cattle industry dictated. For instance, if the company wasn't making profits, that is, paying good dividends, there was a speedup: some cowboys were fired, and the rest had to work harder and longer. Since the purpose of cattle companies was to maximize profits, their working conditions (for instance, the quality and variety of their food) were as poor and their pay as little as possible, and what was possible depended on how compliant and disorganized the work force was and how many experienced unemployed cowboys were seeking work.

The economics, politics, organization, and culture of cattle raising differed from range to range—for instance, for many reasons the industry in
Montana developed late, and Colorado had farming ranches and consequently smaller ranches earlier than elsewhere.[22] But we can generalize
about most ranges. The two big employers of cowboys during the cowboy
era were the trail contracting companies and the range cattle companies.
Other branches of the cattle industry, like stockyard promoters, meat packers, the cattle commission merchants (brokerage houses for buying and
selling and later financing cattle and ranch land) did not employ cowboys
as workers.

At first ranchers took north herds of their own and, for set fees, cattle
of neighboring ranchers; but after only ten years (1875) more than two-
thirds (100,000 cattle) of the annual droving was done by transportation
agents or trailing contractors. Of all the Texas cattle trailed north in twenty-
five years, only 10 to 15 percent was done by ranchers who raised the
beef they trailed.[23] These trailing contractor companies were typically owned
and run by partnerships of Texas entrepreneurs, often of brothers, and
often of cattlemen who were ranchers or became ranchers after trailing.
Since the profits were immediate and great, for the few who succeeded
of the many who tried, there wasn't the need for the massive capitalization
that turned range cattle companies into Eastern-financed joint-stock companies in the eighties. The half-dozen or so big companies that did most
of the business were the ones who managed by their efficiency and ruth-
lessness to survive the huge losses of the periodic panics and depressions
endemic to uncontrolled capitalism, mainly that of 1873, when prices for
beeves at the railhead plummeted. As businessmen their concern was for
profit, and their trail bosses had to protect that profit above all else, which
meant protecting the herd: "In an emergency like the present," said a
cowboy about collecting strays after a stampede, "our foreman would
never give a thought to anything but the recovery of the herd. Our comfort
was nothing; men were cheap, but cattle cost money."[24] Even friends of
the trail contractors in the same social class perceived their lack of concern
for their cowboys: Joseph McCoy, the famed inventor and promoter of
cattle trading at railheads, wrote that many trail contractors "are apparently
indifferent to the health and comfort of the cow-boys in their employ."[25]

Like all successful capitalists, the big trail contractors pursued profit, but
the partly Western ownership of this part of the industry and the cowboy
origins of some of the contractors kept them—maybe—a little more re-
sponsive to the needs of their seasonally employed cowboys than were
the managers of range cattle companies, which were owned by Eastern
and European interests: the contractor or his agent after paying the boys

off would sometimes stand them to a round of drinks in Abilene or Ogallala and customarily send them off home with free railroad tickets, which he usually could obtain gratis as a business favor.[26] After less than two decades the trail driving business declined rapidly, mainly because by 1885 most of the states and territories of the Plains, fearing splenic fever, had enacted legislation against Texas cattle.[27]

The range cattle industry on the Great Plains, except for Texas, was mainly created by a gigantic promotional campaign of the railroad companies. Railroad public relations in the form of books, flyers, editorials, reportage planted in newspapers, and the hustling of their far-flung agents sought to get Eastern and European capitalists to invest in Western ranches.[28] The railroads wanted profit from freight and passenger service and sales of their immense land holdings by immigration westward. They held out prospects of huge profits from cheap cattle getting fat by eating the free grass of the public domain, just there for the taking. Eastern and British entrepreneurs responded with millions of dollars in investments. Most were from the northeastern seaboard (Wall Street), but there were many from Scotland, England, and cities in the Midwest, like St. Louis and Chicago. They formed cattle companies in partnership with a Western rancher or owned by themselves and managed usually by a hired Westerner but sometimes by one of themselves. The managers or part-owner-manager built a headquarters ranch house and corral and some line cabins, bought a chuck wagon or two and some cattle and horses, and hired some cowboys and were in business.

But expenses mounted both with the need to buy at least some land to protect access to water for the cattle and with the perceived need to increase the size of the herd to occupy and thus legitimize the extent of the range claimed by the company in competition with the ranges claimed by neighboring ranches. Both these expenses climbed as the land filled up with cows of cattle companies and, to a much lesser extent, the cows of homesteading ranchers. After a time they also had the expense of buying or breeding cattle, which yielded more meat than did longhorns, although the introduction of new herds with blooded bulls had to await fenced pastures to be very effective in improving the breed. Colorado law allowed Texas scrub bulls running at large to be shot on sight.[29] The development of improved beef herds is original under capitalism. Britain, the first capitalist country, was inevitably the first to undergo an agricultural revolution and to "breed an animal to mature early and produce the maximum amount of beef for the least amount of pasture, labor, and feed, regardless of his ability to pull a plow." A hundred years or so later, ranch managers for U.S. and British capitalists introduced Shorthorns, Herefords, Angus, and Brahmans onto the Western prairies.[30] It took capital and capitalism after the Civil War to do so.

Since expenses turned out to be higher than the railroads claimed, by the late seventies the companies, struggling to survive by acquiring more capital, changed from partnerships to joint-stock companies and then sold shares with the same kind of promotional literature and activities that the railroads had used on them, now in the form of company prospectuses, brochures, and ads. By the eighties most cows on the Plains belonged to joint-stock companies.

The range cattle industry of Texas developed differently because of government by counties, the existence of a state police (Texas and Home Rangers), state administration of leases and sales of public grazing land, and a predominance of ranches owned by Texans. We will take the last one first. The percent of out-of-state ownership of cows was less in Texas than in any other state or territory of the Plains. There were, of course, huge foreign holdings: the XIT Ranch was owned by a Chicago corporation; the Matador Ranch was owned by Scottish capitalists. But in contrast to the rest of the Plains, where almost all of the cattle companies were Eastern and European, the barons in Texas, like Charles Goodnight, were mostly Texans (although even he had a Scottish partner). The reason for this local capitalization is, of course, that the industry arose in Texas during early laissez-faire capitalism among local trader-trailer-cow-hunter cattle-men, who, later under corporate capitalism, themselves became the investors in big family cattle companies. Indeed many were cattle barons in several branches of the industry, like Goodnight and George Saunders, who respectively invested in Texas ranches and cattle commission firms the capital they accumulated in trailing, and Shanghai Pierce, who supplemented the capital he accumulated in ranching by profits from trailing. In the more northern Plains, where there were few native cattlemen to finance a brand-new industry, the capital had to come from the East.

The other differences noted above all favored big corporate ranches with fenced ranges and managed herds. As a result, the Texas cattle companies eliminated the competition of the small ranchers and fenced and managed their herds (and workers) far sooner than did the interloping cattle companies to the northwest. The county system of registration of brands, recording of sales, and inspection of herds protected the property of cattle companies. The cattle of a small family rancher would often be legally appropriated or the family rancher arrested on trumped-up warrants by the company's or the cattle association's control of county government. The northern companies had to rely on hired assassins to eliminate nester ranchers and to wait to seize nester cattle "legally" until their associations controlled the commissions of the state or territory. The Texas companies had the Rangers to call on to catch thieves, or family ranchers they designated as thieves, in order to get rid of them. Or they had the institution of the Home Rangers to provide legal cover for their hired posses of terrorists hunting down small competitors. Northern companies had to rely on the private sector—they had to hire Pinkertons, cattle detectives, assassins, and even small armies of gunmen to do the same thing.

Since the state of Texas, as a provision of its annexation, owned and controlled its own public land and developed and enforced laws for leasing and sales particularly suited to the cattle industry, grazing land could be acquired in legal sections and improved over a guaranteed period. Panhandle cattle companies fought the land laws during the eighties, but they didn't know their own interests. With their land defined and protected and their tenure on it secure, the Texas cattle companies line-rode and later fenced the borders of their huge ranches and then cross-fenced them into pastures, each with a watering place provided if necessary by a windmill. As a result they could farm hay, feed their herds, and improve them by selective reproduction with breeding bulls. In contrast, the northern cattle companies were competitively scrambling for free public lands by claiming ranges as big as their herds warranted and as their guns and later their associations could protect. Without the security of land tenure, they could not fence their ranges and manage and improve their herds. But, for all of these reasons, in Texas sooner than on the rest of the Plains there took place the "transition of the cattle trade from the wheeler-dealer aspects of the open range to the more conservative business practices of planned management."[31]

There was not time to develop cost-efficient management of the huge corporate ranches on the Great Plains during the boom years. In fact, the failure of management to reduce costs by production control, mainly through management's greedy blindness to the necessity of feeding and sheltering their herds, contributed to the bankruptcy of most of the giant cattle companies by the end of the century. Thus the work of cowboys outside Texas was not completely controlled during their heyday, another reason why they didn't strike as much as other corporate workers of the frontier and why Texas cowboys struck first. When their work was controlled by scientific management in our century, there were not so many of them; and because they were working on smaller farming ranches with fenced pastures, the work they did had changed fundamentally. But during the heyday of the cowboy, which corresponds with the boom times of the open range cattle industry (the late seventies and the first half of the eighties), and lasting on in a diminished and changing form during the last decade of the century, cattle companies were struggling for control of production. Control is central to management. The cattle companies strove to control their work force and their ranges. They failed to do so not because they were not ruthless enough but because their managers couldn't see the need for a new way of ranching in a West that was filling up.

Beginnning in the seventies, the cattle companies struggled to control their work force and their ranges by regional associations of cattlemen. These associations arose in answer to threats to their cattle and to the public land they claimed. The threat to their cattle was caused by either outright theft (rustling) or more often the appropriation by family ranchers of cows of unknown or dubious ownership (mavericking). The threat to their ranges came from an increasing number of settlers who took up 160-acre legal claims to federal land or, in Texas, took up leases of public land, all of which—and the mavericks on it—the corporations thought belonged to them. Ordinarily a "maverick" is an unbranded head of cattle of whatever age, but, like "dogie," it can be applied to any cattle, so that "mavericking" can simply mean rounding up cattle.[32] When Siringo writes that "some days we would brand as high as 3 or 400 Mavricks [sic]—none under 2 years old,"[33] he uses the word correctly and loosely to mean any unbranded cattle. (In a related usage, a person who is a "maverick" doesn't belong to anybody.) A narrower meaning, the legal one and the one used in this book, designates unbranded cattle *of unknown ownership*, usually calves or yearlings lost or weaned, that is, separated from their branded and earmarked mothers. These, from time immemorial, having no mother to claim them, as it were, belonged to the finder—that is, until some state and territorial legislatures attempted to change custom by appropriating them by law exclusively to the possessing class.

"Stockmen are learning more and more to act together," Theodore Roosevelt wrote in the mid-eighties of his own class. They are, he said self-admiringly, "the pioneers of civilization."[34] He was referring to the Montana Stock Growers' Association, of which he was a member. It had control of all the roundups and indeed influenced most aspects of economic and civil life in the basin of the Upper Missouri. The first such regional organization, the Stock Growers Association, founded in Denver as early as 1867, united large cattlemen in northern Colorado and surrounding ranges to oppose loss of their beeves to trailers and thieves.[35] The Wyoming Stock Growers Association, whose parent organization was founded as early as 1871, came to control Wyoming more tightly and totally than any of the other regional associations.[36] The first in Texas was the Stock Raisers' Association of Western Texas, founded by Richard King's partner Mifflin

Kenedy in 1870.[37] What became "the most powerful organization of cowmen in the world," the Southwestern Cattle Raisers' Association, began in northwest Texas with Charles Goodnight as a founder in 1877.[38] Its single purpose at first was "dealing with cattle thefts."[39] A few years later, when the huge cattle companies, mainly owned by Scottish, Chicago, and Boston capitalists, filled up the Canadian River and Palo Duro regions to the northwest, the managers and owners formed the powerful Panhandle Cattlemen's Association. Its primary purpose also was protection of the property of the big cattle companies, that is, putting an end to "outlawry."[40] In spite of these apparently innocent beginnings, these were not like neighborhood associations against burglars but the beginnings of monopolistic efforts at restricting ranges for big capital unencumbered by independent producers.

Every region of the Great Plains had its stock growers' association formed to protect the interests of the cattle companies by political control over state or territorial government (and in Texas, county government). Their power over political-economic life was in direct proportion to the relative power of the cattle industry in each region. In Wyoming, where the cattle industry was the only industry except for the Union Pacific Railroad, its control was total before 1886 and strong after 1900, the political decline representing the economic slump and partial recovery during the reorganization of the industry. In Colorado, where the economy was more diversified, the stock associations had to share political power with associations of mining and other interests.[41] The rule is simple, of course: the degree to which an industry controls the economy determines the degree to which it controls politics. By this rule, the varied and conflicting interests of the entrepreneurs, both within the cattle industry and between all industries, prevented them from being effective beyond their regional organizations of range interests. They could not lobby as a national industry. Indeed the abortive attempts at forming national cattlemen associations repeatedly failed because of fights between packers and range cattlemen, investors in Southwest ranches and investors in Northern ranches. An attempt at a national cattle trust, that is, a national *economic* monopoly, also failed.[42] These were the formative days of monopoly capitalism, before ways were fully developed for combining conflicting interests into conglomerates and before the government intervened to regulate competition. But on the regional level cattle companies in association were extremely powerful.

Regional cattle associations sought by influencing and electing legislators and packing commissions with association members to make territorial or state law embody association resolutions. They would offer rewards for

cattle thieves and for prairie-grass and barn burners, and they would distribute wanted posters and place wanted ads. They hired their own detectives or commissioned detective agencies like Pinkerton to help apprehend,
scare off, or fairly often simply assassinate rustlers or homesteading ranchers. These detectives were nothing more than hired guns, like Tom Horn,
hit men who killed on a fee basis for the cattle association. Cattle associations hired or commissioned cattle inspectors to watch for burnt brands
in nester ranchers' pastures, on trails and at railheads, and even in out-
of-state stockyards. They could seize for the association all herds it had
declared to be "mavericks" (herds supposedly created by branding mavericks), even though they were clearly marked with registered brands of
honest family ranchers.

The associations brought roundups totally under their control. They
designated the areas covered by the separate roundups, the foreman of
each, and the starting dates of each. They often prevented any nonmember
small rancher from inspecting for and cutting out his brand or sending a
rep to do so. They sought to control all mavericks by preventing by law
with stiff penalties branding before the authorized roundups or indeed at
any time except under the eyes of an official roundup foreman. Also, the
roundup foreman appropriated all mavericks for the association and usually
sold them in herds at token prices only to association members, with funds
accruing to the association. In some cases the roundup foreman would
vent or obliterate brands that the association declared "maverick" or "rustler," burn in the association brand, and sell such cattle in herds to an
association member at nominal prices.

Most of these laws and procedures went beyond protecting industry
cattle to preserving monopoly by opposing homesteading ranchers, who
otherwise would compete for ranges, water rights, and prices at the stockyards. By thus discouraging family ranching, these laws would also make
cowboys dependent on their jobs by making the homesteading alternative
more difficult. Capitalism characteristically tends to create unemployment
so that wages stay down. Here was another motive to oppose shoestring
ranchers—turn them into a pool of unemployed cowboys to keep wages
down. Associations also published booklets with member brands, ear-
markings, and ranges of public land claimed. They lobbied not only in
state and territorial capitols but to a lesser degree in Washington. They
also issued committee reports on labor policy, with recommendations about
setting wages and regulations on the conduct and lives of cowboys.

Cattle company control over workers took some of the same forms that
other industries in the Gilded Age were attempting to impose. But the
work and the workers on the open ranges resisted the application of

scientific management for two reasons. First, the nature of the work itself was uncongenial to systematic hierarchical control. Second, and even more important, the cowboys' culture resisted it. Cattle companies had almost no success in turning cowboys into robots on the open ranges and only a limited success on the huge cross-fenced ranges that survived for a brief time the liquidations and bankruptcies beginning in the late eighties. But they tried.

First of all, for greater control they organized their ranches in a pyramid. They imposed on the range cattle company the earlier merchant capital "structure of branch organization subdivided among responsible managers."[43] The chairman of the board of directors controlled the manager, who controlled the ranch foreman, who controlled the cowboys, cook, and accountant. If the ranch were large, as it generally was, there were as many foremen or wagon bosses as necessary, each supervising about a dozen cowboys and a cook and reporting to the manager. If the large ranch was cross-fenced or otherwise separated into pastures, each foreman had jurisdiction over his own pasture, where he maintained a camp with some bunkhouses or dugouts, a cook house, and corrals and a barn for blacksmithing, feed, and tack.

Management in all industries learned at this time to increase profits by dividing all the labor to be performed into specialized processes, each performed by a worker skilled only in that process. The new worker could thus be paid less than the old worker capable of performing them all. As a further way of dividing labor to increase profits, since some specialized processes required minimum skill or strength, they could be performed by low-paid workers hired from the largest pools of unemployed, women and children. At a glance, one can see that the labor of cowboys could not be divided into tasks like the labor of factory workers. In this regard he is like the general farm hand, who must do all the tasks of farming—plowing, milking, caring for animals, mending fences and farm machinery, and the rest. But he is unlike the seasonal farm worker who does the plantation-like tasks in crews, like planting and harvesting. The cowboy had to do everything related to handling cattle—to drive, hold, cut, rope, tie, and brand, to mention the main categories, each with a score of related tasks. But the industry tried to divide the cowboy's labor as much as the nature of his work permitted. They usually could build on conventional divisions that originated before the period of corporate control. The wrangler had the specialized job of tending the remuda, the saddle horses of each wagon crew not being ridden at any given time. He worked harder and longer than anyone else; he was the bottom of the pecking order and did all the shit work, like gathering firewood; and he didn't have to have all the skills of a cowboy. As a consequence, beginners, apprentice cowboys, and minorities like Mexicans and less often blacks[44] could be hired for the job at half the wages of a regular cowboy. Occasionally an outfit had an even lower job, assistant to the wrangler—the "nighthawk." He was paid even less. Since cooks were hard to get, they received more than a top hand, but we will not consider them here because they are not cowboys—as indeed we will not consider all the other non-cowboy jobs on a big ranch: managers, accountants, blacksmiths, house servants in the headquarters ranch, storehouse keepers, farmhands (on those ranches that raised feed), and security personnel (to use a nice name for hired guns). Bronc busters were sometimes hired just to do that work, sometimes not on a salary but as a kind of piecework, so much per horse. They were often itinerant, and would move on when the job was done. Perhaps proportionately more blacks and Mexicans than Anglos were specialized bronc busters; and Mexicans, at least, could be got cheap, even for this dangerous and skilled work of gentling horses. The only other cowboy job that was separated by task and specialized skill was the foreman or wagon boss, whom we must think of as a cowboy. He received two or three times as much pay as the top hand, shared in doing all the work of the cowboys he supervised (except night herding and work on foot in the branding area) and was usually more on the side of the working class he came from than the bosses he represented. His higher pay represented partly the company's attempt to shift his allegiance from the workers to his employers. But wagon bosses more often than not joined, even led, the cowboy strikes in the Texas Panhandle in 1883 and three years later on several roundups in the Sweetwater, Platte, and Powder River areas in Wyoming.

There was no other separation of tasks based on skill, but there was separation of degrees of experience in a job that required a high minimum skill for everyone employed. Those with the most responsible jobs, like riding point, where the steers were most restless and inclined to break away, received five to ten dollars more a month than the less experienced; those with the onerous and less responsible jobs, like riding drag, where steers were tired and docile but had to be doggedly pushed ahead in the dust, received as little as half the basic wage. The *segundo*, the cowboy put in charge in the foreman's absence, often drew double wages. The belief that all cowboys in an outfit got the same pay is fostered by the myth of the West, which mystifies the class struggle, part of which involved bosses maximizing profits by paying wages as low as the availability of different grades of labor made possible. The modern historian of the industry generalizes the rule: "The number of men employed, as well as the wages paid them, was kept as small as possible by most managers."[45]

There were also variations of wages less dependent on the division of labor or on the division of responsibility than on how many and what kinds of unemployed cowboys were around to hire. When smaller, fenced ranges, pens, branding chutes, and branding tables came in, employers drew from the larger worker pool of the less skilled. Before that time, wages for cowboys stayed pretty much the same for the two decades after about 1875, when the *average* wage got up to its standard figure of thirty dollars a month. This monthly wage was higher in the North, where the season of employment was shorter. Since a dollar a day was twice as much as other agricultural workers earned,[46] the cowboy was elite in that class, doubtless one reason why many sons of farm workers turned to cowboying. Texas cowboys in the early days only received fifteen to twenty dollars a month.[47] About this time, John Wesley Iliff paid forty cowboys on his ranch on the South Platte River twenty-five to thirty dollars a month.[48] Wages declined when calf counts and beef prices declined. In 1886 the Wyoming Stock Growers Association reduced base wages through the ranges it controlled from forty dollars to thirty-five dollars a month, thus causing a fairly general strike at the spring roundup.[49] Two years later, the Union Cattle Company on one of their ranches paid thirty-eight dollars a month for eleven cowboys hired in April for pre-roundup work, less than thirty dollars for about twenty cowboys hired just for the roundup, and fifty dollars in December for only six cowboys kept for the winter work of feeding stock and line riding.[50] So the year-round cowboys, only about one-fifth of all employed cowboys on the northern ranges, received higher wages than the seasonal ones. Trail cowboys got more than range cowboys because of the smaller labor market for that short, single-shot contract work requiring especially skilled and dependable men. Although they could rope better than most anybody else, Mexican cowboys regularly worked for half or less of the base pay because that was what they were used to and the best they could do. But blacks, twice as numerous as Mexican cowboys and constituting about one-fourth of all cowboys, generally received the same pay as whites.[51]

The average wage, then, in the eighties for a non-Mexican cowboy was probably about a dollar a day. This would mean that the average cowboy received less than $300 a year, because his work was seasonal and, for perhaps a third of all cowboys, casual; that is, they were just hired for roundups of two or three months in the spring and the fall. The best comparison for wages is to those of sailors, also unmarried workers in skilled, dangerous jobs who lived away from family and home and whose wages were monthly and included board. Able-bodied seamen on long Pacific voyages received about twenty-five dollars a month during our period, which would be about the same annual wage as that of cowboys because they would lose less earnings between trips than cowboys would between seasonal jobs. (Interestingly, mates received sixty dollars and galley cooks thirty-five, roughly commensurate to wagon bosses and range cooks.)[52] But the cowboy was better off than the average American adult male worker in the eighties, who made about the same $300 but who, unlike the cowboy, had a minimum yearly expense of about $516 for the bare subsistence of a family, several members of which obviously had to work to get by.[53] And he was better off only because, almost uniquely among Western workers, his work required the whole class of employed cowboys to live in all-male groups away from home and consequently to be sheltered and fed at company expense.

If we add on to the cowboy's salary what food, fuel, and rent would have cost him for the average nine months he was employed (52 percent of the income for the average family),[54] then his real dollar salary is over $500, considerably higher than the average industrial worker's salary in 1880 of $345. But the unemployed, outdoor, unmarried cowboy with a bedroll and a rifle to shoot game would not have spent 52 percent of his salary on room and board, except in winter, when he was not cowboying anyway. The cowboy earned way more, however, almost beyond sight more than the shocking $150 a year (with board, in 1880–1881) received by farm laborers. The cowboy, then, is among the better paid workers in the West, far better than his miserably paid kin, the farm worker, only one step below the farmer class from which most cowboys came. And in 1880 farm workers were still almost half of all workers in America.[55] One can understand how young farm boys, coming from the largest class of workers in the country, would dream of becoming what they saw as well-heeled cowboys and how this pool of aspirants provided pressure to keep employed cowboys obedient to their masters.

Cowboys were by no means in an elite wage bracket in comparison to skilled industrial workers, like the very few skilled factory workers who made four dollars a day or railroad engineers who in 1890 made more than three times as much as cowboys. (Baggagemen and firemen made about the same as cowboys.) But the cowboys' $300 per year as fed and housed bachelors was better in 1890 than railroad brakemen ($212, shockingly low for the danger involved), flagmen ($224), and railroad laborers ($124, mostly Mexican).[56] Since they got a little more than the less-than-subsistence wage of the average American worker, they were constantly threatened by wage cuts, especially after the end of the cattle boom in the mid-eighties, when rigid economies were instituted by the industry. They were also threatened by those who wanted to be cowboys not only because of the glamour of the image but because of the better-than-average pay, as low as that was. Further, the miserably low general wage of American workers as contrasted to the better pay of the cowboy also explains why cowboys continued to go on cowboying, in spite of the treatment by their employers.

Another step of scientific management was to Taylorize production: to take over the skill of the worker, embody that skill in prescriptions of how specialized jobs were to be performed, and to set time minimums for each task. Such production control could work for producing Fords or even fattening steers in feeding pens, but not for breeding calves and fattening steers on a range. But if management couldn't Taylorize the range part of the cattle industry, it could at least exercise some systematic control of production, the essence of scientific management. First of all, the board of a cattle company would instruct its manager to hire fewer cowboys to do the work that larger outfits had done the year before. One former cowboy wrote that in northern Wyoming after the dry summer of 1886, "the working force was curtailed in every way . . . was cut down to one-half."[57]

The movement to disarm the cowboy is relevant here, since one of its purposes was to remove distractions from his work, but disarming goes beyond that. It is part of the effort of all the new industrialists in America to create among their workers moral behavior appropriate to production— sobriety, application, obedience, seriousness, and indifference to personal leisure and pleasure. The movement to disarm cowboys significantly started in 1882, just when management of cattle companies, encouraged by regional associations, began to seek greater control of production of beeves on the range. In the seventies one of the cowboy's jobs was to use his own gun to protect his boss's cows and his boss's range. Now an industry-wide division of labor was to be implemented—cowboys should stick to nurturing cows and leave law and order to specialists. Southwestern cattlemen at the Stockmen's Convention in Caldwell, Kansas, in March 1882, unanimously adopted a resolution against cowboys carrying six-shooters. The resolution was supported widely in the trade press, including the powerful *Texas Livestock Journal*, and the next year the Wyoming Stock Growers Association adopted a similar resolution. In several states, including Texas, cowboys were disarmed by law.[58] And following the recommendations of their associations, many ranches, particularly the large ones, forbade their cowboys from carrying guns. For instance, here is Rule No. 11 (1888) of the mammoth XIT Ranch in the Texas Panhandle: "No employee of the Company, or of any contractor doing work for the Company, is permitted to carry on or about his person or in his saddle bags, any pistol, dirk, dagger, sling shot, knuckles, bowie knife or any other similar instrument for the purpose of offense or defense. Guests of the Company, and persons not employees of the ranch temporarily staying at any of its camps, are expected to comply with this rule, which is also a State law."[59]

Come to think of it, the idea of your average employee of a corporation working with a Colt .45 strapped to his waist was appalling. How could you have compliant, obedient, disciplined, efficiently productive workers if they are armed to the teeth? Keep the weapons in the hands of the forces of law and order. Increasing armies of these forces—rangers, state militia, gangs of goons and gun thugs, Molly Maguire fighters, Pinkertons, U.S. marshals, and Army regiments—were needed in the eighties and early nineties to suppress worker organizing, demands, strikes, resistance to scientific management. Why should cowboys be an exception? Take cowboys' six-shooters away and they would be less independent, all the time threatening to quit and to go into business for themselves, making outrageous demands. Take the equalizer away and they would act like the inferiors that range workers were supposed to be.

It is not generally realized that owner-managers and other company agents who worked with cowboys were ultrareactionary in their politics, and, although they cherished the image they created for themselves of the loyal and dutiful cowboy, down deep they hated cowboys as a class or at the least showed indifference to their needs as human beings. When there were no labor problems and cowboys seemed dutiful and compliant, the owners praised and admired their employees. But let the cowboys resist their exploitation and the owners' abiding contempt for the working class emerges. Six months before the first big, organized strike of cowboys, the trade journal of their employers called the typical Texas cowboy a man of "more than ordinary culture and refinement" who gave "his entire devotion to the interests of his employer . . . *par excellence,* a model in this respect." Half a year later and a month after many of their cowboys went on strike, the owners through the same journal called publicly, although with some verbal deviousness, for a local troup of Texas Rangers to make a "clean job" of "exterminating" the lawless cowboy strikers.[60]

John Clay, the Chicago cattle commission agent, cattle broker, and hard-ass reorganizer of the Swan Land and Cattle Company, is typical of his class in his attitude to cowboys. He hated all cowboys, particularly Texas cowboys, except for a minority of them who became company finks. He almost thought of cowboys as a separate breed. Texas cowboys were thieves by birth: "like many Texas importations of those days, he was a natural born thief." "Occasionally" a cowboy would turn out as well as Owen Wister's Virginian, said Clay, but "the ordinary cowboy usually degenerated, drifted, disappeared, or worse still, became a saloon keeper." Of Texas cowboys who stayed north, "the average run of these men was below par. Many of them left their native state because it was necessary for them to do so. They were . . . handy with their rope, light-fingered in ranch and camp, exceedingly fond of card playing, a bit brutal to their horses, quiet at their work, but noisy and treacherous under the influence of liquor." They got into trouble by idleness in winter, when they were laid off, "and as they generally had a good horse or two they began mavericking, and it was only a step from this to stealing outright." Of a suspected rustler, Clay wrote that "he had that southern cowpuncher swagger, which can only be quelled by the sight of a Texas ranger. . . . A six months' dose of them would have done Wyoming good in the days of which we write [the nineties]." (Note in passing Clay's quite accurate perception of Texas Rangers as cowboy quellers.) Of a tenderfoot range manager of a big Wyoming ranch: "He employed a lot of Texas cowboys, mostly bad men. . . . They handled cattle roughly, just as they did in Texas in the old days. Whenever a steer saw them, they ran." Of another weak-kneed range manager of a big Wyoming ranch: "He lost control of his men and if you wish to be ridden over, stamped upon, get a cowboy to do it, and more especially the brand we employed in those days [1884] in the Sweetwater region [of Wyoming]. They were the real simonpure, devil-may-care, roystering, gambling, immoral, revolver-heeled, brazen, light-fingered lot and yet a dash of bravado among them that was attractive to the stranger. . . . 'In the herd' they were mean and to hesitate with them meant losing. If they bluffed you, goodby to any discipline."[61] Thus the spokesman of tough, strong-arm personnel management in the cattle in-dustry. Given this belief that cowboys were thieving, bullying, violent brutes, it is no wonder that bosses made efforts to tame them by the iron control of management into meek dependency and single-minded application to work, and one of the first steps in their process was, naturally enough, to disarm them.

Then the cattle company insured that its cowboys gave full attention to their job of nurturing beeves by removing other distractions to their work besides gunplay. Again we can use the "General Rules of the XIT Ranch," which were more explicit and formal than most but typical of the sometimes verbal or just understood rules on all big company spreads from the mid-eighties on. The XIT Rules were devised in 1888 by the business manager and the range manager, printed and required by the last rule, No. 23, to be "nailed up in a conspicuous place in the camp." There were seven camps, one in each of the "pastures." Adherence to the rules are "to be considered a condition" of employment. Three rules forbid favorite cowboy amusements—roping wild game, gambling, and drinking:

No. 10:   Employees are not allowed to run mustang, antelope or any kind of game on the Company's horses.

No. 12:   Card playing and gambling of every description, whether engaged in by employees, or by persons not in the service of the Company, is strictly forbidden on the ranch.

No. 15:   Employees are strictly forbidden the use of vinous, malt, spirituous, or intoxicating liquors, during their time of service with the Company.

Rule No. 10 above not only removes a distraction to work but protects company property, in this case company wild game and company saddle horses. Lots of other rules are designed to protect company property, like No. 8: "The killing of beef by any person on the ranch, except by the person in charge of the pasture, or under his instruction, is strictly forbidden. Nor is the person in charge of a pasture allowed to have beef killed, unless it can be distributed and consumed without loss. And all hides of beef killed must be taken care of and accounted for. It shall be the duty of each person having beef killed to keep a tally of the same and report the number, age and sex killed to headquarters every month"; No. 9: "The abuse of horses, mules or cattle by any employee will not be tolerated"; and No. 13: "In case of fire upon the ranch, or on lands bordering on the same, it shall be the duty of every employee to go to it at once and use his best endeavors to extinguish it." Other rules make economies, like limiting hospitality to travelers and to freighters (abolishing the grub line) and conserving company grain and grass:

No. 17:   Employees of neighboring ranches on business are to be cared for at all camps, and their horses fed if desired (provided there is feed in the camp to spare); but such persons will not be expected to remain on the ranch longer than is necessary to transact their business, or continue their journey.

No. 18:   Bona fide travelers may be sheltered if convenient, but they will be expected to pay for what grain and provisions they get, at prices to be fixed from time to time by the Company, and all such persons must not remain at any camp longer than one night.

No. 19:   Persons not in the employment of the Company, but freighting
          for it, are not to be furnished with meals for themselves or feed
          for their time at any of the camps on the ranch, but are expected
          to come on the ranch prepared to take care of themselves.

Other rules merely provide for control over what happens on the ranch,
like the catchall one, handy for the company in another way to be discussed
below, excluding undesirables (No. 20: "Loafers, 'sweaters,' deadbeats,
tramps, gamblers, or disreputable persons, must not be entertained at any
camp, nor will employees be permitted to give, loan or sell such persons
any grain, or provisions of any kind, nor shall such persons be permitted
to remain on the Company's land anywhere under any pretext whatever")
and procedures for hiring and firing and transferring from one wagon to
another (Nos. 1, 2, 3, 4).

Most striking are those rules which appear innocuous but are really
designed to control the loyalties and dependence of cowboys:

No. 5:   No person in charge of any pasture, or any work on the ranch,
          or any contractor on the ranch, will be permitted to hire any one
          who has been discharged from the Company's service; nor shall
          anyone who leaves an outfit, of his own accord, with the intention
          of getting employment at some other place on the ranch, be so
          employed except by special agreement.

This blackballs all fired cowboys and those who transfer between wagons
or camps to avoid being fired. Nos. 6 and 7 provide grounds for firing a
cowboy who is trying to run his own herd on his own nearby ranch, which
would require only registering a brand, leasing some acres, building a
dugout and a corral, and buying a few horses and cattle.

No. 6:   Private horses of employees must not be kept at any of the camps,
          nor will they be allowed to be fed grain belonging to the Company.
          No employee shall be permitted to keep more than two private
          horses on the ranch and all such horses must be kept in some
          pasture designated by the ranch manager.

No. 7:   No employee shall be permitted to own any cattle or stock horses
          on the ranch.

Look at the consequence of these rules. A cowboy is immobilized because
he does not have his own horse among the remuda of his wagon. Since
the headquarters pasture where he may keep a horse is inaccessible,
probably a day's ride away, he can't visit his nearby home ranch at night

or return his own strays which he has found during the day's work, unless in the unlikely event his wagon boss would allow him to use a company horse for such purposes. Of course a Panhandle cowboy can't run his own brand on the ranch of his employer. But the rule in effect prevents him from owning a ranch—it allows him to be fired if his cattle stray onto XIT range or even graze just over an ill-defined boundary. If a cowboy who owns a neighboring ranch has cattle that stray onto the XIT range, he can be fired, blackballed, and never rehired. Blackballed, he cannot even be his own rep at XIT roundups, because the rule providing for reps (see No. 17 above) specifies that reps must be "employees of neighboring ranches," thus excluding cowboys with their own brand, and indeed all single-family ranchers—that is, limiting reps to the big cattle companies. Besides, fired cowboys under Rule No. 3 are "expected to leave the ranch at once." If he returned looking for his strays, he would be classed as a "disreputable" person under No. 20 (see above) and kicked off the ranch. The effect of these rules goes beyond control of workers in the workplace to determining what they cannot do with the rest of their lives, namely, have a family and a ranch of their own. Further, as a final control, workers are required by Rule No. 16 to inform on each other: "It is the duty of every employee to protect the Company's interests to the best of his ability, and when he sees they are threatened in any direction to take every proper measure at his command to accomplish this end, and as soon as possible to inform his employers of the danger threatened." Thus, even if you didn't own your own brand you were supposed to rat on a fellow cowboy who did, because an XIT cowboy moonlighting as a family rancher is clearly a threat to "the Company's interests." The rule (No. 22), requiring employees to excel in "good behavior, sterling honesty, and integrity, and general high character" by adhering to all the Rules, merely records in the disgusting phrases of American big business the determination that all cowboys be straight-arrow company men.

So cattle companies tried to control events off their ranges by ranch rules. They went further by discouraging shoestring settlers. Most settler or homesteading ranchers were former cowboys, whose very American desire to have their own spreads was so general and went so deep that it recurs in the popular myth to this day. Indeed the desire for independence intensifies as the percentage of the self-employed steadily decreases with the progress of capitalism. In *The Gunfighter*, Jimmy Ringo (Gregory Peck), casting about for a way to salvage a wrecked life, accepts as a future model the young family ranchman he meets in the saloon. Can anything be more true to the American Dream?

GREGORY PECK AS JIMMY RINGO IN *THE GUNFIGHTER* (1950)

The bartender is Mac (Karl Malden). At the same bar, Ringo later drinks with Johnny, a young married cowboy who tells him about how he is establishing his own ranch. Later Ringo tells his friend Marshal Mark Street (Millard Mitchell) that he wants to leave the outlaw's life and, like Johnny, have a little spread of his own.

In any case, cattle companies and their associations were fiercely hostile to all settlers, particularly those who owned a brand and ran cattle. There are exceptions to this rule—for a brief time Montana was one such—but they only prove it. Cattle companies came to think of all nesters as thieves to be exterminated. This attitude, characteristically contradicting the cowboy's dream of his own spread, also became part of the myth: a small spread is both to be coveted and discouraged. The first middle-class, slick novel with a cowboy hero romanticizes and justifies in its most basic structure this corporate attitude and practice: the Virginian endangers his relation with his sweetheart by lynching a blackballed cowboy for his boss. Owen Wister spoke for the big cattle companies, who fought and hated their cowboys even more after they fired them than they did while they employed them.

If you were an ex-cowboy in the eighties trying to establish a spread of your own, this is the situation you'd find. To put it in the then current language of the Plains, you wanted to be a *ranch*man and live on your ranch, not a *cattle*man and own cattle absentee. All the public domain would be considered to belong to the cattlemen by customary, though not by legal, right. All the roundups would be organized and controlled by the big companies through their cattle associations, from which you were barred from membership as a small settler. You wouldn't want to join anyway, because they were the enemy and were out to get you. In prairie states and territories the cattle associations controlled most of the institutions of government, which protected the interests of the absentee cattlemen. If you were daunted by the odds against a small ranchman in one area, you might move to another, like along the Pecos in the New Mexico Territory or the Powder River tributaries in northern Wyoming, where you could have a better chance because the old barons, like John Chisum, and the cattle associations, like the WSGA, had not achieved total control. But wherever you went on the Plains, you'd have a tough time of it.

Say you found a little valley with 160 acres for a homestead along a creek. You found the acres unclaimed in the land office. You'd be pleased if the valley didn't have too many cows in it belonging to a nearby ranch of a big cattle company and if your acres were near a single entrance to the valley where you could ride line on your cattle. So you'd file your claim, register your brand, build a cabin and corral, and get a bull or borrow it and buy cheap a few lame she-cattle which were so bad a trail driver couldn't deliver them. And you'd work this beginning of a herd with five or six horses you had acquired over the years when you were a cowboy. You would need a little money for this beginning, but not much.

But if you burnt your legal brand on some mavericks that strayed into your valley you'd be violating the law, which prohibited all brandings except at association roundups. All legal roundups were association roundups. And even if you weren't seen, you could be fingered by cattle detectives working for the big companies or by sheriffs who were their creatures. You couldn't *buy* mavericks collected in the roundups because the foremen sold them cheap only to the big companies. If you missed some of your own cattle, you couldn't go to the roundup and cut them out from the gather or prevent them from being rustled by the association. You weren't big enough to put a wagon with food and bedding into the roundup. As a blackballed cowboy, you wouldn't be welcome at the company wagons, even if you brought your own string of horses. Besides, you'd be effectively barred from the roundup by its foreman, who was appointed by the association and looked out for its interests. Your brand wasn't recognized anyway, because it didn't appear in the only brand book, the one printed by the association, and you had no money left to advertise it in the local newspaper. Thus you not only couldn't buy cheap cattle but you couldn't protect what you already owned. In fact, you couldn't even keep it. The association could at any time declare your brand "maverick" or "rustler." Then a sheriff and his posse of duputies could seize your whole herd, impound it, sell it, and give the money to the big companies of the area. That was the Texas method. Or the agent of the association, the cattle inspector, under orders from the state cattle commission, could seize and sell for the profit of the association any cattle you sent to market either at the railhead or at the stockyards in Omaha or Chicago. That was the Yankee method. If you persisted in being a little ranchman, a big cattle company would offer to buy your brand—that is, put you out of business. In fact, if you had a brand when you were a cowboy, you might already have been approached. If you refused to sell it, the cattle company could strong-arm you and your family and take your property by court action. In the end, you might be bushwhacked by a professional gunman, like Tom Horn or Frank Canton, who killed on commission for the cattle association.

In other words, you as a ranchman in the eighties and nineties would expect to be treated by the cattle associations in the same way the little greasy-sack outfits of the seventies were treated by the individual cattle barons, like the notorious Print Olive north of Austin. The only difference was that now in the eighties the barons were incorporated, absentee, and organized. They institutionalized the private violence of the old days. Only when their institutions didn't work would they resort to the old ways, as when they invaded Johnson County with a private army. Of course, this all describes what the capitalists did to their cowboys and ex-cowboys; in the next chapters we shall see what the cowboys did to them in return. For in spite of these draconian measures taken against them, lots of ex-cowboy nesters managed to achieve, for a time, the very American dream of having a little spread of their own.

Cowboys Fight Back

I'll treat them like a yeller dog,
As they have treated me.[1]

The popular notion of paternalism in the cattle industry, of consensus between ranch house (or boardroom) and bunkhouse (or chuck wagon), of cowboys' deference to their employers is one that has long needed refutation. It is strange that no historian of the West or of the cattle industry has bothered to clear the matter up before. It is not strange that the popular myth of the West sees paternal relations on the ranch. The myth obscures the class struggle to gratify popular longings for a preindustrial community. And the myth of the cowboy is just part of the myth of the West, which led its famous theorist Frederick Jackson Turner to invent the "free conditions of the frontier," where "free land promoted individualism, economic equality, freedom to rise, democracy." The West offered the workers of Europe who were "bound by the chains of social class . . . the chance for indefinite ascent in the scale of social advance."[2] Idealist history, responding to the popular myth, frees the U.S. frontier from the class struggle that has determined all the rest of recorded history.

Both myth and indeed most written history present the cowboy as willingly, eagerly, and joyously subservient to his boss, usually a pioneer rancher. Just a word from the old Indian-fighter and all his hands are happily off to face fierce storms, cross blazing deserts, and fight bands of dangerous gunmen. They'll even shoot sheepmen and sodbusters without batting an eye, if the boss tells them to. Neither discomfort, hardship, nor long hours lead cowboys to complain to the boss, let alone quit or threaten to. Cowboys never ask for more pay, nor do they protest when they are let go at the end of the season or when they are only hired for a few weeks of fall roundup and shipping. In fact, they don't seem to be aware of or concerned about what a fair wage is. They offer complete loyalty and unquestioning compliance because their interests are one with their bosses'. There is complete consensus between the cowboys and their employers. There is no conflict or tension within the social process of the ranch or the trail. The foregoing exaggerates, but it offers the essential tendency of what the myth of the popular media presents, what most historians accept without much questioning, and what most of us believe.

Almost all history is written from the top, that is, from the viewpoint of the minority class who are the public figures. Thus, such history, in the interest of preserving the status quo, which benefits the possessing class, obscures any basic contradictions in the system and presents, as in the case at hand, cowmen as patriarchs and their cowboys as feudal retainers. But a few considerations will show how unlikely a proposition this is. Where were the patriarchs of the Plains? The few who existed soon gave way before the industrial revolution. We've already seen that the big bosses of the range were absentee entrepreneurs on the governing boards of corporations. The old barons of the sixties soon lost their feudal power and took partner-investors to form cattle companies in the seventies and incorporated into stock companies in the eighties. There were exceptions, but that was the pattern. And even the few old barons, whose reigns were fleeting, were not able to subjugate their cowboys.

At the beginning of the cowboy era the industrial revolution was at least a generation old. The rule of the day was control of the work force by regimentation through economic fear (specters of unemployment, threats of discharge, docking of pay), not by utilizing nonexistent patterns of social fealty. Richard King and a few other cattlemen near the Rio Grande were exceptions, with their exploitation of feudalized Mexicans and colonialized Tejanos. Cowboys were never feudalized. Of the black cowboys who had been slaves or freedmen, few brought with them any forelock-touching, shambling subservience. They became cowboys to avoid just that kind of degradation. The few domestic blacks who had been brainwashed into toadyism became the bodyguard-valets of the short-lived barons, like Old Bat for Slaughter, Ikard for Goodnight, and Nigger Jim Kelly for Print

Olive. There were few feudal social relations in the antebellum South. On the plantations of Austin's colony, slaves revolted and ran away. And whatever few Texas feudal relations lingered on after the war as a "patriarchal tinge" soon passed away in the ruthless scramble to accumulate capital during Reconstruction, which reduced all social relations to economics, to "the cash nexus."

Farm boys, mainly from Texas but many from other Confederate states, became cowboys not only in pursuit of the colorful, macho life-style but in flight from the poverty and degradation of their landless farm families in perpetual thrall to furnishing merchants under the crop lien system. Thousands of poor farm families from the Old South in the seventies flooded into Texas seeking farms on the edge of the Plains.[3] They came ridiculed as hayseeds and with "inherited forms of deference" conditioned by years of standing hat in hand with requests for furnishings before the tyrant merchant who owned the unplanted crop and who controlled the ledger book, eventually to foreclose on the suppliant's land. It is no accident that here on the edge of the Texas Plains arose for the first time in America a new kind of agrarian consciousness with the Farmers Alliance in the mid-seventies. Freed from their old degradation they developed "individual self-respect and collective self-confidence, or what some would call 'class-consciousness' . . . a growing political sensibility, one free from deference and ridicule."[4] From this Texas beginning north of Austin emerged in the next decades the powerful movement of populism that stirred the South and swept the plains and prairies of the Midwest and the Far West and increasingly achieved unity with the industrial labor movement. From this poor farm class came cowboys, some too young to be influenced by the forms of deference of their parents in the decade after the war and many of the rest carrying with them the new class consciousness of their parents during the boom years of the cattle kingdoms. We can no longer see the West during the last quarter of the nineteenth century as full of populist farmers in league with industrial workers, fighting the owning class, and at the same time see their offspring, the cowboys, alone of all workers, as the deferential and deluded minions of their corporate bosses.

There's another source for class conflict on the Plains that hasn't been noticed, besides the one emerging from the sufferings of the crop lien system. Farmers and their sons from the South who migrated and took jobs as cowboys or went into family ranching on the Plains had already acquired class consciousness by their fight for free grazing rights in their home counties in Georgia and Alabama. Many hated the owning class because stock laws established to benefit the big landowners had forced them to migrate, most of them bringing their stock with them to a new home on the Plains. Further, they all came to Texas (or Kansas or western Nebraska) with the expectation, based on long custom, that they had a natural right to run cattle on all unfenced land. When the cattle companies and their associations in time tried to keep employed cowboys from owning private herds and to eliminate ex-cowboy nesters, the resulting class warfare on the Plains was intensified by memories of Eastern and older Southern populist feelings against the efforts of the planter class to take away common grazing rights.

Some knowledge of this class struggle in the emerging New South is essential to understanding the concurrent class struggle on the Plains between cowboys (and ex-cowboy nesters) and cowmen. Although Southern land ownership remained in the same hands after the war, large-scale private property in the new capitalist South was threatened by small family farmers, both white and black, grazing and hunting on unenclosed land in accordance with ancient and cherished customary rights. A poor family could exist independently in a cabin in the piney woods or on the edge of coastal pine barrens by hunting and fishing and grazing some hogs and cows. Not only did planters want to possess outright what they considered their own forage and game, but, even more important, they wanted to create a large farm-worker class wholly dependent on wages so that they could replace their former slaves with cheap labor and thus make the transition to a capitalist economy. To eliminate small yeoman farmers, who depended on hunting and grazing, the planters used their power to pass laws taking away these customary rights. And the ensuing fight brought small farmers together, black and white, in united opposition to the owning class. The fight continued into the nineties, with increasing imposition of stock laws and migration west of small farmers. "Upcountry farmers resisted the attack on common rights more successfully than did poorer whites and blacks in the Plantation Belt," where most of the big landowners were. And the struggle contributed to the beginnings of Southern populism, to the defense of a "vision of the Revolutionary heritage that associated freedom with economic independence and tyranny with massive concentrations of wealth and power," as some expressions of opposition to the stock laws testify. "The woods were put here by our Creator for a benefit to his people"; and "we as poor men and negroes do not need the [stock] law but we need a democratic government and independence that will do the common people good," wrote Georgia farmers in 1885.[5] A Southern farmer who fled this oppression and, seeking freedom, turned cowboy couldn't fail to experience a bitter déjà vu when his employer's agent told

him he couldn't run his own cattle or his former employer's agent told
him he couldn't have a little spread of his own. All capitalists are kin in
claiming all nature for their own, and capitalism rapidly prevailed after the
war, spreading south and west. But so were common and shared ways of
resistance among the people—community support of illegal foraging in the
planters' woods in the South and illegal branding up of mavericks on the
Plains.

Cowboys hated their big bosses (not their wagon bosses) and regularly
resisted them. Of course the hate was not always intense, nor even completely conscious, but existed in a spectrum from sullen and smoldering
resentment to breathless rage. The anger often went beyond feeling to a
recognition, however fleeting, of cowboys' exploitation. An apparently loyal
old cowhand, telling in a cattleman's trade journal about some hardships
that he and some black cowboys went through in the old days and about
how no one would now believe it, breaks out with this almost involuntary
radical slogan: he and his cowboy pals were risking death *"trying to care
for the other man's wealth."*[6]

Even the songs collected (and, as is charged, edited and reconstructed)
by John Lomax, who as strongly as anyone else upholds the tradition of
capitalist-worker consensus, contain evidence of class struggle. The songs
often go beyond laments over the conditions of work—its boredom, pain,
danger, and loneliness—to protests against exploitation and bosses. Here
a cowboy complains of the short work-year in the North:

> Work in Montana
> Is six months in the year:
> When all your bills are settled
> There is nothing left for beer.

("The Texas Cowboy")

In a similar vein, another song details the injustice of being in debt to the
boss on payday, a resentment felt so sorely that the singer resolves to sell
his saddle and quit the trade:

> We rounded 'em up and put 'em on the cars,
> An that was the last of the old Two Bars.
>
> Oh it's bacon and beans most every day,—
> I'd as soon be a-eatin' prairie hay. . . .
>
> I went to the wagon to get my roll,
> To come back to Texas, dad-burn my soul.

I went to the boss to draw my roll,
He had it figgered out I was nine dollars in the hole.

I'll sell my outfit just as soon as I can,
I won't punch cattle for no damned man.

("The Old Chisholm Trail")

Another cowboy remarks that his boss wants him to die for the herd:

The cowboy's life is a dreadful life,
He's driven through heat and cold;
I'm almost froze with the water on my clothes,
A-ridin' through heat and cold.

I've been where the lightnin', the lightnin' tangled in my eyes,
The cattle I could scarcely hold;
Think I heard my boss man say:
"I want all brave-hearted men who ain't afraid to die
To whoop up the cattle from morning till night,
Way up on the Kansas Line."

("The Kansas Line")

Another is about high-pressure hiring practices for what turns out to be a rotten job:

You may go to Stamford and there see a man
Who wears a white shirt and is asking for hands;
You may ask him for work and he'll answer you short,
He will hurry you up, for he wants you to start.
He will put you in a wagon and be off in the rain,
You will go up on Tongue River on the U-S-O range.

You will drive up to the ranch and there you will stop.
It's a little sod house with dirt all on top.
You will ask what it is and they will tell you out plain
That it's the ranch house on the U-S-O range.

("The U-S-O Range")

The song continues about the bedding of "some blankets rolled up on the floor" and the grub of beans and cold rice and beef. Another, about freighters but a popular song among cowboys (they often took bullwhacker and mule-skinner jobs as casual employment), presents an employee who wants to get a job in hell, where he can roast his bosses, Livermore and

Meyers, the freight contractors:

> But I want to die and go to hell
> Get there before Livermore and Meyers
> And get a job of hauling coke
> To keep up the devil's fires;
> If I get the job of singeing them,
> I'll see they don't get free;
> I'll treat them like a yaller dog,
> As they have treated me.

("Freighting from Wilcox to Globe")[7]

Then there is a cowboy variant of a buffalo-hunter song about the murder of a boss for nonpayment of wages:

> Well, now the trip is ended and we reached Ben Johnson's
>   farm,
> The first old bronco I tried to break, by God, he broke my
>   arm.
> While punchin' the damned old longhorns, our lives, we had
>   no show,
> There was Indians to pick us off in the hills of New Mexico.
>
> Now the round-up's over and Ben Johnson would not pay,
> He said we'd been so extravagant that he was in debt that
>   day.
> But we showed him about the punchers, that old bankrupt
>   would not go,
> So we left Ben Johnson's bones to bleach in the hills of
>   Mexico.

("The Hills of Mexico")[8]

You can imagine the satisfaction and sense of personal power this song of wish-fulfillment gave to cowboy singers.

Another whole group of songs is even more explicit in treating of the class conflict. Some present just a bitter awareness of the differences between the quality of the life of the classes:

> The cowboy's life is a dreary, dreary life,
> He's driven through the heat and cold;
> While the rich man's a-sleeping on his velvet couch,
> Dreaming of his silver and gold.

("The Dreary, Dreary Life")

Some songs refer to the double legal standard by which bosses but not cowboys are allowed to build their herds by branding stray slicks and the practice of paying cowboys to steal for their bosses and commit perjury in court on the bosses' behalf:

> It's Jim Farrow and John Farrow and Little Simon, too,
> Have plenty of cattle where I have but a few.
> Marking and branding both night and day,—
> It's "Keep still, boys, my boys, and you'll all get your pay."
>
> It's up to the courthouse, the first thing they know,
> Before the Grand Jury they'll have to go.
> They'll ask you about ear-marks, they'll ask you about brand,
> But tell them you were absent when the work was on hand.
>
> Jim Farrow brands J.F. on the side;
> The next comes Johnnie who takes the whole hide;
> Little Simon, too, has H. on the loin;—
> All stand for Farrow but it's not good for Sime.
>
> You ask for the mark, I don't think it's fair,
> You'll find the cow's head but the ear isn't there
> It's a crop and a split and a sort of a twine,—
> All stand for F. but it's not good for Sime.

("Jim Farrow")

The song contains a wealth of lore about branding and earmarking and ways of stealing cattle, but the main point is that the cowboy singer can't increase his "few" cattle by the big rancher's methods: the Farrow brothers are paying their cowboys to steal neighbor Simon's beef and to perjure themselves in court to protect their boss.

Another song on the same subject of the double standard about cattle theft tells of trail boss John Garner, who instructed his cowboys to gather strays on the trail:

> We would round them up at morning, and the boss would
>   make a count,
> And say, "Look here, old punchers, we are out quite an
>   amount;
> You must make all losses good and do it without fail
> Or you will never get another job of driving up the trail."
>
> When we reached the Reservation, how squirmish we did feel,
> Although we had tried old Garner and knew him true as steel.

And if we would follow him and do as he said do,
That old bald-headed cow-thief would surely take us through.

("John Garner's Trail Herd")[9]

Here the singer's admiration for the trail boss being "the biggest cow-thief that ever tramped out there," in spite of Garner's threat to blackball cowboys who wouldn't steal for him, shows the common acceptance of cattle theft by cowboys as demonstrating initiative and toughness.

There are lots of cowboy songs that show admiration for outlaws, particularly those who, in folklore at least, steal from the rich only and don't forget their class origins. Like Jesse James:

Jesse was a man, a friend to the poor,
He never would see a man suffer pain;

And Sam Bass, the cowboy who turned bandit after his first trail drive:

Sam first came out to Texas a cowboy for to be,—
A kinder-heart fellow you seldom ever see.

Sam made it back to Texas all right side up with care;
Rode into the town of Denton with all this friends to share.

Four more bold and daring cowboys the rangers never knew,
They whipped the Texas rangers and ran the boys in blue.

And cowboys celebrated in song the English highwayman in the Robin Hood tradition who bought the horse Black Bess "to plunder the wealthy":

No poor man I plundered
Nor e'er did oppress
The widows or orphans,
My Bonnie Black Bess.

("Bonnie Black Bess")

Finally, we'll include the entire lyrics to the wonderful song "The Cowboy," because it is about a cowboy turning from wage labor to ranching on his own by mavericking. The first part is about the cowboy's lonely life:

All day long on the prairies I ride,
Not even a dog to trot by my side;
My fire I kindle with chips gathered round,
My coffee I boil without being ground.

I wash in a pool and wipe on a sack;
I carry my wardrobe all on my back;

For want of an oven I cook bread in a pot,
And sleep on the ground for want of a cot.

My ceiling is the sky, my floor is the grass,
My music is the lowing of the herds as they pass;
My books are the brooks, my sermons the stones,
My parson is a wolf on his pulpit of bones.

And then if my cooking is not very complete
You can't blame me for wanting to eat.
But show me a man that sleeps more profound
Than the big puncher-boy who stretches himself on the
    ground.

The next part justifies, in spite of his friends' warning, his looking out for
his own interest as a would-be married man by stealing cattle to build his
own herd:

My books teach me ever consistence to prize,
My sermons, that small things I should not despise;
My parson remarks from his pulpit of bones
That fortune favors those who look out for their own.

And then between me and love lies a gulf very wide.
Some lucky fellow may call her his bride.
My friends gently hint I am coming to grief,
But men must make money and women have beef.

He's going to follow "consistence" by being a thief like the rich, ignoring
the double standard, and he's not going to "despise" "small things," like
picking up a daily stray slick or two for his herd. In the last part he justifies
his intent to rise from his lowly position as a cowboy, who is a scapegoat
for all the evils of society, to being respected like the earlier herdsman
King David—and he'll do it by owning, like the patriarchs of the Old
Testament, "a big brand":

But Cupid is always a friend to the bold,
And the best of his arrows are pointed with gold.
Society bans me so savage and dodge
That the Masons would ball me out of their lodge.

If I had hair on my chin, I might pass for the goat
That bore all the sins in the ages remote;
But why it is I can never understand,
For each of the patriarchs owned a big brand

Abraham emigrated in search of a range,
And when water was scarce he wanted a change;
Old Isaac owned cattle in charge of Esau,
And Jacob punched cows for his father-in-law.

He started in business way down at bed rock,
And made quite a streak at handling stock;
Then David went from night-herding to using a sling;
And, winning the battle, he became a great king.
Then the shepherds, while herding the sheep on a hill,
Got a message from heaven of peace and good will.[10]

The last two lines seem to express a Christian viewpoint, but most cowboys were hostile to Christianity, indeed all religions. Teddy Blue testified that 90 percent of the cowboys were "infidels" because of their life: "after you come in contact with nature, you get all that stuff knocked out of you—praying to God for aid, divine Providence, and so on—because it don't work."[11] Cowboys associate religion with settlers, perhaps why the cowboy turned settler-rancher in the above song shows some religious thought at the end.

Let's consider the double standard of honesty on the range before going on. There is one standard for honesty about property for cowmen, another for cowboys, the hired help. Bosses can steal and cheat and be grossly dishonest in the business of accumulating capital, but a cowboy can't put his brand on a slick stray or two. It's the old story that only the big thieves, the robber barons, can get away with it and are even admired for their cleverness, individualism, aggressiveness in "sharp business practices." Cowboys mavericking, when they weren't doing it on commission for their bosses, were usually not organized and, unlike the cattle industry, were never supported by the state. Cattle on open ranges in combination with a capitalist system led inevitably to thievery. Perhaps only in long-established communal societies are cattle secure without fences or herders. Raiding warriors would steal them, but not neighbors. The patriarch Jacob had no problems with mavericking Jews. Nor did Black Kettle with horse-stealing Cheyennes. In contrast, industrializing Texas after the war strained the old early capitalist system of brands, registration, inspection, and stockmen's meetings. It wasn't mavericking cowboys or the few self-serving ranch managers and wagon bosses or the few organized groups of rustlers, like Billy the Kid's gang, that strained the system but the energetic big thievery of competing capitalists, like the Pierce brothers, who started "poorer than skimmed milk" but with "lots of cheek and a branding iron"[12] and in a few years sold their ranch for $100,000. "So long as the ranch was unfenced . . . no owner of land or cattle could control his own property," said a contemporary.[13] Since a small ranchman could not possibly keep track of his strays if he was unfenced, and since the big outfits, having capital, fenced first, the small rancher to survive would replace his strays, mavericked from him by big companies, by mavericking himself from them. The point is that the big thievery that cowboys saw daily as accepted business practices of their bosses led them to feel free to commit a little version of it on their own. They were socialized into thievery, as we all are to some extent under capitalism.

Here is an amusing account of the origin of the double standard in relation to cows and to class conflict told by an evangelical Christian cowboy who wrote a temperance tract in the early nineties about his recollections of life on the early Texas frontier. He simplifies for purpose of wit, but he tells the essential truth:

> After the war, when the poor, half-starved, weather and war-beaten fellows returned, those who had left cattle went to work to make up for lost time, and those who had none, to get even for their four years of service. And it soon became a sort of general scramble as to who should get the greatest number, and on account of thousands of cattle having become wild and unruly because of neglect a very general licence was granted, or rather taken, to kill and eat when one was hungry. Thus it was that the majority of people who lived in the West became involved in branding Mavricks [sic], and killing strays, which at that time was not looked upon as stealing, but a kind of pull dick pull devil, the devil-take-the-hindmost sort of way of securing all the cattle one could. . . .
>
> The circumstances leading to a change in the laws may be briefly stated as follows: A great many of the active and better equipped among the scramblers began to accumulate large herds, and as there were no pasture fences then, they were compelled to turn their cattle loose on the range. The less thrifty and more extravagant classes refused to recognize the rights of the growing nabobs to have their unbranded calves left alone, while they [the nabobs] were still keeping up their old game of branding Mavricks indiscriminately, and the little fellows thus antagonized their former associates. The consequence was the wholesale thieves, now grown powerful, had the legislature pass laws making it an offence

against the peace and dignity of the State to brand and mark a
calf that didn't belong to him. [Texas made stealing cattle a felony
in 1873.]

Then began the battle that for years waged unceasingly until
the big fish swallowed up the little ones. We had as a result the
cattle king and the common cow-puncher. The real difference
being that the king no longer had to do his own stealing, for he
was able to hire the cow-puncher to do it for him, and if the poor
cow-puncher presumed to steal a little scrub for himself once in
a while, the king wouldn't kick unless someone tried to raise a
fuss about it. If he could settle it without too much noise he would
do it, and thus add one more link to the poor boy's chains with
which to hold him in line. If there was too much noise about it,
the king turned honest and sent him down East to work for Texas
[the penitentiary].

The same cowboy moralist in his early tract gives this account of trick
counts, by which cattle entrepreneurs would steal from each other:

A cow-man, in making a large delivery, say of four or five
thousand cattle, they were run into a corral in bunches of say
two hundred and fifty for road-branding, a brand that would
designate them as the property of the purchaser, and if he happened to be a man unused to the cattle business, as many were,
they would brand all in the pen and then count them out and
run in another bunch, they would make it in the way [i.e., do it
in such a way as] to run in, close to time to quit for the day, a
greater number than they could brand, and brand only part of
them, leaving a mixed bunch in the pen over night. During the
night they would steal out and drive in twenty or thirty head of
those that were already branded and counted, putting them in
the pen with the mixed bunch, finish up next morning and count
them out again, thus making a clear steal of all they could run
in during the night. They would keep this up until they had
finished branding, when, perhaps, they had recounted two or
three hundred cattle. This was called slick work. I have an idea,
however, that very scrupulously conscientious people would call
it stealing by wholesale. That is really the proper name for it.[14]

What did the simple hired cowhand see from his lowly position? He saw
the wagon boss provide for the cook by slaughtering only beef that bore
a brand other than his big boss's. "The distinction between 'mine' and
'thine' . . . became so loose that perhaps the majority of ranch people

followed the custom of killing only other people's cattle for beef."[15] He saw large-scale capitalist mavericking in cow hunts for cattle to drive north. An old cowboy dryly recalls details of such a hunt in Texas: his boss paid local ranchers for cattle marked with their brands but "cattle that had no brand or mark—well, that was not our fault. But it was remarkable the way these cattle persisted in following the herd. Naturally our sympathy was with them."[16] Another old Texas cowboy recalls working for Read and O'Connor in 1873: the outfit "gathered cattle around Matagorda Bay. There were a thousand head of beeves, and seven hundred of them had O'Connor's brand on them." But they branded them all with a road brand and took them to Wichita for delivery to Shanghai Pierce.[17]

Cowboys heard about and ruefully chuckled over the huge heists of their bosses. In the fall of 1871, Shanghai Pierce had fled north as a fugitive from justice because he'd lynched some *little* mavericks in Matagorda County; while there he cheated a greenhorn U.S. Army receiving agent by a trick cattle count (at which he was expert and famous) out of 118 beeves in a herd of about a thousand.[18] This was outright theft but was treated as an amusing testimony to his sharp business acumen. The great John Chisum was a *big* cattle thief. He secured powers of attorney to drive many brands from Texas to the Pecos. He executed notes for the payment of these cattle, but holders of notes in Texas could not collect because he was in New Mexico Territory. Sometimes other more cunning *big* thieves would steal from Chisum: Hunter and Evans, Kansas City cattle commission men, bought 50,000 head from Chisum with his own defaulted Texas notes, which they had purchased for a few cents on the dollar. Once, at least, Chisum turned to outright rustling: he lost a herd to Indian raiders so he replaced it by gathering another on the border of Texas "without regard for mark or brand," an act so blatant that Charles Goodnight, who stood out among his fellow cattlemen for his scrupulous ethics within a thieving system, refused the "stolen stock."[19] Cowboys would also know about gigantic thieves in Washington who later became corporation cattlemen and came down hard through their associations on petty lawlessness and mavericking—like U.S. Senator Stephen W. Dorsey "of Star Route fame," who boodled thousands of dollars on railroad mail contracts and used the loot to get himself a big spread in New Mexico Territory, where he became prime mover behind the Cimarron Cattle Ranchers' Association's and his own trade journal *New Mexico Stockmen*'s campaign against petty "cattle thieves."[20] The hypocrisy of this big thief noisily hunting down little thieves was not lost on the ordinary cowboy.

Cowboys saw a great deal of rustling by big stockmen on each other, an activity so widespread in the early eighties in Colorado that the local cattlemen's association had to tighten up the roundups and hire twelve additional brand inspectors to police its own members.[21] An old cattleman from Del Rio, Texas, gives this testimony of depredations among the owners:

> Stealing got so bad that in 1875 a line was formed from the upper line of Karnes County [just southeast of San Antonio], across to the upper line of Frio, on the Nueces. It was made up of 75 or 100 armed men who cut the trail herds from south of that line for their own cattle. Big handlers of cattle from the north would sometimes send riders down to look for *their* cattle. These men went on legitimate business, but they'd drive off all the cattle they could, regardless of whether they were theirs or not. This got so bad that they had to keep this line up for about a year, cutting all the north-bound herds, and they had to hang several men before it stopped. This line was maintained by the cattlemen to the south of it, and a lot of trouble arose over it.[22]

Such large-scale rustling by big ranchmen, sending out outfits of cowboys to steal for them, occurred many times before 1875 too. Cowboys saw and were paid to take part in most of this wholesale capitalist rustling and other forms of business embezzlement and larceny on the Plains during the early years, the time of the real pioneer barons—like Conrad Kohrs (Montana), R. C. Keith (Nebraska), the Patterson brothers (Wyoming and New Mexico), and John Wesley Iliff (Colorado, Wyoming, and Nebraska)—before the coming of the big corporations with their associations. These associations regulated the operations of the big cattle companies and prevented them from self-destructive thievery against each other while facilitating and legalizing their operations against family ranchers. But cowboys' memories of capitalist rapaciousness in the seventies lingered on and influenced their conduct.

This conduct, sometimes just to oppose their employers, sometimes also in support of their own interests, is of two kinds, often overlapping: (1) on the job as employees, and (2) as ex-cowboy independent ranchmen. Both kinds can be seen as the cowboys' contribution to the developing American tradition of worker opposition to exploitation by capital during the industrial revolution, from name calling and anticapitalist graffiti to industrial sabotage and slowdowns, from strikes and demonstrations to throwing stones and shooting gun thugs. The cowboy variety of resistance is distinctive because cowboys worked in smaller groups (an "outfit" is ten to twelve men), to which they showed, as distinct from what they showed their bosses, an intense loyalty; they were a self-conscious worker elite and had (like machinists) more pride in their craft than most; and, most important, they had, uniquely among workers, an alternative to wage labor because of

CHARLES SIRINGO AND WILLIAM S. HART

The date is probably 1925 when Siringo was living in Hollywood. In Riata and Spurs *(1927), Siringo said that it brought back memories when he walked down to The Water Hole on Cahuenga Avenue between Sunset and Hollywood boulevards "to see the movie cowboys and cowgirls with their silver-mounted spurs and high Stetson hats." Hart was being eclipsed by Tom Mix as the Hollywood cowboy hero. This production still was probably taken at Hart's standing set on his Newhall ranch home during the filming of the town shots for* Tumbleweeds *(1925).* (COURTESY OF THE SAN ANTONIO MUSEUM ASSOCIATION.)

the Homestead Act—they could use their skills on their own spread as an independent rancher in competition with their former bosses. Their old bosses made being an independent competitor difficult, in most cases almost impossible—but the alternative to wage labor existed and shaped the quality of their resistance.

First, then, how did cowboys get back at their bosses on the job? They could exchange words and blows if they were lucky enough to have a resident, working boss, as when a disgruntled cowboy after words with Richard King for cursing his men got into a fistfight with him.[23] There were acts of revenge, to release months of pent-up resentment. When Siringo decided to quit the LX Ranch, he went out in style. After a trail drive, his stingy bosses sent him as wagon boss with a small outfit back down the trail to gather strays. The weather and countryside being nice, he decided to turn it into a paid vacation. His outfit took a month to gather eighteen head, and while collecting they lived it up on delicacies purchased from grangers, lots of fresh eggs and butter. When he returned, he presented his account book, obviously padded, to one boss ("Jay Gould would groan under the weight of these bills"), who refused to pay in spite of Siringo's threats, but he did manage to collect from the other partner. He ended up "a few hundred dollars" to the good.[24] Two cowboys went to a ranch in Texas seeking work. The boss said no and charged them fifty cents apiece for dinner. As they left the ranch, they cut out a prime three-year-old steer and with a red-hot cinch ring ran a big brand on him: "MEALS 50¢"![25]

On other occasions resistance went beyond revenge to job control. After procedures for handling cattle became pretty well standardized in the later seventies, cowboys would refuse to work faster and longer or more dangerously than conventional standards dictated. These work codes for all cowboys' collective good were like the factory workers' codes of "a clearly determined stint, or level of output," a measure of production that workers would not go beyond without being called a "hog, a runner, a chaser, a job wrecker."[26] With cowboys, production control by adherence to work codes often included refusal to take unconventional risks or undergo unusual hazards. Cowboys would often refuse to work or refuse to take a job if their employers were trying to reduce production costs in the following ways:

• If a single rep had to cover too many roundups or too big a single roundup for his home ranch;

• if the trail herd was too big for the number of cowboys in the outfit;

• if the scattered or drifted range herd was too big for the number of cowboys in the roundup;

• if the mount for each cowboy in the remuda was too small to provide fresh horses;

• if the remuda had too many wild horses that had to be busted every day (without the specialized help of professional bronc busters).

There aren't many records of cowboys refusing to work beyond conventional standards. The reason is that managers knew the codes and were reluctant to violate them for fear of labor troubles—because they knew they couldn't get away with it. But there had to be some refusals and protests to force managers to limit their rapacity and thus to establish some control over them. For instance, Siringo and the only other Texas cowboy in a trail outfit going to Kansas "finally bolted," that is, quit the job and rode away, because they received nothing extra for taming "wild horses" in the remuda.[27]

Here's a firsthand account of a work-code violation on one ranch of the St. Louis Cattle Company—an insufficient mount or string on a drive in Texas, aggravated by thin clothes in cold weather and double night duty

"COWBOYS CHECKING A STAMPEDE," KERRVILLE, TEXAS, 1881

This wood engraving in a national newspaper, like most early illustrations, shows cowboys using long whips instead of ropes or quirts to manage cattle, a survival on the Great Plains of earlier Southern and Eastern methods of raising cattle. Kerrville is west of Austin on the Edwards Plateau. (COURTESY OF THE DENVER PUBLIC LIBRARY, WESTERN HISTORY DEPARTMENT.)

"A REFRACTORY STEER"

A wood engraving in Harper's Monthly Magazine, June 1885, from a drawing by the young South Carolina artist Rufus Zogbaum, who went West for subjects before Remington and, like him, romanticized cowboys. (COURTESY OF THE DENVER PUBLIC LIBRARY, WESTERN HISTORY DEPARTMENT.)

for the stickers after half the outfit quit:

> The Company had sold some 3500 head of yearlings to be delivered at Clarendon, Texas. 'Twas the middle of November when we started and cold—oh boy! We cut them into two herds. What made things worse, old man Beal [the ranch manager] had about twenty-five four-year-old mules he had broke in the summer; rather, he had them staked about a week and rode them four or five times. He give the boys two mules apiece, but some of them could not ride them hardly, as every time they would get down the mules would jerk away from them. Then a man or two would have to run down the mule to catch it. . . . They was ten of us when we started, but the awful cold and them mules together caused all but five to quit. The boss, three hands and the horse wrangler was left. I was driving the drags, flanking on both sides, and had my horses rode down. I told the boss I wanted to ride some of those extra horses that those boys had been riding that had quit, and he would not allow it. I told him if he didn't I'd quit too. He laughed at me; said I was afraid to quit. I told him I had done quit. He was not going to let me have a horse to ride back, but I took one more out of the herd, put my bed [roll] on him, got on the other and put back to the ranch. I quit on the head of the Pease River in the Matador Pasture. I was full of standing guard half of the night, fooling with them mules when the ice was two inches thick, in my summer clothes. I knew they was other jobs.[28]

There are lots of references to slowdowns, threats, intimidating behavior, and collective defiance among cowboys displeased with their pay, bosses, or work conditions. Probably only a small percentage of such acts of resistance were recorded—the wagon boss seldom including accounts of them in his letters to the owners. For instance, there are those occasions when all hands and all horses in the outfit have worked themselves to the point of utter exhaustion and there is an unavoidable work stoppage. One cowboy kept a diary of a trail drive in 1866. After an entire day getting a herd across the Red River, with one cowboy dead by drowning and several others nearly so, there is a stampede that very night, with the result that "Many men in trouble. Horses *all* give out & Men refused to do anything."[29] Such refusals to work were obviously common but would not often get into company reports or the foreman's notebook. We can only guess what acts of resistance lay behind the complaint of one manager in his weekly letter of "lazy, slovenly cowhands."[30]

Another manager in Wyoming, who hated cowboys, recorded in a journal his relief when his employees left the headquarters ranch: "A crowd of cowboys who had been lying around the ranch waiting for the roundup moved out, which was a great relief." When he joined them on the roundup, he made this entry: "They were not cordial at all. They have been talking about shooting me all winter because I have been made the scapegoat of the attempt to reduce wages. I expect I shall live through it, but it is unpleasant being scowled at and talked at by the blackguards."[31] In a memoir another manager recorded his first reception at the ranch where he was in charge of 1,500 cattle and a group of cowboys: the cowhands "as if by concerted agreement" decided to test him; they openly disobeyed his orders and spent the entire day jeering and idling through their work. (He fired all but two and hired a new outfit.)[32] John Clay, the hard-boiled Chicago commission man put in charge of reorganizing the Swan Cattle Company, wrote to the secretary of the Wyoming Stock Growers Association recommending a new manager on a Swan ranch as being able to "manage" his cowboys better than the former one, who had "one revolt after another." "This [failure to manage cowboys] will have to cease or we will be in worse shape than the cattlemen in Johnson County."[33] (Clay wrote this letter eight years before the association chose to undertake a military invasion of Johnson County because the cowboys in north-central Wyoming *had* become unmanageable.) In his famous memoir, Clay recalls visiting the fall roundup that year on another Swan ranch where he witnessed acts of insubordination in his own presence: "At noon time there was a gambling game for a half hour or more, Long Jim Brown dealing the cards. Gatlin, the foreman, while not playing, looked on unconcernedly. His duty was to pitch the cards into the creek." Back at the ranch, Clay paid off the cowboys. One refused a check, demanding cash. He didn't get it. Gatlin had to go as foreman because "he had a bad gang around him." But when Clay replaced him, the new foreman found the cowboys on the ranch "seemingly loyal" but "inwardly hostile" and quit and fled in fear of his life after being "shot at through the window." So Clay got a real tough foreman, a former Pinkerton and Molly Maguire sleuth, for next spring. Nevertheless, here we see an effective although crude and temporary early form of job action, a variant of the customary cowboy testing of all newcomers and tenderfeet: support a popular foreman and get rid of an unpopular one by terrorizing the latter into quitting. Clay, who managed personnel for many ranches, doesn't support the myth of the faithful and obedient cowboy: "Men come and go; in fact, the ordinary rider is a good deal of a moveable individual. They love fresh pastures and new scenes."[34] What was behind the threat of JA cowboys at the head of the Red River to kidnap a wealthy Anglo-Irish owner and his wife and hold them "for ransom" in the early eighties? Goodnight, the Irish owner's partner, finally got a "troup of cavalry" to protect them during their visit. The threat might have been more an early form of job action, before procedures were worked out, than mere cowboy lawlessness (as the historian reports it).[35]

As a way of increasing their wages illegally, that is, extracting real wages more in accord with the value of their work than their payday wages represented, cowboys would run maverick brands. A cowboy would register his own brand and burn it on any unbranded cattle he would come across. He wouldn't even have to incriminate himself by carrying a running iron on his saddle but would use a cinch or girth ring carried in his chaps pocket and held when red hot with a green stem cut for the occasion. He'd have to have a way of collecting and hiding the cattle so branded— either a confederate, say a brother, who would do it for him or a small ranch nearby to which he could drive his new calves or yearlings after hours if he had a sympathetic wagon boss who would allow him to use a company horse. Siringo ran his brand on so many cattle that later drifted and mixed with other herds that he gave up the practice in despair of collecting them. Another account says he gave it up when "the big chief," Shanghai Pierce, heard of the operation.[36] He was tempted into the practice when he discovered his wagon boss at it! Many other cowboys tried it for themselves, because their own big bosses paid them bounties to burn company brands on all mavericks found anywhere.

Running a maverick brand while working as a day laborer for another is the cowboy equivalent of "high grading" in a rich mine, also a common practice in the West. A miner would conceal on his person and smuggle out of the mine high-grade ore worth anywhere from thirty to ninety dollars a pound, while officially working for, say, three-fifty a day. Miners stole ore cooperatively and sold it through their own assayers.[37] The miner would claim some of the riches of the mountain for his own, just as the cowboy would claim some of the riches of the Plains for his. One wonders if there were similar high-grading-like operations among lumberjacks, teamsters, and railroad workers in the West to raise their wages to subsistence levels. In any case, cowboys had a unique opportunity to increase their real wages covertly by appropriating their employers' property, sometimes in organized and cooperative ways, or, more exactly, appropriating what their employers, backed up by associations, *claimed* as company property, namely, *all* the unbranded cattle on the range—just as mining companies claimed all the subsurface minerals.

"I ran a maverick brand on the head of Double Mountain Fork, on the OO Range" (Texas South Plains, near Lubbock, in the late eighties), an old cowboy recalled without shame for the Trail Drivers of Texas. "O. J. Warren was the owner. It got so big I lost my job and had to change my brand."[38] Teddy Blue's best boss through 1884, the manager-part-owner of a St. Louis–based cattle company, fired his favorite wagon boss for running private cattle.[39] The practice was widespread although outlawed for the most part by the cattle associations. Montana (save only during 1884–85) was one exception in allowing employed cowboys to buy maverick brands. In most other regions the practice was outlawed, by which is meant that if a cowboy was caught by the manager, he would be fired and blackballed and his small herd put under the surveillance of an association detective. It should be noted that employed cowboys seldom ran brands on horses, just cattle. Stealing horses was too dangerous without organized confederates, hidden corrals, and established hideout camps on an outlaw trail to distant markets—like the operation in the recent movie *Missouri Breaks*. The Wild Bunch did this, but few working cowboys had such connections.

And then there were real cowboy strikes of all kinds—organized, wildcats, slowdowns, walkouts (or *ride*outs if the strikers had their own horses), and sit-downs. The best business historian of the cattle industry says that "there were *many* labor strikes on the range."[40] We are referring here to strikes of working cowboys on the range in the eighties, not the numerous strikes of cowboys who were rodeo and Hollywood athletes and entertainers in the 1930s. The fact of numerous cowboy strikes impresses people as strange, unbelievable because we have been taught that cowboys had the same interests as their bosses. People who know of one strike tend to call it unique because they think of it as the exception that proves the rule about loyal idiot cowboys. Siringo, who ought to have known better through his operations for the Pinkerton Agency, called one in the Texas Panhandle in 1883 "the only cowboy strike pulled off in the history of the world."[41] Another cowboy who was a striker in the labor action Siringo refers to as unique also called it "the only strike among cowboys that I ever heard of."[42] Even the historian of the Johnson County War calls a famous strike of at least four roundups in 1886 "the only cowboys strike in the history of the northern range."[43] But there were lots of others if we think of strikes as including work slowdowns or halts other than those highly organized and premeditated strikes that involved several roundups. At least there were strikes in the 1880s through the fall of 1886, the period of recovery after the depression of 1873–1878, when the cattle industry boomed, was most highly capitalized, and was attempting more than at any other time to accumulate capital by squeezing cowboy workers with speedups and cutbacks.

The first seven years of the eighties also correspond to the most active organizing of the populist, trade-unionist Knights of Labor. One historian of the West claims that the Knights of Labor had "gained many recruits among discontented cowboys in Texas and Wyoming."[44] She gives no supporting evidence, but there is plenty around, heretofore unnoticed. The historian of the Great Southwest Railroad Strike of early 1886 found that cowboy assemblies of the Knights of Labor existed over the "entire Western Texas plains" and that many of these assemblies wrote supporting the railroad strikers to the investigating congressional committee.[45] At the height of the Knights' influence, in 1885 and 1886, there were thirteen local assemblies in Denver with a membership in that city alone of over 3,000, and dozens more local assemblies meeting weekly or once or twice a month in smaller towns of the surrounding Plains, including Butte City (Montana); Cheyenne, Laramie, Carbon, Rawlins, and Rock Springs (Wyoming); North Platte (Nebraska); Pueblo, Sterling, Golden, and Coma (Colorado); Ogden (Utah); Las Vegas and Las Animas (New Mexico).[46] When Local Assembly 2487 was reorganized in Cheyenne in the spring of 1884, more than a hundred new workers joined at the public membership recruiting meeting, including some cowboys, as this labor newspaper account by a reporter who was there testifies: "The Stock monopolists of Cheyenne expressed no little anxiety over the excitement [about the membership drive]. They were very much concerned about the report that the cow-boys were going into the organization, and the indications are that their fears were warranted."[47]

In the spring of 1886 the Denver *Labor Enquirer* reported the identity of the Knights of Labor organizer of cowboys: "John H. Sullivan, a cowboy since he was 12 years old, has been studying the working of labor organizations with a view of bringing into the Knights of Labor the 8,000 or 10,000 cowboys on the plains."[48] The following winter the same John H. Sullivan, "a cowboy of singularly handsome face and figure, with the frankest of blue eyes," found work as "Bronco John" in a touring "dime museum" (midway or arcade show) which was in Cincinnati in early December. He sat among other "terribly bored" cowboys in traditional garb on a raised platform and, as part of each show, gave a speech to each audience denouncing "capitalists in general and . . . ranch-owners in particular." The gist of his repeated and very earnest speech, delivered with "homely, natural pathos," was that cowboys "are distinctly members of the non-possessing and yet producing and distributing class, that they are as much at the mercy of the capitalist as a New or Old England cotton-operative [mill worker], that their supposed 'freedom' is no more of a reality than his. . . . that the cowboys, as a class, are beginning to recognise these facts, are becoming anxious that the general public should know them, and . . . are desirous, through the medium of either the Knights of Labor, or some other working-class organization, to connect themselves with the mass of the laboring class and with the general movement of that class against the tyranny of their employers." He gave the same estimate of the number of working cowboys as the Denver news release of the previous spring and claimed that "no class is harder worked . . . and none so poorly paid for their services," and that so many cowboys are " 'awakening to the necessity of a league of their own' that a Cowboy Assembly of the K. of L. or a Cowboy Union is sure to be started in the near future." He also spoke of the blackballed cowboys turned nesters struggling against maverick laws imposed by "the terrorist regime of the ranchers" whose association "steals all unbranded cattle."

Sullivan seems to have had a special purpose in this winter public relations tour: to appeal "to the newspapers of the East that they should do what the Western ones were afraid to do and state clearly the case of the cowboy, their complaints, and their demands." Each time he finished his speech he invited interested members of the audience to get in touch with him. And he had a "little pamphlet" to distribute.[49] One wishes that a copy of this pamphlet had survived, and we can't help but admire this radical cowboy organizer, who used a seedy traveling midway show and the Eastern fascination with cowboys and the West to expose the cattle industry's monopoly of the Plains and stranglehold on labor. Sullivan's dream of a national cowboy union was never realized, not because of cowboy backwardness or individualism but because cowboys were turning nesters, and because the unionization of a whole section of agricultural laborers was premature by almost a century. But, as we shall see, cowboys led the way for rural workers in organized resistance.

There is evidence that when Powderly, the Master Workman of the Knights, turned his organization away from the National Trade Unions and other socialist labor organizations by his stand against the Haymarket anarchists and his antiboycott and antistrike policies, some cowboys were with the most militant faction that opposed him. One cowboy wrote this letter to the *Labor Enquirer* in support of Joseph Buchanan, popularly known as "Buck," who was the Western leader of the radical faction in the Knights:

> Dear Enquirer: I send you the picture of one of us. He is h--ll
> on "mutual assistance" [i.e., boycotts and strikes] but don't go
> much on blind *obedience*.
>   P'raps that's wrong, but then most of us *free* Americans *are*
> that way, thank God!
>   Here's our style: [woodcut of a cowboy on a *buck*ing bronco]
> We are Buck's, and don't you forget it.
>
>   [signed] Maverick.

The editor's comment on this letter reveals how the cowboys' popular
reputation of independence, which was formed even this early, can be
reconciled with radical populism:

> A cowboy is a peculiar Western institution. He not only thinks
> for himself but acts as well. He rounds up a good many things
> and doesn't let himself be rounded up ordinarily unless he knows
> the reason why.
>   Eastern tenderfeet who dwell in palaces ought to take off their
> coronets when they come West; Eastern slaves living in hovels
> learn here to ride instead of to be ridden.[50]

The International Workers' Association, of German Marxist origin, spread
from San Francisco east to Denver by 1883—where Buchanan's *Labor
Enquirer* became its organ and where the Rocky Mountain Division of
IWA's North American section had its headquarters.[51] Perhaps among the
many German immigrants to south-central Texas there were IWA members
who spread their organizing west and north from San Antonio, but this is
difficult to document because the organization was secret. The man who
in the seventies became the leading popularizer of Marxism in America,
Adolf Douai, after a year in prison for leading the 1848 revolution in his
hometown in Germany, came to Texas and edited an abolitionist newspaper in San Antonio for three years.[52] So there were radical European
ideas on the southwest Plains even in the fifties.

In the eighties there was a general movement to bring together populist
granger and antimonopoly societies. At a state convention the Texas Farmers' Alliance in 1885 appointed a committee to meet a Knights of Labor
committee at Dallas "to draft resolutions and bring about the effective
union" of the two organizations.[53] Like the later Industrial Workers of the
World, which came after the cowboy era, the principal strength of the IWA
was in the West, and one of the pledges of new members was to "assist
the alliance between the industrial and agricultural producers,"[54] which

would include, of course, cowboys. Cowboys on a visit to town and during long winter months of unemployment might well have been persuaded to join. The many Western railroad and mining towns in the eighties had lots of workers organized into trade unions—typographers, carpenters, bricklayers, machinists, railroad men, coal miners, even women with Knights of Labor local assemblies in unions of printers and laundry workers.[55] Cowboys could not possibly have been unaware of or aloof from this organized struggle against capital on the frontier. The struggle affected everyone.

Indeed, the historian of organized labor in Texas in the eighties believes that cowboys were the first of all frontier workers to confront corporate capital. Commenting on the cowboy strike against five cattle corporations in the Texas Panhandle in 1883, Ruth Alice Allen, professor of economics at the University of Texas in Austin, wrote, long enough ago, one would imagine, to have been heard by this time, that cowboys, "rather than the miners whose struggles have filled pages of labor history, were the legitimate precursors of the western labor movement. The cowboy, due to the nature of his work, became more completely cognizant of the growing disparity in attitudes and wealth between his employer and himself. If the cowboy's day had not already ended, because his industry was passing away beneath him, it would probably have been the hired cattle hands rather than the miners and the lumberjacks whose resentment echoed menacingly through the history of the West."[56] In her history of the Southwest Railroad Strike against Gould, Professor Allen again asserts that on the frontier "the first overt attack upon the corporation came not from employees congregated in towns but among the ranch workers of the [Texas] Panhandle country."[57] In an earlier, unpublished study Allen generalized even more strongly: "No two groups were more basically antagonistic in interests and attitudes than the cowboys of the western plains and the joint stock company. The cowboys were . . . the first group of workers in the West to feel and resent dominance by corporate employers with its hired bosses of impersonal owners whose primary aim was the delivering of profits."[58] Allen's placing of cowboys in the vanguard of the labor movement on the frontier has been ignored because her image of cowboys contradicts the dominant image of the culture and because her values are obviously left-wing.

Certainly inspired by, if not necessarily organized by, the trade and industrial labor union activity of the time, cowboys struck for higher wages, usually without prior notice, at the time of the spring roundups after the wagons had left the ranches and at the time they met at the determined starting points. It would be easy to plan ahead during the winter months because the time and the starting points of the roundups were by law set in advance. Clay remembers one at the spring roundup of 1884 on the lower Powder River in Wyoming: "half a dozen or more outfits met [at the starting point]. The cowpunchers . . . struck for higher wages. They had said nothing when engaged or on leaving for the meeting point. . . . The foreman . . . after some show of resistance lay down and granted the demands of the boys."[59] There is no evidence that this strike was timed to coincide with strikes at or to spread to other Wyoming roundups, but there might well have been some at adjacent roundups that failed to get into managers' reports, memoirs, or the minutes of association meetings. Clay, a general manager for all the ranches owned by the Swan Cattle Company, reports another kind of strike, a wildcat on a single ranch in the fall, where the cowboys could quit without much loss if their demands were not met because they faced being let go soon anyway. The trick was to time it when their labor was essential for a short period:

> We went up [from the 71 Quarter Circle ranch in the Sweetwater Valley in central Wyoming near the end of September 1884] to meet the beef herd as it moved down the Sweetwater. There had been a roundup below Crook's Gap and we had several more to make on the lower reaches of the river before trimming the herd and starting for Rock Creek, our shipping station on the Union Pacific Railroad. . . . About one o'clock we started the herd towards the ranch, about 600 beeves and some old cows. It was a fine clear day after the storm and the cattle spread out like a fan to graze. We pushed them gently down the creek and all was seemingly going well. About half afternoon three boys rode up to me saying they wished to talk to me. Although the foreman is the man they should have addressed, they passed Gatlin up and Shorty Brown dived into his subject at once by saying that they wanted their wages till the end of December instead of being paid off as was the custom when the fall work closed. If this request was not granted, they would quit at once. It was rather a trying moment, because we had a herd of beef just about ready to start to market, but there was just one answer. "Quit now if you wish. We can't grant your request." They turned their horses, gave a cowboy yell, waved their Stetsons in the air and made a bee-line for the headquarters. One by one the other boys, except two, came up, made the same demand and promptly galloped off to the ranch. Eight of them, I think, resigned in this prompt manner.

Clay, the foreman, the assistant foreman, and three scab cowboys managed to move the herd to the corral at the ranch. At the ranch Clay paid off the cowboys who had ridden off, now joined by the three scabs, probably frightened into solidarity, and they all terrorized the manager and foreman that night: "After the settlements were all made it appears they met in the big bunkroom. There was a good deal of talk about lynching or licking or tar and feathering, and as a prelude they fired off their revolvers." Clay slept that night with his rifle at hand and the windows barricaded. The next morning after breakfast the cowboys caught up "their private horses, consisting generally of two head [for each cowboy], packed their bed and other belongings on one of them and saddled up the other. There was a bit of pow-wow, but first one and then another pulled up the river toward Signor's" (a general store, road ranch, and reputed headquarters of the rustling element). The three defected scabs remained to help Clay, the foreman, and the ranch hands called in from making hay at the horse camp (minus the foreman of the horse-camp outfit who quit in loyalty to the strikers) to hold the herd for a few days and then to move it to the railroad. Clay ends the account with a revolting Horatio Alger–type parable "of the industrious and idle apprentice,"detailing how *the strikers* never amounted to anything, "drifted downward" and how the *"men who stood by"* prospered in corporate management or became little capitalists themselves.[60]

There were doubtless a great many of these wildcat strikes at the end of the season when herds had to be moved to railheads and when cowboys had little to lose by riding to the headquarters ranch, collecting their money and property, and riding to town on their own horses if they had them. They would be blackballed, but many were following the dream of becoming homesteading ranchers anyway, were sick of being exploited by managers like Clay, and saw their cowboying days drawing to a close. Probably some of them, seeing the overstocked ranges, untended herds, and aware of likely bad winters, foresaw the bankruptcies and retrenchments the greed of the corporations was forcing on themselves, and the consequent unemployment in the offing. So they made their risky moves while corporate profits were temporarily high, or seemed to be from account-book cattle counts.

There were big strikes in at least four of the spring roundups in central and north Wyoming in 1886. The strike activity was caused by the association's reducing the basic wage for cowboys by five dollars per month, generally but not completely complied with by ranches. A cowboy who worked for a ranch in the upper Powder River roundup district, which met at the mouth of the Crazy Woman River, later reported the strike in these words:

> As soon as the roundup started a strike was organized. All work
> was stopped and word sent to the different managers that no
> work would go on until they agreed to pay the former wages.
> They were caught at a disadvantage, work had to be shoved
> forward, they were obliged to brand their calves and gather beef,
> and as they had no time to get more men, were obliged to comply
> with the demands of the strikers and restore their wages.[61]

This account suggests that the strike was organized on the spot at the
meeting place of one roundup by all the cowboys from the different ranches.
But there is no way to tell at which roundup the strike started because all
the roundups in the region were connected by the system of neighboring
ranch representatives. If representatives of ranches in adjacent roundups
were not getting the demanded wages, they'd be sent back to their headquarters ranches to demand it of their managers, not allowed in the roundup
unless they got it, and in the meantime "the boys worked their cattle while
they were gone." If they came back with a refusal, they were ordered out
of the roundup "with threats of bodily harm," a Cheyenne newspaper
reported, and their company's calves remained unbranded. As a local
paper gleefully noted: "the other boys refusing to work any cattle of the
outfit, CY cows with maverick calves are now running around here as
thick as the flowers that bloom in the spring, Tra-la." (The CY Ranch was
owned by Joseph Carey, then president of the Wyoming Stock Growers
Association, later governor of Wyoming, and finally U.S. Senator of the
new state.)

A Montana newspaper reported this strike in a different roundup, the
lower Powder River:

> When roundup No. 23 met on the south fork of Powder River
> on the 10th inst., the boys concluded to strike for $40 a month
> all around. This was done by the men who were already receiving
> $40 who disapproved of the idea of men working by their side
> for $35 and as low as $30 per month. Not a wheel moved until
> the foremen submitted to the terms made by a committee from
> among the cowboys, to the effect that *no man* should work on
> roundup 23 for less than $40 a month [emphasis added].

The strike committee of Roundup 23 decided that "no man" would include
"no rep" from cattle companies in adjacent roundups.[62] Thus the rep
system and cowboy solidarity provided a unique way for cowboy strikes

to spread from one workplace to another. It is known that the strike spread to two more adjacent roundups in the Sweetwater-Platte area, and it probably spread much farther. A newspaper in northeast Colorado reported in May that of the cowboys in "the northern country . . . not a man is left on the range."[63] The wage demands of the strikers were met, and the roundup work went forward, but later in the summer the association pressured member cattle companies to reduce the wages of and eventually discharge and blackball cowboys who had struck. Carey was so ignorant of cowboys that he wanted harsher measures—he wanted to arrest the strike committees on the roundups who had barred his underpaid reps. They were to be charged with "committing a breach of the peace." But his barred reps indicated that they would not betray their comrades by swearing out a complaint before a justice against their fellow cowboys, and the matter was dropped.[64]

The most famous of cowboy strikes took place three years before the northern one we have been looking at. This was in the Texas Panhandle in the Canadian River valley, with the strike headquarters near Old Tascosa, twenty-five miles northwest of present-day Amarillo. John McCarty, the popular historian of the strike, says that it didn't involve many cowboys, that it was an "ill-starred venture" doomed to "complete failure" because of cowboy frivolity and aimlessness, that although it was inevitable because of cowboy discontent, it was a spur-of-the-moment protest made during just one randomly selected spring hunt for drifted cows.[65] Journalists and historians copying this account accept his interpretation, evidently eager to reinforce the popular notion that cowboys who go on the prod over the inequities of class are feckless misfits, not your mainline, died-in-the-wool cowboys, who are, as we all know, not real bright and are loyal to the death to owners.

The brief account of the strike by Lewis Nordyke, in his history of the range from the viewpoint of the Texas and Southwestern Cattle Raisers' Association, illustrates the typical treatment:

> In March of 1883, at the booming cowtown of Tascosa in the Texas Panhandle, two dozen punchers on the LX, LIT and LS ranches, all big outfits, handed their bosses a written ultimatum— higher pay by April 1 or a strike. The ranchers didn't meet the demand and the leather-pounders pulled the first cowland strike in history. They camped at the edge of Tascosa, hoping to halt the spring work and thereby realize their demands. They had a little pile of money to sustain their strike. Girls from the dancehall

part of town visited them a time or two taking along a supply of whiskey for sale. The strike fund was soon exhausted, and before long the men were back in the saddle at their old wages.

It was no trouble to hire cowpunchers. Adventurers were riding in daily, and there was a dribble of settlers who were willing to work for cow outfits at wages even lower than those the cowboys were drawing.[66]

But Ruth Allen, the first and more disinterested historian of the strike, on whom McCarty and Nordyke and all the rest are without recognition dependent, treats this early labor action seriously and sympathetically. Indeed, as we have seen, she treats the cowboy strikers as workers in the vanguard of the labor movement on the frontier.

The strike was a serious labor action and was recognized as such at the time. The Denver *Labor Inquirer*, the voice of labor in the West, on April 7, 1883, reported it under "Labor Notes": "The cowboys in the Pan Handle of Texas are striking for an advance from $30 to $50 per month." The strike eventually involved the cowboys and many of the wagon bosses of the five big squatting, unfenced ranches with Eastern and British financing—the LIT (Prairie Cattle Company, a Scottish syndicate), the T-Anchor (controlled by the Gunter-Munson Company, also involved in land speculation), the LE (Reynolds Land and Cattle Company, with backing from Alliance Trust of Scotland), the LS (Lee Scott Company), and the LX (owned by Boston financiers Bates and Beals). The strike began at the principal spring roundup near the mouth of Frio Creek, where three of the five companies (LIT, LS, and LX) had wagons rounding up drifted cattle. All three of the wagon bosses at the roundup and twenty-one cowboys signed the strike ultimatum.[67] This was *just the time* when the owners would feel the financial pressure the most. More than three hundred cowboys[68] eventually walked out when the strike spread to the line and pasture camps of the giant ranches and to the wagons and bunkhouses of the smaller ranches and included six out of the ten cowboys of the only fenced ranch of the region (Frying Pan of the Glidden and Sanborn Company) and spread as far away as the Tierra Blanca to the south, where there were twenty striking cowboys. U.S. Labor Commissioner statistics show that wages went up from the miserable $25 or $30 a month by more than 40 percent after the strike,[69] although most of the original strikers did not enjoy this benefit, because their jobs were taken by imported scabs and they did not come back to work as wage-earning cowboys in the area. Further, the striking cowboys wanted more than the double pay-raise they demanded in the ultimatum: $50 per month for cowboys and cooks, $75 for wagon bosses, or no one will work after a week; during that week, a walkout and gathering at the strike headquarters, where food will be provided; after the deadline, scab cowboys will "suffer the consequences."

This was the most ingenious plan for a strike that could be devised at a time when there were few conventions for this kind of agricultural labor action: the strike to begin at *the* spring roundup; prior support assured by at least one wagon boss of three of the five giant cattle companies involved; a popular leader—Thomas Harris, a part-time ranchman, a wagon boss of LS, with money connections in town to provide food for strikers if collected funds ran out; an immediate walk-off but a week's time to gather more cowboys at a headquarters camp by taking the ultimatum signed by respected cowboys to other ranges in the area; the promise of food for strikers and the vague threat of "consequences" to scabs after the deadline; the issue of wages, which every worker felt deeply as a grievance. This was altogether brilliant in conception, and it probably worked out just the way the leaders and most of the strikers wanted it to, in spite of the almost insurmountable difficulties of such an operation, like bringing wagons and remudas back to headquarters so that strikers could pick up their own horses, providing horses for strikers stranded on their ranches because they didn't have their own, and keeping strikers busy with strike-related activities but away from shootouts and vandalism, which could bring in the hated Rangers. The strike fund was not "gambled and guzzled, and danced away,"[70] as historians claim without a shred of evidence, falling all over each other in their eagerness to vilify the striking workers. The written demand promised "board" for only thirty days, which was easily provided by donations (it cost little to feed a few hundred cowboys for a month, and there were sympathetic merchants, farmers, and small ranchers to make contributions of food) and was offered to induce cowboys to quit. In fact, there is evidence of widespread local sympathy for the strikers among all elements of the community, a characteristic of workers' struggles in industrializing the United States.

Most cowboys who quit did so because they were fed up with syndicates and wanted to fight back, even though they knew they would likely never be hired back at all, let alone at double the wages they were earning. They were prepared to quit cowboying if necessary. The deliberately outrageous demand for *double* the going wages was a sign that other issues were involved, like the right to run cattle of your own and to be your own rep at roundups. The local sheriff said that the leader, Tom Harris, had "enough cattle of his own that he doesn't have to work for wages," and that, although the strikers didn't know how to insert it in the written statement, one of the demands was that small herd owners "be allowed to own and run our range cattle on the premises,"[71] that is, on the public lands claimed by the cattle companies. The strike was a joint action between small independent producers and wage laborers, who were frequently the same people. The strike was a declaration of class war, a populist regional war against foreign capital, and an appeal for all cowboys to join in on the side of the little ranchman. It said to all angry, frustrated cowboys who could understand language, "we're through *forever* selling our skills and labor to the big corporations squatting on thousands of acres of our land, chasing or buying out the family ranchers, and putting their brands on all the slicks on the range. We're going to take our share of the pie, using the same table manners you do."

The strike got lots of cowboys off the job and into small ranching, either as ranchmen or hired hands on shoestring ranches, and into mavericking operations, some organized into cattle pools, one organized by the leader of the strike, and associated loosely in a common cause for mutual protection. A nonstriking cowboy on the way back to his home ranch from Colorado remembered meeting a group of thirty "real cowboy strikers" around two wagons in September 1884, which was *eighteen months* after the beginning of the strike, just over the line in New Mexico Territory, where they "had been rounding up their remnants of cattle and were on the alert for spies and officers." They were "trying to gather their cattle and dispose of them as best they could." There is no suggestion in the account that the cowboy observer considered the cattle stolen. Since they were barred from the "company roundups," they were disposing of their cattle "as best they could" through a "neutral" rancher in New Mexico willing to buy cattle with brands owned by striking cowboys. Back in Tascosa, in the saloon owned by Jess Jenkins, Tom Harris's brother-in-law, he learned that the "strikers" were still "holding out," and he heard rumors that the strikers had spies to find out who the syndicate men were and were compiling a death list. From the sheriff he learned that Tom Harris led the strike and maintained "good control" over the forty to fifty cowboy militants who hated the "organized companies, some . . . foreign," with "costly managers and bookkeepers who live on and drink the best stuff money can buy." The strike was in a "windup" stage, "the companies . . . fast winning out against the strikers by driving them out of the Panhandle." Besides relocating in the community just over the state line to the west, "others had gone to the Pecos." Blackballed cowboys were still rounding up and claiming their cattle in the official roundups. But the cattle companies divided the loyalties of cowboys and put nester ranches out of business by allowing "men eligible to work the roundups" to gather and buy strikers' cattle. "It got so warm that when the roundups started last spring part of a ranger company was ordered to work with the roundup. They also borrowed Pat Garrett from New Mexico and had him in charge of a bunch of gun men." The sheriff credited Tom Harris's "coolheaded" control over his men for preventing what could have been "the bloodiest cattlemen's war that was ever fought."[72]

This unique eyewitness account of the situation a year and a half after the strike began makes clear that a protracted, potential "cattlemen's war" between striking cowboy ranchers and company managers followed the work stoppage and walkouts and was locally considered part of the strike, even after scab cowboys replaced the strikers and work continued as usual. (The sheriff's letter at the time speaks of "an ugly cowboy strike that has been on for more than a year now.")[73] Further, we note that striking cowboys, now blackballed, were cooperating in organized ways and with important support from the community to protect their holdings, even if it meant countering company terror and spying with armed self defense and finally relocating in New Mexico. What the cowboy observer doesn't seem to know is that the outfit he encountered just west of the state line was part of a new "cowboy syndicate," an incorporated pool of strikers' herds organized by Tom Harris, worked and managed by strikers themselves and supported by shareholders in the business community and by sympathetic working cowboys.[74] Cowboy syndicates seem perfect for uniting salaried and independent producers with community support in a continuing struggle, a truly remarkable strategy in a very early trailblazing strike against corporations in industrializing America, perhaps the first rural strike against them, and certainly the first to bring together the interests of wage and independent workers.

The strike wasn't just a walkout for higher wages but the first organized protest against big business on the Great Plains. Ruth Allen long ago declared to anyone willing to listen: "That the interests of cowboys as wage earners were not clearly differentiated from those of small cattle owners shows the unity [of independent producers] with the labor interests of the decade." Indeed this strike prefigured the unity of the Knights of Labor and the Farmers Alliance a few years later, particularly in Texas. "The joining of small owners with laborers may indicate bewilderment as to interests," Allen continues, "but in this also the cowboys were not unique. The entire labor movement was subject to the same incomprehension which stemmed in large part from the agrarian strain . . . as well as the great Utopians. And why should not cowboys be agrarian?"[75] Why shouldn't cowboys long for a little spread of their own? The strike expressed that longing.

The strike was a success if not interpreted too literally—that is, if we see it as a dramatic and forceful move to attract a lot of cowboys and small ranchers into a protracted war with the corporations. Twentieth-century commentators call the strike abortive, short-lived, and a failure because they consider only the meaning of the word *strike* now, as it has evolved over a century or more of labor history—a work stoppage to achieve job benefits. In the early eighties in the Texas Panhandle, long before modern strike practices and strategies had developed, a *strike* meant a struggle of cowboys against cattle companies that only began with quitting wage work but continued with cooperative activity in raising and marketing cattle and in defense against the companies' opposition. The striking cowboy ranchmen did not actually lose the war that they called a strike until years later. A careful student of this strike, Elmer Kelton, wrote a fine novel about it, *The Day the Cowboys Quit*, which unfortunately provides an unhistorical upbeat ending, the triumph of democracy and the populist rancher, an ending that ignores the continuing class struggle and the increasing hegemony of the capitalist class. He shapes history in the novel to fit his interpretation, expressed by a character-spokesman: "The old-time cowboy is finished, but the days of the big ranches are numbered too. This is going to be a little man's country."[76]

Kelton later defended this interpretation in a history journal: "The cowboys were blacklisted from work on any of the big outfits, but a great many stayed around anyhow. They settled in the Panhandle towns. Many took up land which the big ranches had been using. Some started their own small cattle brands or continued the brands they had had before, and which had been one of the big bones of contention in the first place. They had the sympathy of most of the other small settlers, and together they became a formidable political force. In many Panhandle counties they became the *dominant* political force. They shaped Panhandle history for generations."[77] Kelton is thinking wishfully that small Texas ranchmen controlled their own destinies. There is evidence that big capital finished taking over the Panhandle in the years after the strike just the way it did everywhere else.

That the cowboys and their families eventually lost the war is more a testimony to the superior strength of big capital supported fully by the state, including the Texas Rangers, than an indication of cowboy frivolity. All rural laborers lost that war. But the immediate "strike" was not lost until the companies drove the last nester from the Panhandle. Further, this first organized strike against cattle companies gave other cowboys the idea, although not for several years realized on this very Texas-size scale. For instance, in the fall of the year when the Panhandle strike began, twenty-six cowboys in Kansas struck against the Comanche Pool Ranch owned by Hunter and Evans. They straightway were fired and replaced by scabs, but most were going to be laid off for the winter anyway, probably the reason they chose this time to demand a raise.[78]

What the striking cowboys of the Canadian River did after they quit in March 1883 is what more and more cowboys on the Plains were going to do. But they led the way: they did it first, they did it together, and they did it with intelligence and gallantry. Their lives are unsung, except in Kelton's novel and in Ruth Allen's short chapter, and in a recent scholarly article in a regional historical journal that tries to see the strike from the cowboys' point of view.[79] Even the great working-class hero, Tom Harris, the leader, who should be more famous than Billy the Kid of the Lincoln County wars, awaits his biographer. You can't spit without hitting lengthy, worshipful accounts of the barons and businessmen who opposed Harris. But nary a word on the *popular* leader on the other side. We don't celebrate our working-class heroes unless they are outlaws. We still hear about martyrs of labor like Joe Hill, the Haymarket Eight, and Sacco and Vanzetti because industrial workers took them to their hearts. But Martin Irons, leader of the Southwest strike against Gould, and the brave heroes of cowboy wars, the ones on the side of the people like Tom Harris of Oldham County, Texas, and that other great Texan, Nate Champion, who spent the last ten years of his brief life in Johnson County, Wyoming, remain unsung. We can't hear them through the myth that celebrates only the outlaws and the imaginary feudal serfs and has no place for honest cowboy militants.

Cowboys as Homesteaders

I always wanted a cow ranch and a wife.

—*Teddy Blue*[1]

What did cowboys do when they had had enough and quit or went on strike and got blackballed? If they decided to remain in the business of raising cattle, they joined in a class war, recognized by everyone as a class war, by increasing their own herds. They branded mavericks. They entered, as an Omaha newspaper said in 1891, referring to murders of settlers in Johnson County, Wyoming, a "bitter conflict which raged incessantly between large and small owners as classes for six years." Seven years before, in 1884, the Omaha account continues, a "maverick law" resulted in "the little fellows" being "compelled to collect their cattle as they could" because of what was called the roundup "boycott," whereby cowboy ranchers were not allowed to work their cattle in official roundups. Blackballing and roundup boycotts by cattle associations forced nester ranchers into mavericking. The whole situation is described with unusual candor by the official historian of the Wyoming Stock Growers Association: "The big ranchers blacklisted those who thus came into competition with them; that is, they barred the upstarts from Association roundups. The men thus

ostracized then got together with their sympathizers and other small operators and rounded up what they called their own cattle."[2]

We see the same situation described from the other side in this simple
and straightforward account of what happened to unemployed cowboys
in Johnson County after the spring of 1887. It is by a cowboy recalling
the time of his youth.

> With a surplus of cowboys, some drifted back down into Texas.
> Some drifted into the small, pioneer towns and started into some
> kind of business of their own. But the largest per cent stayed.
> They took land by a squatter's right or some kind of right, and
> became nesters starting up a cattle business of their own. When
> they started to branding a few slicks or mavericks, they were
> called rustlers. These nesters or rustlers pooled together and ran
> a roundup wagon of their own.[3]

A cowboy in the Canadian River region of Texas in the early eighties
described the situation simply in these words, which are taken from a
typescript of an interview with him in the late 1920s, here published for
the first time:

> The LS people [i.e., the owners of the Lee-Scott Co., head-
> quarters of the giant squatter-ranch fifteen miles southwest of Old
> Tascosa on the Alamocitos: L. C. Scott, the Wall Street financier;
> W. M. D. Lee, the part-owner/manager] were against the majority
> of the people. They were opposed. It would be hard to tell all
> the reasons. Every man felt he was as good as another or a good
> deal better. Some of those people carried the impression that
> because they owned a certain number of cattle they had a pre-
> cedence over somebody else, and that did not go at all. That
> accounts for some of it. Some of the people that were killed had
> been playing state officers and they were paid by the state and
> by the cattle companies. I think they were too close with stealing
> [that is, meddling with maverick operations]. At that time cattle
> were outside, loose, and cattle growing up when they were a
> certain age they would get separated from the cow. It was cus-
> tomary in the cattle country to brand everything as theirs. In a
> good many cases they did not have a right to them. They called
> them mavericks. That accounted for a good deal of the stealing.
> Sometimes they were wrong and sometimes they were right.
> There was not a large amount of stealing in there. The big cattle
> companies would brand stuff that was not theirs and if caught

up with they would say, "We made a mistake." But if another
man branded one of the cattle company's they would say, "That
is mine, and you stole it." There was quite a bit of hard feeling
toward the big companies on the part of the majority of cowboys.
I never had any inclination to feel that I was one of the rustlers.
Those people went ahead and did what they did, but I had no
interest with them. They did not burn brands very often. They
mavericked mostly. Some of the people are living yet who did
it, so I won't mention any names or the brands that were burned.[4]

Another old-timer summed up the situation thus: "Men ordinarily honest
stole cattle from the big outfits and did not consider it dishonest but an
act justifiable in a war of the classes."[5] The range struggles of the eighties
and early nineties were between rich and poor, a war of the classes,
cattlemen against blackballed cowboys with greasy-sack shoestring ranches.
They involved fence cutting and sheep slaughter but were not fence and
sheep wars in themselves. The corporations, having money, fenced first,
and often fenced public land; cowboy ranchers cut the fences when they
intruded on their ranges. The cattle companies hated sheep as competitors
for free grass and sometimes ordered their cowboy employees to drive
them off or destroy them; but cowboy settlers often turned sheepmen
themselves.[6] The popular notion that cowboys hated sheep and sheepmen,
like so much of the Western myth, reflects the wishes and interests of
cattlemen.

When this class war burst out into open violence with small armies on
both sides in Johnson County in 1892, the Denver *Rocky Mountain News*
wrote an editorial summarizing the decade-old conflict as one between big
cattle companies (or barons and kings) and settlers or *ranch*men (as distinct
from nonresident *cattle*men):

> When the true history of the range cattle business, since the date
> of its first conflict with the vanguard of Western pioneer husband-
> men, is written, it will disclose a record of intimidation, oppression,
> pillage and outrage perpetrated upon the latter by the big cattle
> companies that will arouse the just indignation of all fair-minded
> readers.
>
> The late raid upon the agricultural settlers of Wyoming, with
> the design of frightening them from their homes, by demonstrat-
> ing that there was no security to life for those who encroached
> upon the government domain which had been appropriated by
> cattle kings, will bring this subject forcibly to the attention of the
> country. It may result beneficially to Wyoming and to the Rocky

mountain country generally by attracting settlers by thousands to fertile and well-watered sections that are now monopolized for grazing purposes without any legal right whatever as against the right of the homesteader or bona fide occupant. The cattle baron can assail the actual settler with no weapons that are lawful, and is obliged to rely on such means as are calculated to discourage settlement by making it dangerous and unprofitable. He has never wanted for agents to perform that kind of service among the reckless and devil-may-care class who find their way into the range business.

To the attempted justification of jayhawking and murderous proceedings carried out by hired ruffians, on the plea that the object is to recover stolen property or arrest the thieves, every informed person knows that for one head of stock stolen from the big companies by the loose characters that are found in border settlements, as they are also found in our centers of refinement, one hundred head have been swept into the large herds and lost to their rightful owners, the ranchmen. The big companies have been the despoilers with exceptions that by comparison are not worth mentioning.

It should be understood that while the actual settler can only lawfully claim the land he takes up, as a preemptor or home-steader, and what he can acquire by purchase, he has a moral right to the use of the surrounding open range for his stock as against the stock of non-resident cattle barons or non-residents of any kind. This is the common law of the West, and the right has been enjoyed and enforced by rural settlers since the first immigration across the Alleghenies a century and a half ago. Of course that right cannot have much value while herds by thou-sands, owned by people in the large cities of Europe and America, are roaming over the plains. Such a herd would eat the grass bare and tramp it out for miles about a settler's home in a day or two.

Is it any wonder that while the occupancy and improvement of the country under the land laws is unreasonably resented by the cattle barons, the settler regards the big herds in proximity to a home or a settlement as a destructive nuisance and its owner as a trespasser? And measured by the custom of the West, and by every rule of equity and fair play, the settler is right. The conclusion is that upon the approach of the bona fide occupant the big ranch herds should be retired, and the small owners, in

banding together for mutual protection against the lawless mach-
inations of cattle corporations, will most assuredly merit the good
will and moral support of all honest and law-respecting people.[7]

Cowboys were drifting from the bunkhouses to their own dugouts or
cabins. There were far fewer jobs after mid-decade, particularly after the
die-outs of the winter of 1886–87 forced the mismanaged cattle companies
out of business and almost all into sharp retrenchments. Unemployed
cowboys became small ranchers, many with radical populist politics. When
the main Western labor spokesman, Joseph Buchanan, went down from
Denver to give the principal address at a supper-dance of the Knights of
Labor in Las Animas, New Mexico, one Friday evening in December 1886,
he didn't try to recruit cowboys into labor unions but pitched an antimonopoly line to small ranchers. Although the comrades had billed his
speech as "The Labor Question," he addressed "every cattle raiser" who
was threatened by "Phil Armour, the butcher prince." "There were in the
audience owners of herds who had felt the power of this man Armour
within the past few months." Buchanan spoke to a large group that filled
the Town Hall, including a delegation from La Junta and men who "had
come from the range 8 and 10 miles away." Everybody he met that
weekend was "friendly to Socialism" and at least "two score" were friends
of the "Chicago Anarchists," then in jail awaiting execution.[8]

The Northern New Mexico Small Cattlemen and Cowboys' Union was
organized, evidently by the Knights of Labor, in 1886. Capitalists were
pointedly excluded: "no cattle owners who employ more than two men"
could join. Most of the eighty cowboy ranchmen who joined at the first
meeting depended on income from seasonal work for the cattle companies.
The cooperation between wage earners and small producers, indeed the
identity of the two among cowboys, characterized this period in American
history. The Knights had always had an ideal of a cooperative commonwealth made up of independent producers, and they had always worked
for cooperation between workers and family farmers. On the other side,
the Farmers Alliance was seeking support from wage laborers. Cowboys
alone formed a class of wage workers who in increasing numbers were
also part-time independent producers in the same craft, that is, nester
ranchers, a most suitable group to organize around the currently strong
populist principles of solidarity. Thus this Cowboys' Union at the first
meeting demanded "living wages" for the five months' working season of
the average cowboy and a priority for themselves over "import[ed] cheap
labor." (This reference seems to indicate that the cattlemen of the Northern
New Mexico Stock Growers' Association were importing Mexican or Te-

jano vaqueros to replace blackballed cowboys.) At the second meeting two weeks later, the union proposed a monthly wage scale that was weighted in favor of experienced and seasonal cowboys, who made up the greater part of the membership.[9] Almost at the same time the Knights were forming this Cowboys' Union, a newspaper in northwest Colorado reported that "the cowboys of Wyoming are forming a Knights of Labor assembly," which probably organized a union much like the one in New Mexico.[10]

The increase of nester ranchers created an eddy in nineteenth-century United States economic history. The century shows the rise of capitalist production and the decline of petty independent production—of farmers, small manufacturers, artisans, teamsters, and builders who based themselves on self-earned property and their own or, at most, their families' productive labor. During the last three decades of the century there was an "increasing hegemony of northern capital over independent commodity production," that is, over family units of agricultural settlers, small businesses, and small manufacturers. After Reconstruction in 1877, Southern capital joined the hegemony. Populism arose as a movement of the small agricultural producing class to resist the pressure of rising rail rates, shortage of credits, crop liens, mortgage foreclosures, and manipulated commodity exchanges. But populism did not succeed long in stemming the tide of capitalism and the crumbling of the small independent producing class.[11] Small nester ranches pretty well disappeared in the early years of the present century, either bankrupted or absorbed or converted into modern fenced ranches—smaller, more scientific, more specialized, and more locally financed than the sprawling corporate squatters of the 1880s.

Thus when the cowboy quit or was fired as a day laborer and began building a small spread of his own—a movement quite common in the eighties on the Great Plains, he for a brief time held at bay the development of corporate cattle production during a period when elsewhere capital's independent-producer competitors were rapidly crumbling. The movement was retrograde—against the general tendency: for a period during the last decade and a half of the century the general rise of modern capital was slowed by homesteading cowboys, who later, with the rapid decline of family ranches, returned to the mainstream by either becoming capitalist cattlemen themselves or, much more commonly, returning to the class of wage slaves. Consequently, we can add another quality peculiar to the history of the cowboy. Not only was he unique among all United States workers in that public land and roaming unmarked cattle allowed him to quit his job and go into business on his own but in that, alone of all workers-turned-independent producers, he held back, however briefly, the course of the cattle empire of his old bosses. Indeed, as an independent producer, he contributed to its demise in its form of untended, unfenced herds. But the end of family ranching inevitably followed the end of the open range: a quarter-section homestead did not provide pasture and hay to produce enough beef cattle to support a family by yearly sales. And few family ranchers could afford to buy additional acreage to make the business possible, nor could they lease public land for grazing small herds, because government leasing policies always favored big cattle owners. When the family rancher could not make ends meet by augmenting his own with adjacent open range, he sooner or later had to quit and leave the industry once again exclusively to the capitalists. He lost the fight for independence in the end, but so also did almost everybody else.

There are no separate figures, but we can reasonably assume that the independent family ranchers went the same way as the landowning family farmers who worked for themselves, although most of the latter were in thrall to banks and merchants—from 75 percent independents in 1880 to 64 percent in 1900 to 52 percent in 1940 (this last figure is just from Kansas) and so on in accelerated decline until today, when there are very few. Farms became fewer and larger (5.9 million in 1947 to 2.9 million in 1970, the average doubling in size), and small farms declined in number by half in only fourteen years (farms with less than 100 acres from 3 million in 1950 to 1.4 million in 1964).[12] (These statistics are only suggestive and doubtless don't indicate to what a great extent agribusiness since the 1920s has put family ranchers out of business. But they are the best available because corporation disclosure laws prevent research into land central- ization. As the historian of United States populism explains, "large scale property ownership in America is a legal secret"; information about it is "first, not available, and second, its non-availability is not a subject of public debate" since "cultural hegemony" sanctions land centralization.)[13]

What about the class consciousness of the cowboy-turned-rancher in the eighties? If he simultaneously turned a would-be capitalist upon reg- istering his claim and his brand, where is the class war of the Plains? The fact is that he kept his cowboy-worker loyalties, and because his old em- ployers continued to harass him, although now in different ways suited to his new role as competitor, he continued to think of capitalists as enemies. For a time anyway. The seductions of success, very much less common than failure, would characteristically lead a few to class betrayal in time. In other words, blackballed cowboy nesters continued to participate in the class struggle. Before those so inclined—as many probably were after a time—could ally themselves with the owning class, they were in most cases wiped out by the triumphant march of big capital. The change from wage earner to small rancher would result in some changes of material interests that would coincide with those of his old bosses—like a common passion for land, with an attendant imperialist hostility to native possessors, such as American Indians and Mexicans, and a common desire for low freight rates and high prices for his beeves. But since nester cowboys were not in the market for hired labor, they would not share capitalist attitudes to workers and capital's endeavors to create labor surpluses. (Indeed, capitalist need for labor surplus provided another motive beyond competition for ranges in its campaigns to drive settlers out of business and back into the labor market.) The old culture of hostility to absentee bosses, with their foppish tents and servants and Havana cigars, reinforced by feeling the effects of new draconian measures against nesters, overbalanced any shared interests with big owners and operated for a time to produce class war on the Plains.

Sometimes a cowboy's work would put him in a position to pick up a good-sized herd quickly. An old cowboy recalled in notes he made for his biographer how he assembled his first herd. In 1883 the Western Kansas Cattle Growers Association posted him and another cowboy in a log cabin by the Western Trail in the Cherokee Strip to cut out "all range brands belonging to our Association members that were picked up in the through trail herds." During the peak of the season in June and July as many as twelve herds of 2,000 to 3,000 cattle would pass their inspection point daily. Our young cowboy took to buying the "give out cattle," the

> little leppies, some yearlings, and others that were not able to travel up the trail. Some would have sore feet, some were sick or crippled. These cattle would be eventually left along the trail anyway, so I began to dicker the trail bosses out of them. I bought them cheap, and had the trail boss write me a bill of sale on whatever paper we had handy in our pockets, an old envelope or the back of a letter, the edge of a newspaper or magazine or the blank pages torn from the front and back of a brand new book. After branding these cattle with my own brand, I would throw them back in a little valley I knew where there was a spring and the grass was good, not too far from the YL Ranch [the ranch of his employer]. . . . So my enterprise grew, and I was soon initiated into the mystic economic system by which cattlemen made money appropriating livestock on the range, a practice that was carried out through their hired help. The only difference I could see was that I was doing my own work, riding for cattle like they did in the early days in the brush of south Texas, after

the Civil War. My activities were similar in every way to those of the Association members, and I, too, was prospering through my own initiative.

At the end of the season he sold his herd for $1,800 to a new ranch to the west of the YL. Later he had to flee Oklahoma Territory to avoid being sent to jail for this and similar operations as a ranch foreman, "getting some good stuff" to add to his own herd.[14]

The controversy over whether the cattle companies own all the mavericks was clearly laid out by an editorial condemning the invaders of Johnson County, Wyoming, in the Denver *Daily News*:

> For many years the maverick—a calf following no particular cow—became by the law of the ranges the property of the owner of the brand with which it could be first branded, and the custom was common for range cattle owners to stimulate their employees to scour the plains for such animals by paying so much a head for all branded with the employer's brand—the price ranging between $5 and $7. During all those years that disposition of mavericks was considered perfectly honest as it undoubtedly was, since such animals belong to no one, or what amounts to the same thing, it is impossible to trace the ownership. But with the advent of settlers, when there was a chance that others than the agents of the cattle barons might brand these strays, laws were enacted at the instigation of the latter by which the custom theretofore followed and honored was decreed to be dishonest and under which all mavericks should thereafter be sold exclusively for the benefit of the cattle kings.
>
> Wyoming has such a law and its operation sweeps into the hands of the cattle corporations not only the mavericks that presumably belong to their own herds, but also such mavericks as may rightfully belong to the herds of legitimate settlers and small stock owners, for it is forbidden under severe penalty to brand such animals except when it is done officially at the regular round up, when they are sold for the benefit of the cattle barons' association under conditions that preclude all but men of means from bidding.[15]

Here we are concerned with the new independent producer who increases his small herd by burning his brand on and cutting his mark in the ears of weaned this-year calves and occasional yearlings who escaped the irons and knives of the previous roundup. We are not here concerned with early Texas and New Mexico hunts for wild cattle to build trail herds or to skin for their hides. Nor with cowboys paid either wages or bonuses by a corporation for putting company brands on range mavericks. Nor even with all the devious and time-honored ways of creating mavericks or with outright brand burning or rustling—although we shall shortly deal with those activities as escalations of the class war. Nor are we concerned with butchering of cattle owned by corporations, destroying the hide, or at least the branded portion of it, and selling the meat to retail butchers and road ranchers. We are here concerned with the cowboy who typically has put his brand on some mavericks while still working for wages and has boarded them on his boss's range for so much per head per year or has sequestered them somewhere or knows what herd they're in and can cut them out for himself when he gets an opportunity to trail them to a part of the range he thinks of as his own. He now has decided to become a rancher himself. Most often his old and his new work overlap—he is for several years a winter ranchman and a summer cowboy. And he now increases his herd, begun while he was a wage earner, not only by branding the calves of his own cows but while doing so keeping his eye peeled for mavericks, branding them as his own when he happens upon them, and adding them to his herd.

One Texas cowboy turned rancher jokes about how he began: "The laws of Wyoming required a man to brand his calves before they were a year old and as a great many of the cowmen violated that law . . . I adopted some of those neglected yearlings and put my brand on them so that cowboys would know whose they were. And also to increase my herd."[16]

Our cowboy-ranchman may even ride out in search of mavericks on a range he knows the roundup has missed this year or in a valley it regularly misses every year. Or he may ride out a few weeks or days before the roundup sweeps the ranges near his own and brand up mavericks before the roundup does. All of this is illegal, as is even branding calves of his own she-cows, we should remember, but only because the cattle companies make the laws to keep the would-be ranchman out of business. And he'd better smell a potential maverick's breath for milk and not make a mistake about putting his brand on one that afterwards turns out not to be weaned from a mother he doesn't own. The two tagging along sporting different brands could send him to prison. But he's forced into this dangerous and illegal activity of mavericking because he can't buy mavericks or even attend the legal roundup to collect his own herd and brand his own calves or yearlings. As yet, although he's a lawbreaker he has done nothing "dishonest," or, to avoid a word that has little meaning in the system in which he is operating, he has done nothing contrary to ancient range convention that allots mavericks to finders. He hasn't, in short, put his brand on an animal he *knows* belongs to another, even if, as is usually the case, the "other" is an impersonal, absentee capitalist.

He will probably take the next step, from mavericker to rustler, because he's already outside the law and because he's pressed to the wall by the cattle companies. The step is tentative, and generally doesn't proceed beyond occasional rustling on the side. The first step is to *make* mavericks. He does this in lots of ways. He can make them by "sleepering." He rides out in front of the roundup by a day and moves some cows with calves around in back of it so that they will be missed and not branded. Then he returns after the calves are weaned, brands them, and drives them to his herd. Or he creates a maverick by "hair branding." He finds a big unbranded calf still following a mother who wears the brand of a neighbor cattle company. He runs that company's brand lightly on the calf so that the hair is quite visibly burnt but no scar is made on the hide, and he cuts the company mark on the ear or ears. The roundup will not cut out the calf for branding because it is apparently marked already. The cowboy-rancher returns before the next roundup and puts his own brand on the now slick yearling and alters the ear mark to his own. Or he can use another form of sleepering: cut the ears of a calf to match its mother so that a rider in the roundup checking from afar will think it is already branded. Then the rustler picks up the calf after it is weaned, burns his own brand on it, and reshapes its ears to his mark. Or he creates a maverick simply by killing the mother. Or he does so by forcibly separating a calf from its mother and preventing it from rejoining her in numerous ingenious and some very cruel ways. For instance, while driving a small herd north from Texas, when the cowboy owner "met up with any unbranded calves, he'd rope the cow, run a hot ring between her toes so she couldn't keep up with him and neck the calf to one of his own cows."[17] But he would be caught dead to rights if he let a calf sporting his brand return to its cattle-company mother to become a walking testimony against him.

All of this is dangerous, but he has to do it to exist as a small rancher. Some few cowboy ranchers took the next step in rustling to brand burning. Probably not many of them burnt brands, because if you got caught the evidence was clear enough for conviction even in a court friendly to home-steading ranchers. There's your brand burnt over another brand for all the world to see, if all the hair were picked clean away for a clear look, or even if the cow in question were killed and skinned to expose the old brand on the flesh side. But there are ways to minimize the dangers of discovery. Our cowboy-rancher now turned brand burner could change some company brands to his own by using his running iron to complete lines and make new ones. To take some famous examples of brand burning of the giant XIT herds by surrounding Panhandle and New Mexico ranchers, we can cite Boxed XITF 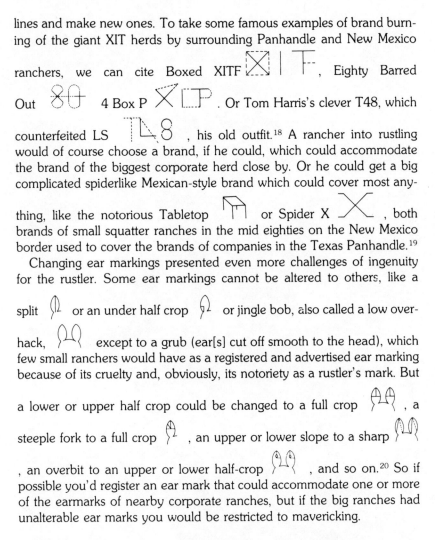, Eighty Barred Out 4 Box P . Or Tom Harris's clever T48, which counterfeited LS , his old outfit.[18] A rancher into rustling would of course choose a brand, if he could, which could accommodate the brand of the biggest corporate herd close by. Or he could get a big complicated spiderlike Mexican-style brand which could cover most anything, like the notorious Tabletop or Spider X , both brands of small squatter ranches in the mid eighties on the New Mexico border used to cover the brands of companies in the Texas Panhandle.[19]

Changing ear markings presented even more challenges of ingenuity for the rustler. Some ear markings cannot be altered to others, like a split or an under half crop or jingle bob, also called a low overhack, except to a grub (ear[s] cut off smooth to the head), which few small ranchers would have as a registered and advertised ear marking because of its cruelty and, obviously, its notoriety as a rustler's mark. But a lower or upper half crop could be changed to a full crop , a steeple fork to a full crop , an upper or lower slope to a sharp , an overbit to an upper or lower half-crop , and so on.[20] So if possible you'd register an ear mark that could accommodate one or more of the earmarks of nearby corporate ranches, but if the big ranches had unalterable ear marks you would be restricted to mavericking.

Rustling, as distinct from mavericking, was not practiced to any great extent by settlers because the many cattle detectives employed by the cattle companies made it too dangerous for homesteaders, who were proving up their claims (and so were not as mobile as the few full-time rustling gangs had to be) and who were limited by family responsibilities. Rather, they would enter into cooperative arrangements. At a fairly low level of organization, one could execute a raid on the legal roundup, from which you were debarred, in order to recover settler cattle. Two managers

of big companies describe the situation in Wyoming during the early nineties:

> These men worked together with sufficient force, armed with Winchesters and revolvers so as to intimidate the owners and even the foremen of the outfits. They did their work openly— going so far as to wait until the roundup was made and then tying down and branding anything they chose.
>
> The men working for the cattle outfits seemed to have an understanding among themselves that they were being paid so much a month for working, not fighting, and it was up to the owner or manager to do his own fighting.

This kind of forceful incursion into official roundups would not, of course, be possible without the class loyalty of wage-earning cowboys to black-balled cowboys turned ranchers.

> It is told of Al Allison [partner of Jack Flagg's Hat outfit near Buffalo, Wyoming] that one day he rode up to the wagon of a roundup on the Antelope range and addressed the owner, "Mr. K, you've got some of our cattle in that roundup and I'd like to go in and cut them out." He was observing the outward form of range etiquette, he was asking permission, and besides he was armed and no one cared to stop him. He thereupon rode into the herd and cut out a sizable number of big unbranded calves. [21]

Intervening in the official roundup can be combined with an unofficial roundup consisting of a single wagon.

> Robert Tisdale was rounding up on his range, when he found himself camped across a creek from an independent roundup being conducted by Nate Champion and his friends. Next day,

---

TEXAS COWBOYS TURNED RANCHMEN IN JOHNSON COUNTY, WYOMING, ABOUT 1890

Helena H. Smith in her book on the Johnson County War identified the man on the right as Nate Champion, but several local historians disagree. Most probably they are partners in Jack Flagg's Hat-brand outfit and the man in the middle is Al Allison, brother of Texas trail boss-turned-family-ranchman John Tisdale, murdered by a gunman in the employ of the Stock Growers Association in 1891. (COURTESY OF THE AMERICAN HERITAGE CENTER, UNIVERSITY OF WYOMING.)

76 WAGON, WITH NATE CHAMPION

The identification is uncertain. "The 76" was the main brand of the British-owned Powder River Cattle Company, the largest operating in Johnson County. At its peak in 1883, the 76 put six wagons into the regional roundup (of twenty-seven wagons total). Nate Champion from 1882 was a cowboy and wagonboss for the Bar C and EK, two other British corporate operations in the County, but was blackballed in about 1888 for running his own cattle. The first mounted man on the left has been identified as Champion by an old-timer. (COURTESY OF THE AMERICAN HERITAGE CENTER, UNIVERSITY OF WYOMING.)

after Tisdale and his men had gathered fifteen hundred head of wild range cattle, Champion and his men rode out leisurely on fresh mounts, armed to the teeth, and ignoring Tisdale's cowboys completely, they proceeded to rope, throw and tie all the calves, after which they scattered the remainder of the herd.[22]

The historian leaves out of this account that the calves belonged to the settlers and would have been stolen by the roundup foreman if not reclaimed by Champion's outfit, which was composed of cowboys turned ranchmen.

Another cooperative method of rounding up your cattle and getting your share of mavericks was to form a partnership of some ranchers and so have the means to send a wagon, by threat of arms, to the official roundup, from which you were legally barred as not being members of the stockmen's association. A sympathetic foreman might welcome you and your partners as offering skilled help in the roundups and hope that the big ranch managers didn't hear of it. And you could offer other small ranchers repping for themselves the use of your wagon (the other wagon bosses would be forbidden by their employers to do so). Jack Flagg, a blackballed cowboy in Johnson County, wrote a newspaper account of such an action:

> There was one more wagon added to round-up that spring [the Upper Powder River roundup in 1889]. I had been out to so much trouble gathering my cattle that I determined to start a wagon. I had before this sold to Martin Tisdale, Lou Webb, Thomas Gardner, and W. H. Hill each a one-fifth interest in the Hat brand which I owned. I had bought the brand from W. E. Hathaway of Powder River in the fall of 1886, it had been on the record in Buffalo for two years prior to that time. We each of us owned a string of horses, and we had a team and wagon, and so, as we only had to hire a cook, we concluded that the cheapest way would be to put a wagon on the round-up.[23]

The young wrangler for the Hat brand wagon in the spring roundup of the next year later recollected his impressions of his first job, interesting because his account shows that the wagon for the partnership of five nesters was used by other nesters in the roundup, the beginnings of a cattle co-operative or nester cattle pool, a populist form of organization that was becoming fairly common on the Great Plains.

> The morning after I reached the nester wagon, I took over the job as a horse wrangler. There were about forty head of good saddle horses in the cavvy, or remuda. Each partner had his own string of cow horses. In my string there were three ponies, a rather tall flea bitten bay, a little old bench-kneed brown that wasn't worth a damn, and a small strawberry roan that was a real saddle pony. At first I was a little homesick and some disappointed. When I hired out I supposed it to be herding horses on some ranch. At first I was a little spooky, with the cowboys all having some sort of gun in a holster on their cartridge belt. Some of the tough-looking guys were wearing two six-shooters. With most everyone being nice to me, it was only a few days 'till I felt right at home among the cowboys. These five men of the nester wagon

BAR C WAGON, WITH JACK FLAGG AND NATE CHAMPION, 1884

The identification and date are uncertain. The Bar C was one of the British cattle operations in Johnson County. It liquidated in 1889. Jack Flagg came up from Texas in 1882 and for several years cowboyed for the Bar C. Another Texan, Nate Champion was a wagonboss for the Bar C in 1884. Flagg was blackballed at the end of 1886, Champion two years later. They are probably in this picture; but since no other authentic picture of them survives, it's difficult to determine who they are. Champion was locally remembered as "stocky" and was twenty-seven years old in 1884. Is he the seated cowboy in the center with a pipe in his hand? (COURTESY OF THE AMERICAN HERITAGE CENTER, UNIVERSITY OF WYOMING.)

were using the hat brand on their cattle. They were all top cow hands who knew the cow business and range conditions. When the winter of 1886–87 hit the country, they probably were among those who were out of a job. They pooled their wages, located a claim on the Red Fork of Powder River, and started up in the cattle business. They were not cattle thieves. They were just small cattlemen or nesters, no different than 80 percent of the nesters and grangers. They probably would brand a maverick or slick when one crossed their path. The HAT wagon worked right along with the cow outfits. They were, though, not allowed to work the roundup until the cowmen were through. There were always nesters at the HAT wagon, gathering up their own cattle, branding up their calves. The cowboys and nesters were quite friendly. It was the foremen or managers of the cow outfits who were bitter towards the nester. They were all in the maverick game. Some of the managers or foremen for the cow outfits had their own private brands, and in one way or another were building up their herd of mavericks.[24]

There were other ways for nesters to band together for their collective strength and welfare. Groups of nesters went beyond the Hat brand type of partly co-op, partly partnership cattle pool. They formed collective cattle companies or incorporated pools or "cowboy syndicates" which bought the herds of blackballed cowboys and used their work in return for shares in the company and, to take advantage of the general hostility to the cattlemen, offered shares also to those local merchants and even working cowboys who supported nester cowboys. A "cowboy syndicate" was composed of nester-cowboy herds worked and self-managed by nester cowboys. Or it could be used as a legal cover to continue individual family ranch operations. An example is the "Tom Harris Syndicate," which, as we have seen, helped cowboys during the 1883 Panhandle strike.[25]

A "Cowboys' Cattle Company," a joint stock company selling shares to "cowboys on the range," formed in Colorado in 1884, was still shipping herds two years later. Another cooperative way for cowboys to become cattle owners appeared a year later in Montrose, Colorado: a "mutual benefit association organized for the purpose of jointly herding its members' stock" and thus to "place the cowboy on his old footing" as a "cowman and live stock owner." A cowboy could buy shares, but the big innovation was that he would receive a share for "every animal turned over to the company" and after every five years receive back five head for every head put in.[26]

Also, cowboy nesters did what grangers had made a common practice: they established "claim clubs" which hired counsel to protect members' homestead claims and preemptions from conflicting claims and boundary disputes contrived by the well-paid lawyers of the cattle companies. Nester ranchers or grangers wrote individually and organized letter-writing campaigns to the Secretary of the Interior or to government agencies attacking large cattle companies or even reporting a cattleman for fencing "100,000 acres of choice hay land" and for bribing the "land agent."[27] There were some efforts to market beef cooperatively: for instance, in 1888 the Dallas headquarters of the Farmers Alliance together with the Knights of Labor sought to organize a "cooperative system of refrigerating and distributing beef . . . to get a fair price for beef and reduce the price to the consumer."

Realizing that they had to have capital to get started, they rather surprisingly approached the Texas and Southwestern Cattle Raisers' Association which not surprisingly refused to give them any help.[28] In the only cowboy state or territory with a truly mass-based populist movement, Dakota farmers and ranchers developed cooperative commodity exchanges as early as 1884, and four years later there was a territory-wide exchange.[29] Such cooperative financing, marketing, and purchasing systems were the keys to populist organizing because they would benefit people where they could feel it most: increase their income by circumventing the established economic structures. But one can imagine how livestock commission firms fought the rival American Livestock Commission Company, the first experiment in cooperative multistate livestock marketing, organized by the Kansas, Missouri, and Nebraska Alliances, with some help from the Grange, in 1889–1890.[30] And the few such cooperatives that nester ranchers organized were soon destroyed by the powerful opposition of all the non-producing and monopoly elements of the cattle industry: cattle companies, livestock commission companies, railroads, meat packers, ranch supply manufacturers and distributors, and banks. The failure of the co-ops left ranch families only the illusory hope of national monetary reform through electoral politics. And, of course, their turning to the silver movement and the People's Party diverted their energies and thus contributed to the failure of the cooperative movement.

At a different level of organizing, farmers and ranchers formed local alliances and held independent roundups. Such, for instance, was the Northern Wyoming Farmers' and Stock Growers' Association, formed at a large meeting of settlers and small stockmen in Buffalo in late 1891, as described by Jack Flagg in his newspaper account:

> The small stockowners then determined for their mutual benefit to organize and form for their protection, an association. A great many of them claimed that the large owners had been driving out of the country and shipping their stock from time to time. There is a law on the statutes that makes it a fineable offense for an outfit when moving cattle, to drive off of its range an animal belonging to another party. The big outfits had never respected the law, and had time and again driven cattle off in their herds that they would be moving through the country, belonging to farmers, and turned them loose many miles from their owner's range. In the majority of cases these cattle would never be recovered and on the range where they were turned loose, no owner could be found for them when they were rounded up the

next year, as the farmers owning them would not be able to have a representative on the different round-ups looking out for them, and they would be called strays and would be shipped and the money turned into the [Wyoming Stock Growers] association.

The object of the farmers and small stock growers in forming an association was mainly to guard against that way of losing their stock. The night of Oct. 30 was set as the time for holding the meeting in Buffalo to organize. About all the stock owners were present, and the by-laws having been read nearly everyone present joined. John R. Smith was elected president and Dr. J. C. Watkins, secretary and treasurer. The by-laws required every member to report any crookedness seen on the range to the association, and any one of the *big* outfits found driving stock off the range was to be prosecuted [emphasis added].[31]

This organization of small agricultural producers in subsequent monthly meetings took legal steps to recover money lost because of the Wyoming Stock Growers Association's seizure of settlers' cattle in Omaha stockyards. And in open defiance of the law, they planned an independent roundup for the next spring. The roundup went forward, although delayed by late snows, in spite of court orders against it—one U. S. marshal was shot dead while serving an injunction, and posters announcing the prohibition were "so obliterated with derisive shots from six shooters" that they were un-readable.[32]

Such local organization of nesters and grangers to fight against and protect themselves from the state and county cattlemen's associations were common in the early nineties. For instance, there was an association of small stockmen set up to rival the Owyhee County Stock Association (Idaho) for the purpose of bringing "to justice some of the perjurers and assassins . . . in the employ of the stock association."[33]

We should not be surprised about cowboys and farmers working to-gether. During the populist era, cowboy nesters regularly teamed with the grangers to fight the cattle companies and their associations and to promote their own interests. There is no foundation to the popular belief that cow-boys hated farmers. Cowmen hated them, cowboys did not. They shared the same culture, since cowboys came from farm families in the South and Midwest. They shared a clear class interest with grangers now that they were all small independent producers striving together to survive in a political-economic system that favored the rich and to protect themselves from the cattle companies, who fought their claims on public land, on mavericks, even on their right to exist. Besides, the family ranchers farmed too; unlike the cattle companies, they realized the need to grow hay for wintering their small herds, and they usually kept a milch cow or two. So the cowboy rancher and his family cultivated fields, planted and cut and pitched hay, milked cows, and dug fence-post holes. His work had become more diversified and more like that of farmers. Finally, cowboys courted and married farmers' daughters.

A cowboy in 1882 resisted his boss's orders, endorsed by the regional association, to steal grangers' livestock in the Neutral Strip (present-day Oklahoma panhandle). He wrote:

> Cowboys were friendly by nature to the grangers, and looked to them for the courtship of their pretty daughters on an otherwise womanless range. We cowboys were young men, many of us just boys, and lonely as could be for womenfolk. So a settler's daughter . . . looked mighty good to our eyes after what we had seen at the end of the annual beef drive to Dodge City. Most of the settlers were hospitable and treated us boys as though they thought there was yet a chance we would be good citizens one day. This treatment gave us a chance to learn some of the social graces by mixing around with worthwhile people.[34]

It is not clear to what extent the militancy of small ranchers was organized by state and territorial Farmers Alliances and inspired by lecturers from the National Farmers Alliance and Industrial Union, although we do know that lecturers in the national organizing campaign in 1890 were active in Montana, Wyoming, and Colorado.[35] Agrarian populism was, of course, becoming strong during the late eighties and early nineties, just the time that cowboys were proving up their claims and becoming family ranchers. It was on the edge of the Great Plains in the hill and prairie country northwest of Austin, Texas, that migrant poor Southern farmers, dispossessed by the crop lien system, first formed "a new people's politics." Perhaps some were small ranchers. The embryo group in Lampasas County, Texas, "The Farmers Alliance," itself collapsed in 1880 because of premature third-party moves and sectional loyalties, but the Alliance ideas spread north on the frontier and resulted in 120 sub-alliances in twelve counties in Texas in the next two years.[36] From there the movement grew, Alliance lecturers educating workers about cooperative ways to independence (purchasing, marketing, even manufacturing); about the necessity of a farm-labor coalition; and finally about changing from Alliance-endorsed Democrats and Republicans, the so-called "fusion tickets," to People's Party candidates.

The attempt to organize a National Farmers Alliance club in Johnson

County, Wyoming, the year before the invasion "met with little success," but Alliance clubs were organized in seven other towns in Wyoming that year, including Lander and Tie Siding.[37] In Lincoln County, New Mexico Territory, like Johnson County a section where small ranchers were struggling to survive the corporate ranch campaign against them, the Farmers Alliance was strong after 1888 and by 1890 had its own newspaper, *Liberty Banner*. These Anglo Lincoln County ranchers were really small. Jasper Coe, president of the county chapter of the Farmers Alliance in the late eighties and in 1890 the territorial Alliance president, had four horses and three cows and property assets of $940. His brother Frank had twenty-two horses and eighty cows. Through the Alliance newspaper they attacked Republican support of the "Cattle Association monopoly" of the public domain and the "system of land fraud" by which original Mexican land grants purchased by Anglo land companies could by fraudulent court action be made to cover entire counties. There was a similar Alliance chapter for small ranchers in Colfax County to the north combating Senator Dorsey's 10,000-acre spread. But the racism of these political alliances doomed their effort as populist forces because most of the population, the Mexicanos, were excluded.[38]

Alliance activities on the Plains entered electoral politics in the early nineties and organized a coalition of small farmers and ranchers and industrial workers into the People's Party. This organizing effort in effect brought Alliance rural families together with the workers of the old Knights of Labor movement into a third political party with local clubs and candidates for office. The People's Party was strong in the cattle-raising states and territories, and its platform emphasized economic equality by breaking monopolies. The People's Party attracted the support of many nester ranchers. For example, in Wyoming, where there were more nester ranchers than grangers, a state committee of the People's Party was set up in June 1891. In Laramie in the same year, the local club adopted the platform of the St. Louis People's Party convention of 1889. There were clubs about that time also in seven other towns, mostly along the Union Pacific tracks, because at this time the support was largely from industrial workers. But the stockmen's invasion of Johnson County created a great swell of opinion not only against the Republicans but in favor of the populists. In Johnson County itself the whole Republican County Committee resigned and its chairman joined the People's Party and edited a populist paper in Buffalo, the *Free Lance*. Newspapers in Sundance and Douglas turned populist.

In June 1892 at the People's Party state convention in Laramie, with six counties represented, among which were Crook and Sheridan in the north with large nester constituencies, delegates adopted a platform to repeal all laws favoring the Wyoming Stock Growers Association, to reclaim public land and hold it for settlers, and to investigate both the invasion of Johnson County and the "Cheyenne Republican Ring." The question of whether to put up People's Party candidates or fusion Democratic candidates divided the antimonopoly forces, with the radical old Knights of Labor workers along the Union Pacific route supporting the former and the more traditional northern ranchers and farmers supporting the latter. Nevertheless, in the off-year election, when the Republicans were swept out of office and the Democrats (mostly fusionists) and some Populists were swept in, the ranching areas in the north supported strong antimonopoly candidates. Two Populist representatives won in Johnson County.

In adjacent Sheridan County, a former Greenback activist, Lewis Cass Tidball, won as a Populist and was made Speaker of the House. Tidball, a founder of the People's Party in Wyoming, a strong antifusionist, perhaps the strongest and most lasting force for radical populism in Wyoming, was himself a rancher, first in Montana and after 1883 in Sheridan County. Tidball had the support of small farmers and ranchmen and their wives, and he and Sheridan County remained Populist even when the Republicans were back in control about four years later and the People's Party was virtually dead. Of the four Populists elected to the State House in 1896, three were from Sheridan, Tidball among them. Tidball later became a Debsian socialist and edited a paper in Sheridan, the *Independent Press*, described in 1903 as "an uncompromising Socialist publication."[39]

The conclusion is that in Wyoming ex-cowboy nesters tried to protect their interests for several years by supporting a third political party. They did the same in the other ranching states and territories too, with varying degrees of success. Texas and Dakota were particularly strong. In Montana, the People's Party ran a strong third to the two major parties in 1892, and in the next year Colorado elected a Populist governor, Davis H. Waite.[40] That working people were not successful in creating a lasting political party devoted to their interests is less an indication of their weakness than of the strength of the impediments the system raises to such a party.

Fortunately, there were other cooperative ways of surviving than electoral politics. The cattle wars were mostly between family ranchers and corporate cattle companies—not, as the popular myth presents, between rival barons over range rights or grangers against pioneer cattle barons (like *Shane*), or cattle barons against sheepmen. These wars were mainly the class struggle in its most militant and violent form. They were usually forced on the nesters by the giant cattlemen, who looked upon them as a nuisance because they claimed some mavericks and some range. In Johnson County the nesters acquired their share of mavericks and branded their own calves by any means necessary. Some even made up for past inequities by casual rustling. In response the cattle companies and their Association, which controlled the government, hired cattle detectives to survey nester herds, brought indictments against nesters declared rustlers, and seized herds at railheads or in the cattle yards in Omaha or Chicago. The nesters countered by bringing joint suits for the return of seized herds, packing juries to acquit neighbors charged with rustling, and forming associations of their own to conduct independent roundups. They also cooperated in finding new markets and driving herds to them well away from railroads and from syndicate agents. This all was the protracted six-year war (1886–1892) within the system, only occasionally punctuated by gunfire—a throwdown at a roundup foreman's wagon, a potshot at a cattle inspector. Earlier range wars, like the one in Lincoln County, New Mexico Territory, never had the opportunity to go through this legal, nonviolent stage.

When intimidation did not make nesters go away in Johnson County, the Association hired assassins and gun thugs to lynch and bushwhack nesters thought to be "ringleaders" and finally, in what seems today an act of desperation, sent in a small army of Association ranchmen and Texas hired guns to take over the county, execute the rustlers, and establish their own kind of law. The nesters and grangers responded by spontaneously creating a citizens' militia under the direction of a popular sheriff to repel the armed invaders. After this was accomplished, they tightened their control of the government of the County and repudiated all friends of the Association and the Cheyenne Ring, the Populist name for the political-financial cabal in the capitol. They had won the immediate battle, although not the longer fight against the economic laws that eventually eliminated small ranchers. What the armed invaders couldn't do, economic progress and the agricultural revolution took care of.

The coincidence of the end of the war, or, more exactly, the decision of both sides to lay down their guns for a while, and the Populist political activity in the 1892 election campaigns is probably not just accidental. For a time there seemed to be a new way to fight "the syndicate," as nesters called the corporate ranches and their Association: with ballots, not bullets (to use a catchphrase generally meant to discourage militancy). A darker interpretation is that the populist movement acted to defuse popular discontent by giving the illusion of a remedy within a system that structurally benefits only the rich.

It was different in the Lincoln County War. There, in the southeast corner of New Mexico Territory, the conflict had four stages, of which only the third and most colorful has entered the popular mind. The first, soon after the annexation (1846), was between Anglo ranchers from Texas and the Mexicano native sheepherders who for more than a hundred years had used the land communally and considered it theirs.[41] After Anglo ranching drove out Mexicano sheepherding, the second stage was a class fight between John Chisum, who claimed the whole Pecos valley and its tributaries from Texas to Fort Sumner, and a swarm of nester ranchers who wanted bits of it. The third stage was between rival capitalists in which both sides attracted mixed popular and ethnic support that thus obscured the national-racial and class basis of the first two stages and also obscured the increasing control by big capital. In this third stage, which alone has entered the mythology of the West, Chisum and the cattle barons fought the interloping entrepreneur Lawrence Murphy, who was taking over the reservation and army beef contracts through political connections with the Santa Fe Ring. Murphy allied himself with the big merchants and the law in Lincoln, and some Pecos ranchmen and the border rustlers who supplied them came to his side to fight the barons. Chisum and his British capitalist associate Tunstall hired cowboys, like Billy the Kid, as mercenaries, had some support from small Anglo ranchers and farmers, and even got some help from the Mexicanos, who wanted to fight the Santa Fe Ring connection. But we are not concerned with the first national-racial fight, nor the famous one over which capitalist got the beef contracts, but with the fight between the big and small ranchers in the early seventies. The nesters were taking Pecos ranges and mavericks, so Chisum hired warriors to make them leave. And the small ranchers fought back.

An old cowboy who worked for Chisum before the "war," and whose father was one of these small ranchers, gave this simple account in an interview in 1927: "The war started by the big fish wanting to eat up the little ones. . . . The first move they [Chisum and Tunstall] made looked like they aimed to kill out the little men. They hired a bunch of men. I think they had 62 or 64 to kill or run the little men out. They gathered all the loose-footed men coming from Texas. Many of them came with trail herds [that is, as hands or themselves bringing in small herds of stolen cattle]. They started out to put out the Seven Rivers people . . . so Beckwith . . . and the rest of the little fellows banded in together."[42] After Chisum moved out, the struggle continued in its fourth and final stage between the nesters, now organized under the Farmers Alliance, and the companies who replaced Chisum. But it was no longer called a "war" once Billy the Kid became a fugitive. Cattle "wars" involve posses of armed men in pitched battles. Typically, after the big shootout, the defeated party lies low for a time and then raises the level of violence. For instance, after the Wyoming Stock Growers Association army was defeated in northern Wyoming, the cattlemen waited for two years before a faction within the association hired Tom Horn to execute some nesters.[43] Violence against nesters continued, but it was not a "war" because only one gun thug was involved.

Most of the conflicts between cattle companies and nesters never had a "war" stage, although they were marked by regular acts of violence. The conflict along the Canadian River in the Texas Panhandle after the 1883 strike, already described in part, raged on for three or four years before the huge corporations like the XIT completed the fencing of their land. The strike was so successful that many of the small army of blackballed cowboys that it had created became full-time nesters, branding up mavericks mainly from cattle drifted southeast from New Mexico and Colorado but occasionally rustling company cattle by creating mavericks and even by some plain brand burning. They worked together in these operations and protected themselves with a cattle pool that offered shares to cowboys and to a community of ranches of blackballed cowboys right across the line in New Mexico, a haven for nesters pursued by Rangers and sheriffs' posses. The Panhandle Livestock Association retaliated by hiring Pat Garrett to lead a posse of hired gunmen called Home Rangers, first to disarm the blackballed cowboys and then to arrest them for theft and to seize their herds with papers supplied by a rigged grand jury. Big ranches like the LS also hired special gunmen (what today we call "security forces") to terrorize the nesters, and there was even a small shootout (small as compared to Lincoln County, 1878, or Johnson County, 1892) early in the spring of 1886 in the streets of Tascosa between the LS gun thugs and the nester ranchers and their town supporters.[44] That little exchange of shots ended the struggle because the Texas county and state government, more than those in other states and territories on the Plains, facilitated the corporate takeover of the ranges by legal means backed up by Rangers and sheriffs and deputies and private security forces. It is significant that Texas never had a real cattle war. They won't stand for violence over yonder in Texas if it's directed against the possessing class.

Las Gorras Blancas (White Caps) were Mexicano night riders who defended their communal land near Las Vegas, New Mexico Territory, against encroaching Anglo cattlemen and land speculators in the late eighties. With white masks over their faces and sometimes over their horses' heads, they cut fences, burned barns and ranch homes, and scattered stock; they generally avoided taking human life except in a few pinpointed assassinations. The movement spread to neighboring counties. It was political: the Gorras infiltrated railroad workers' Knights of Labor chapters and worked out an active alliance with them, and they were involved in building the first People's Party in the territory and helped lead the party to victory in 1890 in San Miguel, the most populous county. For several years the Gorras had strong popular support, and cases against them in courts had to be dismissed.[45] These Mexicano night riders were mainly sheepherders and small sheep rancheros, not cowboys, but they are relevant here because they fought the cattle and land companies cooperatively in extralegal ways that cowboys were not able to manage. They are different from all the ex-cowboy Anglo nesters on the Plains who were cutting fences and burning the barns of cattle companies in temporary and fragile alliances: Las Gorras were organized, politicized, had an obvious enemy in the Anglo land grabbers and cattle companies, and thus a popular cause with wide regional support, and they made connections with populist groups. Anglo nesters did not have a sufficient racial and community culture threatened by an obvious alien intruder to mount such a sustained and brave fight, both a public one and a nighttime one.

There was, however, temporary, fragmented Anglo resistance, not as principled and populist as Las Gorras, but ideological nonetheless. With the spread of barbed wire, there emerged all over the Southwest secret organizations of small ranchers to cut down company fences intruding on their customary ranges, to burn posts, and to appropriate rolls of wire. Sometimes their names were flatly descriptive, like the Land League, at others more colorful, reflecting their nocturnal activities—Owls, Javelinas, Blue Devils.[46]

After the cowboy nester discovers that even a "war" won't help him, he can turn outlaw. But outlaws who rustled company cattle differ from the cowboy resisters we have been discussing because outlaws don't support a popular cause, even if they don't steal nester cattle and horses. Stealing in itself is not a political act, even under capitalism. When Billy the Kid's gang stole cattle that drifted from the Panhandle, the cattle companies there were hurt enough to send posses out to help Garrett capture the Kid. But Billy the Kid was not a Robin Hood–type bandit, because, though he stole only cattle belonging to big companies, he was not fighting the big owners. He was just riding where the most cattle were. Nor did he distribute to the poor. He had popular support but only because he was successful in hurting the big cattlemen, whom just about everyone hated. Also, by this time Billy was probably imitating his image in the mass media, pretending to be the social bandit that he really wasn't. Traditional social bandits flourished in precapitalist societies, where they "never cease to be part of society in the eyes of the peasants."[47] In capitalist societies, even postindustrial ones, self-serving outlaws who rob the rich are often heroized by the masses who hate the rich. Bonnie and Clyde are late Anglo-American examples. Also, such outlaws begin to create and imitate their own popular image. (Consider Jimmy Cliff, in *The Harder They Come*, posing like a Western outlaw in the photographer's studio, creating images for his own public relations.)

Such criminal bandits can gain the reputation of being social bandits merely by hitting the institutions the people consider the most oppressive. For example, the James brothers developed their legendary reputations as Robin Hoods merely by robbing banks and trains in a country where foreclosed mortgages, bondage credit, high shipping rates, and lavish land grants and subsidies hurt the grangers and nesters or at least impressed upon them the inequities of the system. So, although capitalism was too advanced to create cowboy social bandits distributing to the poor what they gained in fighting cattlemen or knocking over banks or robbing trains (the institutional oppressors of the rural poor), cowboys supported those that they thought were hurting the enemies of the people, and their support influenced the behavior of the bandits. The important fact here is that cowboys *liked* Billy the Kid and Jessie James and Sam Bass and Butch Cassidy. Their support proves the cowboys' antagonism to bosses and the system that supports special privilege and oppresses the poor. Therefore, though we can't claim for cowboy resisters the existence among them of Robin Hood cattle rustlers, we can claim for them a strong class consciousness reflected in their support of the criminal rustlers and bank and train robbers who appeared to be striking a blow against the privileged and oppressive class.

Jesse and Frank James and their gang, the archetypal Robin Hood bandits in Anglo-American myth, were not cowboys of the Great Plains at all but riders of the Middle Border, using the skills and techniques of wartime Confederate raiders, and, like most of their fellow guerrillas, not poor at all but themselves entrepreneurs, "the elder sons of well-to-do slave-holding farmers fighting against loss of property and status."[48] But because they robbed banks, they became heroes to cowboys, many of whom, as we have seen, came from tenant farming families who suffered from the crop lien system. The version of the song about Jesse that John Lomax thought cowboys sang is the one we all know, romanticizing the killer as "a friend to the poor" who "never would see a man suffer pain."[49] Other versions to the same melody contain the line that epitomizes the mythical social bandit: "But he took from the rich and delivered to the poor" (the "but" contrasts with what he didn't do—robbing the poor or frightening "a mother with a child").[50]

Sam Bass, who "ranks just below Jesse as an American Robin Hood,"[51] was a cowboy and is so celebrated in cowboy song: from his home state of Indiana, "Sam first came out to Texas a cowboy for to be,/A kinder hearted fellow you seldom ever see." He was dear to cowboys for his train robberies and because he and his gang "whipped Texas rangers and ran the boys in blue" (federal troops in Texas during Reconstruction).[52] Siringo testifies that "Sam Bass was the hero of more young Texas cowboys than any other 'bad' man, and the song about him was the most popular."[53]

It is more difficult to turn the chief gun on the side of John Chisum's warriors into a Robin Hood, and there is the evidence of one of the most trustworthy of the cowboy autobiographers that "cowpunchers as a class never had any use for Billy the Kid."[54] But the Kid stole company cows and horses, and Siringo shows there were some cowboy sympathizers, including himself, who thought the Kid "kind to the weak and helpless." He says that when the Kid escaped from the Lincoln Court House, nearly one hundred citizens in the street didn't lift a hand or gun against him because they nearly all "sympathized with the Kid,"[55] and Siringo heard the story of the escape from a cowboy eyewitness who could have killed the Kid, "but he wanted to see him escape." Siringo and Big Foot Wallace were rounding up cattle when a man rode up and announced that the Kid had killed two guards and escaped from Lincoln. Wallace gave a Comanche yell, cried out, "Hurray for Billy the Kid," dove headfirst into the muddy water of the Pecos with all his clothes on, and when he came up hollered again, "Hurray for Billy the Kid."[56]

Minority Cowboys and Women Cowhands

The cow-puncher, the American descendant of Saxon ances-tors, . . . for thirty years flourished upon our part of the earth.

—*Owen Wister (1895)*[1]

In *Red River* Tom Dunson (John Wayne) trails his big herd up from southwest Texas. If we look closely, we can see a few vaguely Mexican types among his outfit, but we don't see any black cowboys at all. Earlier, we applauded Dunson when he shot two Mexicans who told him to get off their boss's land. The studied realism of most Western movies conditions us to accept what we see as historically true. In this movie, the voice-over, diary-style narrative of Dunson's sidekick and cook (Walter Brennan) es-pecially encourages this tendency to consider the movie as a documentary of the frontier. We are so caught up in the realistic surface of detail that we fail to notice even gross anachronisms and historical improbabilities, like metallic cartridges for six-shooters several years before their introduc-tion, a trail herd three times the size of the standard maximum and not enough cowboys or horses or chuck wagons to handle such a herd, married cowboys in Dunson's bunkhouse, the arrival in Abilene two years before

TOM DUNSON (JOHN WAYNE) SHOOTS A MEXICAN IN *RED RIVER* (1948)

Cherry (John Ireland) and Matt Garth (Montgomery Clift) help Dunson shoot three mutinous cowboys. Buster (Noah Berry) and Quo (Chief Yowlachie) are watching by the rear of the chuckwagon.

the railhead existed—and, of course, the absence of blacks and the dimness of Mexicans. But popular Westerns are meant to engross our interest and to gross profits, not necessarily to show what happened. To the contrary, they also serve to reinforce bias and justify history. *Red River*, like most Westerns, depicts a frontier where blacks played no active part, save an occasional subservient one, and where the Mexicans were either no account or actively threatening to the Anglo good guys. So the theft of land and labor, even of life, need not be confronted.

The truth of the matter is that one out of three or four cowboys during the cowboy era was either black or Mexicano. The source for this figure is authoritative and the circumstances revealing. George W. Saunders, who went up the trail to Abilene as a teenage cowboy and became in later life the president of a livestock commission firm in San Antonio, founded in 1915 the Trail Drivers of Texas, a fraternal organization open to any white man (or his white male heirs) who had trailed cattle north in the good old days. The organization flourished under his enthusiastic leadership, and in the first volume of reminiscences of members, he concluded his own lively memoir with this estimate of the number of eligible old men to recruit into membership:

> From 1868 to 1895 it is estimated that fully 35,000 men went up the trail with herds, if the number of men computed by the number of cattle driven is correct. Of this number of men *about one-third were negroes and Mexicans*, another third made more than one trip. Let us conclude that one-half of the *white* trail drivers who made one trip have died, and we still have some 6,000 survivors of the trail scattered all over the world, all of whom ought to be members of our association [emphasis added].[2]

Here is a case where Texas Jim Crow helps the historical demographer. Because of their race, the surviving black and Mexicano trail drivers, evidently about 2,000 in 1920, were not eligible for membership in Saunders's association. We learn by his assumption of this exclusion in his calculation that there was one black or Mexican cowboy on the trail for every two Anglos. We can argue with his calculation of absolute figures but not with his authoritative, disinterested testimony about the fraction of nonwhite cowboys. We can assume that the ratio was the same in range work in the South, but we have to adjust for a smaller percentage of blacks and Mexicans on the northern ranges, say, one to something less than three overall. Since there were about twice as many black as Mexican cowboys,[3] we can conclude that, on the average, on all the ranges and trails of the Great Plains, of every one hundred cowboys about seventy were Anglos, twenty blacks, and ten Mexicanos.

1. Vaqueros

Quinientos novillos eran, todos grandes y livianos,
y entre trienta americanos no los podían embalar.

Llegan cinco mexicanos, todos bien enchivarrados,
y en menos de un cuarto de hora los tenían encerrados.

(Five hundred steers there were, all big and quick;
thirty American cowboys could not keep them bunched together.

Then five Mexicans arrived, all of them wearing good chaps;
And in less than a quarter hour they had the steers penned up.)
  —from "Kiansas," an old *corrido* (song) from the Lower
Rio Grande border about a cattle drive to Kansas[4]

These vaqueros were the first group of Mexican *male* workers to be exploited by Anglo-American capital. (Mexicanas had doubtless been employed as house servants before.) They are a part of the Mexicano population of the Southwest, which since the United States's annexation has been colonialized internally on their native homeland and reduced to a sub-proletariat of contracted gang laborers, working for starvation wages in mines, on farms, on railroad beds, and, what is often forgotten, on cattle ranges and trails. Articles Eight and Nine of the Treaty of Guadalupe Hildaldo guaranteed them and their Mexican bosses their land, but the courts, land speculators, military plunderers, and self-serving vigilantes eventually robbed them of almost all of it. Not only did their poverty make them exploitable, but the feudal social relations (*latisfundism*), as they had developed in Mexico, created a culture vulnerable to exploitation by the new capitalist class.

The vaqueros in old Mexico worked on the big cattle haciendas of the northern states, particularly Chihuahua, Nuevo Leon y Coahuila, the southern half of Nuevo Santander (after Mexican Independence, Tamaulipas), and the north-central state of Durango. Unlike our cattlemen, who used public land for their ranges, the hacendados owned their huge estates outright, either by government grant, purchase, or expropriation of Indian holdings. These Mexican cattle kings were European and were conservative in politics, like the Church and the agricultural, mining, and lumbering hacendados; together they dominated the economy of the north, where cattle and sheep were the main products. Each ruled over his estate with absolute power, controlling all the people around him by the institution of debt peonage. These people in the north, the workers on the haciendas, were not Indians but mestizos, because the Indians of the semiarid cattle country were all nomadic hunters and raiders whom the Mexicans killed off or forced into settlements, as the United States did its indigenous nomads like the Apaches. The mestizos of this most southern portion of the Great Plains came from the early Spanish settlements that had attracted Indians over the three centuries of colonial rule—some former nomads, some agricultural Indians kidnapped from the central plateau. This association had created a mixture of genes in the laboring class, *los pobres*, more Indian than European.[5] From old settlements, inside or near these vast estates, came all the near-Indian cooks and servants and craftspeople and farmers and shepherds and unmounted corral, stable, and barn workers, and, of course, the vaqueros. The latter had the most prestige among their fellow peons because they were mounted, like gentlemen; nevertheless, they were enslaved like all the rest by indebtedness to the *patrón*. Further, they were supervised closely by their Creole or light-mestizo corporals (*caporales de la vaquería*),[6] and if they fled from their endless task of paying off their indebtedness, they were arrested for "robbery" and returned for a reward (which was added to their account) by local police or, under dictator Porfirio Díaz, by the Rurales, the federal police army.[7] Since whole communities worked and lived on the hacienda, the vaquero, unlike the American cowboy, could be married and live a more fixed life because he usually had the same *patrón* for life. His wages were fixed so low (in 1804, 28 centavos a day, which is, at the present U.S. rate, 2⅓ cents)[8] that he would never discharge his debt. Virtually all vaqueros in Mexico slaved on haciendas to pay their debts; that is, again unlike American cowboys turned ranchers, there were almost no independent cattle producers, called *rancheros* in Mexico (owners of *ranchos*, small private agricultural holdings) who raised cattle and sheep for market. There were no markets for small producers, and rancheros raised the necessities of life and most often became wage laborers, at least seasonally, by being enticed into indebtedness to the local hacendado. When during the Porfiriato so much of Mexico was sold to foreign entrepreneurs, and when American cattle companies established large ranches, particularly in Sonora after it was taken from the Yaquis, the Mexican vaqueros who worked for them were kept in debt slavery on low wages by Anglo managers exactly like peons on haciendas.[9] Even today, after the Revolution of 1911–1917, to which northern vaqueros contributed so much, they "continue to live in much the same way that they always have" and continue the traditional relations with the now capitalized haciendas.[10]

The cradle of the vaquero in the United States is the southern part of what has been called the "cradle of the Western cattle business,"[11] the diamond-shaped area marked by San Antonio, Old Indianola on Matagorda Bay, the convergence of the Rio Grande and the Gulf Coast (now Brownsville), and Laredo. From this most teeming breeding ground and several lesser cattle ranching areas to the north spread the cows, the cowmen, and the cowboys of the cattle industry on the Great Plains. Most Mexicans settled before and after Texas Independence in the southern half of this area and the area extending beyond it to the west. This is the area between the Nueces River and the Rio Grande—called the Brasada, or the Nueces and Lower Rio Grande valleys, or the Border, or, for the purposes of this book, the Nueces Strip. From the middle of the eighteenth century, it comprised the early Spanish and later Mexican cattle business in the most northern part of the New Spain province of Nuevo Santander. It was called "el Valle" or more popularly "Seno Mexicano" (the Mexican breast or womb), to signify its fertility.[12] Soon after Independence, the Texas quartermaster corps and companies of "independent Rangers" raided the area for cattle.

> After the disbandonment of the [Texas] army, many of the cattle beyond the Nueces were rounded up by discharged soldiers, adventurers, and other enterprising Texans for private ownership, to replace losses sustained during the revolution, or to drive to markets. . . . The Texas "cowboys" raiding into the area west of the Nueces, drove out cattle from the Mexican ranches at Viejo, Anaquitas, Las Animas, San Juan de Carricitos, Noria, San Antonio, Los Fresnos, Colorado, El Mulato, Jaboncillos, Santa Rosa, Mota, Santa Margarita, Santo Gertrudis, San Diego, Los Angeles, El Pato, La Parido, San Patricio, Salmoneño and others, some of which had been abandoned.[13]

Then, in the cruelest justification for rapine in history, these cowboy raiders justified their pillage by appealing to the Texas Constitution, which decreed forfeit the land and possessions of any persons who fled the country without permission to avoid participation in the war with Mexico. If Nueces Mexicans fled the raiders for their lives, their property was forfeit! But later the Mexicans returned to their haciendas and ranchos, and the battle continued between bands of cowboys and vaqueros.

After General Zachariah Taylor used Texas claims to the strip to start the war and thereby achieved Texas control over it, Texas capitalists acquired most of the private ranges and cattle still held by the Mexican landowners; and the Rangers and Anglo vigilantes killed or ran off most of the smaller Mexicano rancheros, leaving landless Mexican day laborers to work for the new Anglo owners. Simply and brutally, Anglo-Texans built an industry by taking over the Mexican cattle business and the Mexicano vaqueros of the Nueces Strip.

Texas historians distort the story of the vaqueros by playing down, in mitigation of Texas imperialism, the conquest of the Nueces Strip. A modern historian of the Texas Republic claims that the hostile Indian action and, after the defeat of Santa Ana at San Jacinto, fear of the Texas colonists caused the owners of "the large Mexican ranches on the southwest frontier" to flee "hastily across the Rio Grande leaving thousands of head of cattle to run wild in the region."[14] A recent Texas historian of the cattle business argues that since the Mexican hacendados and rancheros were destroyed or caused to flee because of the Mexican War, U.S. annexation, and Texas economic penetration, their old cattle and sheep culture could have had no effect on the developing industry: "The Mexican rancheros of the South Texas diamond had very nearly disappeared before 1850."[15] The great Texas historian Walter Prescott Webb explains the Anglo conquest this way: "In the long run the Texans had the best of it, and the Mexicans found the land north of the Rio Grande untenable. They abandoned their ranches and much of their stock and retired from the scene. The Texans pushed out into the cattle country and took charge of what the Mexicans had left behind."[16]

These accounts are typical in their assumption that the Nueces Strip was sparsely populated by squatting rancheros, small sheep and cattle herders with no title to the land, and that the takeover was inevitable and easy. We are left wondering where the vaqueros came from who worked the cattle in the strip and southwest Texas for the new Anglo bosses. Were they the dispossessed rancheros and their sons? Were they all raided or runaways from Mexican haciendas to the south and west? The fact is that most were the vaqueros who used to work for the Mexican hacendados and rancheros of the strip. These vaqueros were a good part of the largest and densest concentration of Mexicans in all the trans–Rio Bravo states of Mexico. A modern Chicano historian puts it simply: "El Valle was the most densely populated [of Mexico's northern states]. Reynosa in 1835 had 15,000 inhabitants."[17] From 12,000 to 20,000 Mexicans lived in the strip at the time of U.S. annexation,[18] many more than lived in all California, ten times as many as lived in Arizona. Only New Mexico had more Mexicans—four times as many—but distributed over many times larger an area.[19]

When we consider the history of the strip, we have to include the whole valley on both sides of the river, from Laredo to the Gulf and the coastal prairies to the northeast, as a single cultural and political-economic unit. The first settlements were just south of the river at confluences of tributaries in the middle third portion, that is, between Ciudad Guerrero (then Revilla) and Reynosa. Here, in the mid-eighteenth century, villas with mission churches were built by rich families, with their sheep and cattle and their dependent families of peons mainly from the two nearest New Spain provinces to the east. The four towns on the south side of this sixty-mile stretch of river each had a mission church, communal land for the dozen Indian tribes who had used it seasonally for hundreds of years, a few settler-soldiers who were commanded by a "captain"—the most influential early grandee—and narrow strips of land, each with a bit of river frontage, called *porciones*, stretching back about fifteen miles to the south, and surveyed and distributed in numbers and size according to the owners' ability to stock them with cattle and sheep and work them with peons. Only the fairly well off got anything, and the richest got the most. A very large majority of the early grantees were Creoles, that is, Europeans born in New Spain. All the land was owned by a few rich Spanish hacendados and by six or seven times as many well-off ranchers, mainly Creole, for whom the thousands of mestizo peons and an increasing number of Indians herded cattle, sheep, or goats.[20]

Across the River to the northeast and north there were more very large haciendas and more small rancheros, many occupying land not theirs by grant, and more ranges operated from camps by overseers and peons of owners living in the villas across the river. In the northwest third there were several very large haciendas working up to thirteen families of peons, raising sheep and cattle. Near one hacienda was Laredo, the only town north of the river.[21]

In the middle section, to the north across from the towns, there were a few huge haciendas owned by rich original white settlers of the towns on the south bank. But most of the land belonged to absentee owners, white residents of the towns across the river who had been using these ranges to graze herds worked by their peons living in huts on the grants. There were also a growing number of mestizo rancheros who had small herding operations going in this dangerous northern frontier and who could never legally own the land they used because they were so poor.[22]

In the lower third, east of Reynosa, and north along the Gulf Coast to the Nueces River estuary (today Corpus Christi), the land was up for grabs in very large parcels to the richest and most influential. Many ranch headquarters were established in this area in the last quarter of the eighteenth century on large grants of a hundred thousand to half a million acres, given to rich Creole residents of the valley. Most of these owners did not establish haciendas on grants but hired majordomos to supervise peons working cattle and sheep from local camps.[23] Examples of these large grants are the 400,000-acre hacienda near La Parra, partly acquired later by Mifflin Kenedy, Richard King's partner, and the Santa Gertrudis hacienda, from which King acquired in 1854 the first 70,000 acres of his later giant ranch.[24] In this area, too, there were lots of mestizo rancheros squatting on unclaimed or unused land.

Although they are just outside the strip to the east, we should consider the later settlements on the coastal prairies. In the 1830s, Martin de León led Mexican colonists to establish large cattle and sheep haciendas near the Guadalupe River in the present county of Victoria. This colony was short-lived, since the Anglo Texas ranchers took it over in the 1840s.[25]

After Mexican Independence, up to five leagues (22,000 acres) of all unclaimed land was sold to any recent settler in the valley with enough "stock to occupy them" at ten pesos a league.[26] These provisions excluded as grantees the many poor squatting rancheros north of the river who owned their land only by customary right. But these post-Independence grants increased the number of moderate-sized ranchos in the strip prior to U.S. and Texas annexation.

The smaller holdings increased over time because the original grants were at first divided among the children, and later the "many descendents simply held the land in common, grouping their houses in small villages around what had been the ancestral home."[27] In relation to the primitive capitalist peonage of central Mexico and the developing industrial capitalist society of Texas, the border society was more pastoral and patriarchal, one in which the hierarchies were determined not only by wealth but by tradition and by family relations to the primitive grantees. These petit-bourgeois landowning rancheros in the valley constituted a social unit almost unique in Mexico, where except here in the Lower Rio Grande Valley and in northern New Mexico, cattle and sheep were raised exclusively on large haciendas.

The vaqueros of the strip before the annexation were different in a number of ways from those working in the hacienda cattle economy to the south and east. They were less peonized—that is, less dependent on or deferential to their *patrones* because there was more opportunity for work with many smaller landowners. They could even quit to run some cattle and sheep on their own and work for wages part of the year (as American cowboys were to do in the eighties), since squatting was common on plentiful unclaimed or granted but unused land. Since one or two resident *patrones* did not control all of life in a large area, except in the north toward Laredo, the system of debt peonage was only partially established. Runaways could find new employment and be relatively free from enforced return to former *patrones*. Peons could become vaqueros, and their sons could even marry the boss's daughter and become rancheros, as this description by a Mexicano Borderer testifies:

> The peon was usually a *fuereño*, an "outsider" from central Mexico, but on the Border he was not a serf. *Peón* in Nuevo Santander had preserved much of its old meaning of "man on foot." The gap between the peon and the vaquero was not extreme, though the man on horseback had a job with more prestige, one which was considered to involve more danger and more skill. The peon, however, could and did rise in the social

scale. People along the Border who like to remember genealogies and study family trees can tell of instances in which a man came to the Border as a peon (today he would be called a *bracero*) and ended his life as a vaquero while his son began life as a vaquero and ended it as a small landowner, and the grandson married into the old family that had employed his grandfather— the whole process taking place before the Madero Revolution [1910].[28]

There was a large proportion of newly arrived vaqueros. The diversified social economy of the Lower Valley attracted vaqueros fleeing peonage in the neighboring Mexican states to the west not only because of more independence and choices but because the political autonomy of the region and the common Federalist sentiments lessened the chance of forced return to the haciendas they were fleeing from. Also, the Lower Rio Grande was among the last settlements of New Spain. The first vaqueros who came east with the primitive settlers had by the nineteenth century all passed away, and their sons and daughters were less peons than their fathers because they were conditioned by a society not completely dominated by a hacienda economy. A recent Chicano historian agrees that the "land tenure practices" of the Lower Rio Grande Valley tended toward "greater egalitarian practices" than, for instance, in New Mexico, where "two percent of the population owned most of the wealth."[29]

If Mexican vaqueros fleeing peonage wanted to remain in their craft, they would not go to New Mexico, which, like the strip, had the advantages of distance, considerable autonomy, and small ranchos, because almost all herding there was of sheep and goats. Anglo Texans brought cattle to southeast New Mexico in the sixties and *displaced* sheep hacendados and sheep rancheros, unlike what was going on in the strip, where Anglos *took over* Mexicano land, cattle, and workers. They would not go to California, not only because of the distance but because after the Gold Rush the economy was dominated by Anglos, the huge majority of the population. They went to the one area of dense Mexican population with lots of cattle operations. At the time of the Cortina War in 1859, 12,000 Mexicans were still living in the strip (compared to 300 Anglos!) in spite of the thousand or more refugees who had fled across the river after annexation.[30]

There is evidence for the existence of many runaway peons in Texas. There were so many of them that Texas slaveholders in 1855 and again in 1857 attempted (unsuccessfully) to work out agreements with governors of border states to exchange fugitive peons in Texas for fugitive black slaves in Mexico. One wonders if this is the first instance of an attempt to round up what later became known as undocumented workers for repatriation. One might also wonder whether the slave owners were prepared to round up 4,000 peons in Texas to match that number of black fugitive slaves from Texas in the north-central states of Mexico at the time.[31]

We can make some generalizations about these Texas and Nueces vaqueros before the cowboy era. They were predominantly Indian mestizos, Spanish-speaking, illiterate, practiced in the skills developed in three hundred years of handling cattle and horses on the southern Great Plains between the Sierra Madres, willing to risk their very lives for personal freedom, accustomed to independence and social mobility but for survival capable of compliant subservience because they were socialized into deference.

These characteristics explain why Anglo bosses perceived their Mexican workers as shiftless and dangerous. They could not see that they were angry and resentful. Joseph McCoy, the celebrated Yankee cattleman who opened the railhead at Abilene, wrote in the first book about the cattle industry that Mexican cowhands murder trail bosses and abuse cattle and are "impudent and mean" unless "the boss keeps them under strict surveillance," in which case many can offer "good, faithful help."[32] So we can see the beginning of the popular stereotype, conceived by the employing class as a justification for their tight control over their cheap but dangerous workers. Another cowboy writer who consistently identified with moneyed people saw Mexican cowhands as possessing "cunning and craftiness" and as rebelling against Anglo leadership if it seemed to be at all weak, even though they would be subservient to "an old *patrón*."[33] Again we see the justification of exploiting a skilled but menacing worker by exerting iron control.

Vaqueros overcame their reputations by working for cut-rate wages and by roping and riding so well. Wagon bosses taught them to handle capitalist cows gently, for a brutal throw could lame a steer and put him off his feed, resulting in loss of weight and thus of value. They taught vaqueros to change horses more frequently than had been their custom, in order to protect the company's capital invested in the remuda. A single story will serve to show how the vaqueros' skill at roping soon became legend. An old cowboy recalled an incident on the trail in the seventies: as a diversion, an Anglo in the outfit tried to outrun and rope an antelope, which doubled back with the exhausted pursuer far behind; as it passed the herd, the boss "told a Mexican to go out and lasso it. He succeeded in doing so in a very few minutes."[34] When McCoy organized his 1868 publicity stunt of shipping buffalo to Chicago in sign-draped railroad cars for an exhibition to attract cattle buyers, he hired some California vaqueros to help the Texans rope the beasts.[35] A cowboy in the 1920s remembered one of his first jobs, on the Scott and Byler range in the Nueces Strip in the early seventies. He and the manager were the only Anglos. His wage was twenty dollars a month, all year. The "Mexicans" all got ten dollars a month, part-time, when needed, except for a small group he called "henetes," who got twelve dollars a month and who were "supposed to ride any horse they might be given."[36] Wages remained shockingly low: "In 1900 a Mexican vaquero's monthly earnings were between $6 and $12 (in Texas)."[37]

Early Anglo ranch managers near the border got their cheap, expert Mexican help from four sources. They could hire the sons of the independent ranchero class of farmer-herdsmen—not altogether the best choice because this kind of help would not be peonized. They could hire wetback vaqueros fleeing peonage in Mexico. They could hire the vaqueros who used to work for the Mexican land grant hacendados or rancheros of the Nueces Strip. Or, best of all, they could bring a whole poor village up from Mexico to resettle as dependents around the headquarters of a new ranch.

When Richard King extended his business from shipping on the Rio Grande to ranching in the south corner of the Nueces Strip soon after it had been annexed and "cleared," he chose the method of mass resettlement from Mexico because he wanted a docile work force. His modern biographer claims he couldn't get local vaqueros at this time because the local settlers were all farmers, not ranchers,[38] which is manifestly untrue—cattle haciendas and cattle ranchos with vaqueros to work them had existed in the Nueces Strip for a hundred years by that time, and their establishment had accelerated after Mexican Independence (1821) because of large land grants by the new government. But wanting a more tractable, stable, and dependent work force than vaqueros out of work from dispossessed Nueces haciendas, runaways from the south, and sons of small Nueces rancheros, King returned from a cattle-buying trip to Tamaulipas leading, like a feudal lord at the head of an *entrada*, a whole village of poor people, more than one hundred men, women, and children, along with burros, chickens, dogs, and carts, back to the ranch "where they could build homes, have jobs and get regular wages paid in cash" in return for their loyalty and servitude. These *gente* called King *patrón*, and they and their offspring were the vaqueros called *los Keñenos* (the King people), who work the cows and horses on this Texas capitalist hacienda to this day. Most of the bosses, although not all, were Anglos.[39] Most vaqueros in the U.S. cattle industry were not, however, peons like *los Keñenos* but were the bold refugees from Mexican peonage and products of the more independent and equal border society.

The land and cattle of the strip changed ownership from Mexicano to Anglo, but the vaqueros simply changed bosses. Texas courts ruled against Mexicano land titles; Anglo lawyers defending Mexicano titles took land in lieu of fees; and rancheros or their widows, threatened by charges of rustling or their cattle stolen or killed, would sell cheap. A dozen years after annexation, the new Anglo owning class were a tiny minority—one out of every forty Mexicanos.[40] The ten out of every twelve or so who chose not to become refugees were mostly workers, but there were a few middle-class Mexicano collaborators, and there were some little rancheros who clung to the thorny brushlands in spite of Ranger and sheriff terror. These Mexican workers, a good portion of them vaqueros, worked now for Anglo cattle companies, but they were not the shifty, peonized sneak thieves that Texas eyes perceived and the U.S. media stereotyped. If an Anglo steals a Mexican's cows, the Anglo justifies his theft by seeing the Mexican as the thief. As an old Mexicano Borderer bitterly comments:

> The cattle industry of the Southwest had its origin in the Nueces–Rio Grande area, with the stock and the ranches of the Rio Grande rancheros. The "cattle barons" built up their fortunes at the expense of the Border Mexican by means which were far from ethical. One notes that the white Southerner took his slave women as concubines and then created an image of the male Negro as a sex fiend. In the same way he appears to have taken the Mexican's property and then made him out a thief.[41]

But the truth about a vaquero's character sometimes even penetrates the deep racism of a typical Texas cowboy. He and his trail boss questioned a border vaquero about his claim to have recognized the track of a missing horse. In reply the vaquero "lifts his hat" and addressed the trail boss politely as "Don Tomas." "We laughed at him. He had been a peon, and that made him respect our opinions—at least he avoided differing with us."[42] Although he regularly calls Mexicans "greasers," this cowboy recognizes in a dim sort of way two truths about border vaqueros: one, that not all Mexican workers are peons; and, two, that some pretend to be. The fact is that most border vaqueros were not peonized, but that experience taught them to behave among Anglo Texans according to the racist stereotypes imposed upon them. A subjugated and threatened minority, while awaiting opportunities for resistance, survives by complying with the expectations of the dominant culture, even to the extent of pretending to the stereotype created by that culture. Thus the border vaquero fulfilled the Anglo's racist perceptions, of which the later stereotypes are just extensions. The formula is simple: the *good Mexicans* are comic little people who really like Anglos and love to serve them (Speedy Gonzales; Cisco Kid's sidekick Pancho; Carlos, the hotel owner in *Rio Bravo*), and *bad Mexicans* are dangerous killers who really hate and want to injure Anglos (all the Hollywood movie roles of Alfonso Bedoya, best known as Yellow Hat in *Treasure of the Sierra Madre*).

Moving on to consider vaqueros in New Mexico, we are concerned only with the open, rolling plains of the Rio Abajo, south of Santa Fe, and to the east the high plateau of the western Llano Estacado and the higher and more wooded Ceja to the north. These were the ancient grazing lands of the buffalo and the home of the nomadic Comanches and Mescalero Apaches. With the passing or containment of both in the seventies, stock raising became the major enterprise of the territory, the great part of it sheep raising, New Mexico's oldest industry.[43] The Mexicano natives were rancheros, who herded sheep and kept a few cattle, or peons on the haciendas, almost all of which raised sheep exclusively until the late eighties, when to compete with the new Anglos there were several large Mexicano ranches with all-vaquero help west of the upper Pecos. These had month-long moving "rodeos" twice a year to brand and separate their cattle. Mexicano families emigrated from the Nueces Strip in the late seventies and early eighties after they had been dispossessed by Anglo Texans and came seeking new homes, particularly in the Cuervo country above Fort Sumner. Sheep rancheros to the south had to have some of the skills of the vaquero, of course, to handle the few cattle they kept. The early very large sheep haciendas on the Llano, like those of Gonzáles and López, employed some vaqueros to handle remudas and small herds of longhorns. And the earlier Comancheros were all vaqueros, of course, because their main business was driving cattle: they traded for cattle stolen by the Comanches from early Texas ranchers in the Panhandle or the Cross Timber area and sold it back cheap to other Texas or territory ranchers or to other Anglo speculators, who, to avoid the pursuing Texas cattle detectives, would hire trail crews, all or mostly vaqueros, to drive the rustled herds north or to California for sale.[44] This kind of illicit traffic ended after about the mid-seventies, but another kind continued in which vaqueros were involved: Mexicano rancheros and newly arrived Texas nester ranchers, either as a casual occupation or a full-time bandit-type enterprise, collected Texas cattle drifted from the Llano and sold it to Anglo dealers, who arranged to move it out of the territory to sell. Unemployed Anglo cowboys, like Billy the Kid, and unemployed vaqueros shared this trade, of course.

Texas cattle began to fill up the New Mexico plains soon after 1848, and some of the larger ranches employed vaqueros for half of Anglo wages. These vaqueros would all be imported from the Nueces Strip or old Mexico because the plains of New Mexico, being sheep country, produced few native vaqueros and because the native workers who could ride and rope were too independent to work at Anglo cattle ranches. The Anglo cattle barons (like John Chisum and the Patterson brothers) and the small Texas farmers and ranching homesteaders were the first to move into the southeastern corner of New Mexico, all Lincoln County at that time. Because of this settlement, the region soon became known as "Little Texas." Then came the big political land-grant speculators, part of or with connections to the Santa Fe Ring, like Stephen B. Elkins (agent in Congress for the Maxwell Land Grant grabbers), Stephen B. Dorsey and his partner J. W. Dwyer (by owning 160 acres on a river in Colfax County, they claimed a range of 10,000 acres of public land back of it), and Charles B. Eddy and George Williamson in Lincoln County.[45] And finally came the cattle companies, owned by Eastern and European investors. All of these large Anglo cattle interests exploited imported Mexicanos as workers and fought and terrorized the native Mexicanos, who considered the plains and water as communal pasturage for their sheep. The political-economic background of the Lincoln County War of Chisum and Billy the Kid fame was a conflict between resident Mexicano sheepmen and interloping Anglo cattle interests. When Anglo cattlemen won in Lincoln County, the struggle became internalized among the victors, populist small ranchers versus corporate, monopoly cattle companies.[46] The struggle on the more northern ranges continued along race and class lines, with the Mexicano small herders organizing against the Anglo land and cattle companies, politically through the Knights of Labor and the People's Party and covertly, as we have seen, for a brief period as the fence-cutting activists Las Gorras Blancas, or the White Caps.

The upper Sonora ranges on the western slopes of the Sierra Madre Occidentales—what is now Arizona—were never settled by the Spanish or Mexicans because of the Apaches, and for the same reason the U.S. cattle industry arrived there late and exploited imported Mexican vaqueros from lower Sonora. And in the last decade and a half of the century, when dictator Díaz sold Mexican land and workers to foreign entrepreneurs, U.S. cattle companies responded by establishing huge ranches with Mexican vaqueros kept in peonage. The California cattle business partly used imported Sonora and Baja vaqueros.

But these considerations take us beyond the subject of the U.S. vaquero during the cowboy era, that is, during the two and a half decades after the Civil War, when the U.S. cattle industry arose on the Great Plains, not without the vaquero's important contributions, and where his image in the popular media emerged. There he came mainly from haciendas in Mexico or from the Nueces–Rio Grande valleys. These proud, brave, and skillful workers deserve but should not expect a better popular image than the media has made of them in justification of American pillage, mistreatment, and prejudice. Some true stories of real vaqueros in America told admiringly and sympathetically would modify the cowardly/sinister or trivial/comic images—if they could gain some popular currency. Perhaps a movie based on Neruda's poetic drama about the social bandit Juaquin Murietta, or about the remarkable life of Juan Herrera, the poor New Mexican ranchero turned populist leader, or perhaps about the life of the nameless drunk vaquero rescued in 1859 from the pistol whipping of a Brownsville Anglo marshal by his *patrón*, Juan Cortina, or best of all about the heroic flight of the great vaquero Gregorio Cortez, recently the subject of a television movie.

Born on the Mexican side of the border, Cortez learned to be a vaquero on ranches in southern Texas, then settled on a rented ranch with his family south of San Antonio. There he shot the sheriff of Karnes County, who without cause had killed Cortez's brother, and, in one of the most brilliant displays of horse and trail and counter-tracking work of all time, eluded and fought off dozens of posses of up to three hundred men each, transported with remudas by railroad to where he had last been sighted, in a ten-day chase of more than five hundred miles all over south Texas. During his trial, he became a hero to Mexican and Mexican-American people. But he is almost unknown to Anglo Americans. Here is a true story of just part of this heroic flight.

> Meanwhile Gregorio Cortez lay in a field, his feet wrapped in pieces of his vest, while the shooting died away at the Robledo house [where he had escaped an ambush]. After a while he crept back to the scene, entered the house, and got his shoes. This time he headed for the Rio Grande. He walked directly south to the banks of the Guadalupe River, about ten miles, to the house of another friend, Ceferino Flores. It was early on the morning of Saturday, June 15. In the two and one-half days since he had killed Sheriff Morris, Cortez had walked nearly one hundred miles. He was to walk no more for several days. Flores took Morris' pistol and hid it, giving Cortez his own. He also gave Gregorio his own mount and his saddle. It was another sorrel mare, the second of three mares that Cortez was to ride in his flight.
>
> He left Flores' house on the mare, pursued by a posse. Bloodhounds chased him across the Guadalupe River before they left off, but the posse stopped to give Ceferino Flores the rope treat-

ment and Cortez escaped. Flores got two years in the penitentiary for his part in the affair.

Cortez was now on his way to the Border. Between early Saturday morning and Sunday evening the sorrel mare carried him from the Guadalupe to the San Antonio River. In a straight line it is less than fifty miles. Cortez traveled many times the distance in those two days and one night. Long afterward all he remembered was riding and riding, doubling back, stopping to shoot, then riding again, circling about, leaving false leads when he could, and riding again.

The little mare was fleet and strong, but by Sunday morning she showed signs of giving out. Sunday noon, as he crossed the Cibolo creek near Stockdale, his trail was picked up by a fresh posse. For the next six hours he galloped, running in circles and zigzags in the area between Stockdale and Floresville, with the posse sometimes less than five hundred yards behind him. About six in the afternoon the sorrel mare stopped and refused to go any further. He had barely dismounted when she fell dead.

Cortez slipped saddle and bridle off the mare, got behind a thick tree trunk and waited. The posse stopped some distance away, dismounted, and broke into small groups, but he managed to elude them in the brush until dark. Then he slipped away, carrying the saddle until he came to a pasture where he saw another mare, a brown mare which looked tall to him, though it has been later described as a "Spanish mare, not much over thirteen hands high."

Cortez saddled the little brown mare, cut the pasture fence with a file, and started on the last lap of his ride. He was just outside of Floresville, about one hundred miles from Cotulla, where he was to leave the mare. His pursuers later estimated that he rode at least three hundred miles in getting from Floresville to Cotulla, through brush and rough country, over barbed wire fences and rivers, in three days.

The little brown mare made a name for herself. Time and again posses sighted Cortez, and every time the mare ran away from them. In the end the posses had to stop for fresh horses. At least six horses were killed by one posse in pursuing Cortez and the little mare.

Meanwhile Cortez moved toward the Rio Grande and safety. The latter part of the chase became a blur, and later he could remember but few details. He would be chased by one posse in one county and run until he lost them, only to have another one pick up his trail and chase him again, often in the direction from which he had come. Hundreds of men were out looking for him.

Aside from the dogs, probably the greatest handicap that Cortez and the brown mare faced was the Corpus Christi–to–Laredo railroad, which had been built in 1882. No matter how much Cortez hid his trail, no matter how he twisted and turned, it was evident that he was moving toward Laredo. Special trains moved up and down the tracks, bearing men, horses, and dogs, which kept in touch with other searching parties by telephone and telegraph. Whenever Cortez was sighted a posse with fresh horses would be transported to the scene by rail. And when his trail was lost, all the pursuers had to do was board a train, travel a few miles in the direction of Laredo, and take up the search again. . . .

From Floresville Cortez rode twenty-five miles along the San Antonio looking for a fording place. When he heard dogs behind, he cut off his shirt tails, blindfolded the mare, and forced her into the river and to the other side. The mare kept ahead of all the horses that chased her, but whenever he could Cortez ran into the brush. He cut across pastures, filing in two the upper strand of wire and making the mare jump over the lower. Several times he rounded up cattle and used them to cover up his trail; and once, desperate with thirst, he did drive a bunch of cattle up to a waterhole near which were several armed men, who took him for a vaquero from a nearby ranch.

But the time came when the little brown mare could no longer go on. She dragged her hind legs when she jumped over fences, and once she cut herself on the wire and began to limp. Cortez rode her into a thicket near Cotulla, took the saddle off, and hung it to a *coma* tree. A posse was right behind him when he entered the thicket.[47]

2. Black Cowboys

Jim Perry, redoubtable cook, rider, and fiddler of the XIT ranch, once wryly remarked: "If it weren't for my damned old black face I'd have been boss of one of these divisions long ago." "And no doubt he would have," a white employee commented.[48]

Although they numbered about one out of every five cowboys in the first two decades of the cowboy era, blacks were invisible in Western movies until the late 1960s and the 1970s, when some producers and writers, encouraged by the civil rights movement, made some changes. A few token blacks appeared in Westerns, like Woody Strode in *The Professionals* (1966), *Once Upon a Time in the West* (1969), *The Deserter* (1971), Jim Brown in *100 Rifles* (1969), and Ossie Davis in *The Scalphunters* (1967). But the popular myth that blacks did not help conquer the West dies hard, and no black actors except Strode are recognized as sufficiently genre actors to be included in any of the standard picture and reference books about Western movies. Further, movies about working cowboys that obviously attempt to be historically accurate, like *Will Penny* (1968), *Monte Walsh* (1970), and *The Culpepper Cattle Co.* (1972), present all white, if soiled, faces above their dusty neck bandanas. The public has been conditioned for so long about all-white cowboy trail and range outfits that movie producers seem reluctant to challenge that image. Even on more popular, prolific, and recent television, where in 1959 Westerns peaked in popularity at twenty-eight different series, "the only case in the entire run of a major TV Western that a black has achieved status as a regular cast member," that is, got regular billing in the credits, was a cowboy played by Raymond St. Jacques on *Rawhide* beginning in the series' sixth year, in 1965, after the death of trail boss Favor.[49] Monte Hellman's realistic *Ride in the Whirlwind* (1967) is typical: the three unemployed cowboys riding south seeking work are all Anglos; the only black is a member of the small outlaw gang they stumble upon.

The lily-white popular vision of the conquerors of our West began back long before movies. The scores of commercial photographers of the West, who made cheaply reproduced scrapbook souvenir and postcard photo prints and graphoscope and stereopticon cards for mass consumption—F. M. Steel, N. H. Rose, C. D. Kirkland, W. J. Carpenter, L. A. Huffman—didn't include blacks in their scenes of cowboy life. The same is true of wood-engravings of photographs or of on-location sketches printed in popular magazines, like *Harper's* and *Leslie's Illustrated Weekly*: nary a black cowboy. The all-black Ninth and Tenth Cavalry could not be ignored by artists, but black cowboys could and were—Remington painted and sketched many black cavalry soldiers but no black cowboys. The "Cowboy Fun" part of early Wild West shows had no blacks, nor were they depicted on the lithograph posters and billboards. Our Western myth began to form early on the very frontier it presented and shaped—and from the beginning excluded blacks.

The veil lowered on black cowboys seems almost impenetrable. Where else but in rodeos does the public see real, living cowboys firsthand, not mediated by the media? Or at least what look like cowboys. And from the beginning virtually all the rodeo cowboys were white. Rodeo has steadfastly resisted integration and remains largely Jim Crow to this day. There are a few exceptions that stand out because of their rarity—for instance, Charlie Sampson, the top pro bull rider on the circuit recently. A member of the Rodeo Historical Society gives the standard explanation: "Negroes were automatically barred from competition because most whites felt that it was below their dignity to compete with a black man,"[50] an explanation that ignores the years of their "competing" with them for jobs on the range and trail. Only a handful of blacks made it into rodeo, notably Bill Pickett, the Texas working cowboy who invented bulldogging as a spectacle and introduced it as an event. Pickett became famous for his spectacular performances at country fairs and so couldn't be denied entry into rodeo in 1902. There were a very few others: Joe Pickett, a bulldogger unrelated to Bill; Jesse Stahl, a bareback bronc rider from California. In 1971 Bill Pickett became the first and only black cowboy in the National Cowboy Hall of Fame, after a three-year struggle against racists on the board of trustees.[51] Blacks had their own segregated annual rodeos in Texas near where they worked (for instance, at Bonham and at Sandy Point), but these received no national publicity and so did not get into the popular consciousness. All black rodeos in Texas were like the numerous small Anglo local rodeos ("pun'kin rollers," as they are called), primarily for local talent from nearby ranches. Although there has recently been a strong revival of black rodeo in a weekend circuit around Houston of riders and ropers with weekday city jobs, these local events leave little trace on the average person's notion of the complexion of the American cowboy.

This phenomenon of willful exclusion by which those historical images that don't agree with racial stereotypes are deleted from the consciousness of generations of Americans deserves further study. Black cowboys are not the only blacks who have been made invisible. The tens of thousands of blacks who fought for their freedom in the Civil War and the thousands in the Revolutionary War and the War of 1812 have been forgotten, not only in the popular mind but in school history texts. During the Civil War "the newspapers and magazines of the day printed regular reports of the recruitment and battlefield activity of the black regiments, as well as articles and interviews dealing with the individual exploits of black infantrymen, artillerymen, scouts and guerrillas, illustrated copiously by journalist-artists at the fronts." But the black soldiers and guerrillas fighting in their own war for their own liberation has given way to the popular image of the "kneeling, grateful slave who thanks the benign Emancipator for the gift of freedom." So the "200,000 black soldiers, organized in 166 regiments of infantry, cavalry, and artillery, together with almost 30,000 black sailors, about one-quarter of the navy,"[52] have as effectively passed from American consciousness as the one-quarter of all cowboys on the Great Plains during the cowboy era. We close our eyes to what we don't want to see: in the case of Civil War fighters, militant and self-determining blacks; in the case of cowboys, strong, independent black pioneers of the frontier.

Students of our culture and history haven't done much better than our entertainers and our media producers, even in the present more enlightened times. Although there are several chapters on cowboys in recent books about blacks on the frontier,[53] the only book-length treatment of black cowboys, published in 1965,[54] merely collects some neglected facts without any interpretation and fails to deal at all with the black cattle workers *before* the cowboy era. The late Kenneth Wiggins Porter alone deals analytically and systematically with the whole subject at monograph length,[55] but an important part of his work on black riders and herdsmen before the Civil War has never been published. The first attempt, in 1940, to inform the public that cowboys were not all white significantly appeared in a fine long essay in the anti–Jim Crow NAACP magazine *The Crisis,*[56] and was ignored—even by historians.

There is some evidence that there were more black cowboys in the first decade and a half of the cowboy era than in the last, that is, that blacks began quitting cowboying earlier than whites. Two recent Anglo historians have reacted with a kind of backlash to revisionist claims that 20 to 25 percent of cowboys were black, but their work can be refuted on factual grounds. One shows 4 percent black cowhands in west Texas in 1880, "far lower than claimed by some historians," but excludes the black concentrations of south and southeast Texas, excludes cooks and wranglers altogether, and excludes cowboys on the trail or between jobs; and he trusts census figures too much.[57] The other, on the basis of his impressions of not seeing many blacks during his survey of nineteenth-century photographs of cowboy outfits, claims that "Negro cowboys may not have been as prevalent as some historians have indicated,"[58] but fails to consider how popular consciousness is created by media artists, in this case early photographers who already were not seeing black cowboys or taking pictures of mixed outfits and whose selective and composed pictures cannot be considered any more an accurate "historical record" than, say, Remington's sketches and paintings or Wister's novel. The same historian sneaks in a second gratuitous and bogus attack on the revisionist estimate of the proportion of black cowboys in his critique of how George Saunders arrived

BLACKS AT A FAIR, BONHAM, TEXAS, 1909

Bonham is seventy miles northeast of Dallas. These cowboys are dressed and equipped with their finest for the occasion, but there is evidence of extreme poverty: the rider in the middle (eighth from left) doesn't have a right stirrup strap and uses a rope tied to the front rigging ring. Perhaps only the working cowboys (about half) are fully equipped with ropes, chaps, and boots; and only a very few have spurs (but observe the huge spiked rowel between the front legs of the third horse from the left). The cowboy on the extreme left alone has a slicker tied behind his cantle and has decorated his horse's headstall with ribbons. (COURTESY OF THE ERWIN E. SMITH COLLECTION OF RANGE-LIFE PHOTOGRAPHS, LIBRARY OF CONGRESS.)

PART OF THE SAME GROUP, BONHAM, TEXAS, 1909

Wanting to show the fanciest cowboy, the photographer Erwin Smith asked the one with spurs and wrist gauntlets to pose dismounted and to present a side view of his horse. There are silver conchas on the split-ear headstall and at the bases of his leather ties on his saddle, a cheap one with stamped, simulated tooling and without a rear latigo and cinch. For contrast, Smith poses the rider with the rope stirrup strap to the right rear. (COURTESY OF THE ERWIN E. SMITH COLLECTION OF RANGE-LIFE PHOTOGRAPHS, LIBRARY OF CONGRESS.)

BULLDOGGING, SUNDAY RODEO, BROOKSHIRE, TEXAS, 1981

Brookshire is thirty miles west of the center of Houston. The rodeo is sponsored by one of the six black cowboy associations which offer three to five rodeos every weekend within a sixty-mile radius of Houston. (COURTESY OF THE WATRISS/BALDWIN-WOODFINE CAMP ASSOCS.)

SUNDAY RODEO, DICKINSON, TEXAS, 1981

This rodeo is twenty-five miles southwest of Houston near the Dickinson Bayou. (COURTESY OF THE WATRISS/BALDWIN-WOODFINE CAMP ASSOCS.)

at his famous figure for *all* cowboys who went up the trail with herds. He doesn't mention in his four-page argument dealing with absolute numbers that Saunders declared *one-third of them were either black or Mexican.*[59] But after taking care of these recent champions of Anglo historiography, some qualifications must be made. Saunders's fraction only holds for the southern Plains and up to the time trail drives dwindled, which was in the first half of the eighties. Thereafter, the percentage of black cowboys probably did fall off. After experiencing the freedom of the frontier in considerable numbers, blacks were quitting cowboying by the eighties, when trail drives (upon which the revisionist figures are based) were rapidly winding down, and when commercial photographers were taking many more pictures than before, and when after Reconstruction and the passing of the frontier, Jim Crow enforced by terror might have caused militant blacks to migrate to Northern cities.

Let us look now at the neglected history that probably cannot ever become as deeply embedded in our national consciousness as the image that comes from the wish-fulfilling and justifying popular culture and mass media. Where did the almost 9,000 black Texas cowboys who went up the trail come from? At the outset, one should remember that since many African societies are based on cattle raising and herding, many captives, particularly those from Gambia, came here with skills in managing cattle which could be put to advantage by slave owners or by the slaves themselves if they ran away. There were several places where black slaves or freedmen or fugitives worked cattle in North America. First and most important, blacks hunted and worked cattle in the savannahs, pine barrens, and tall grass marshes of colonial South Carolina in gangs on cattle plantations. This earliest Anglo-American cattle business on open ranges spread with its predominantly African herders working in plantation-type cow-pen crews, many mounted, all through the pine barrens that extend in a wide coastal belt south through Georgia and northern Florida and west along the Gulf of Mexico into southern Alabama, Mississippi, Louisiana, and finally into southeast Texas. As has been noted before, this distinctive Anglo-Afro cattle raising used dogs, bullwhips, and salt to manage cattle in the East but learned roping and adopted horned saddles from Mexicans in the Southeast. The relevant point here is that there were thousands of black cowboys long before the Civil War in the cattle business of the pine barren belt of the coastal South.[60]

The other centers of black cowboys outside Texas were made up of fugitives from slavery or captured slaves. From New Spain times on, the Seminole Indians on the savannahs of southern Florida raised cattle, and many of the black runaways to this nation became herdsmen, both on foot and horseback. Similarly, the Five Civilized Tribes in the Indian Territory were farmers and stock raisers and employed many fugitive slaves in these occupations. And finally, there were thousands of blacks, mostly from south Texas, who made the perilous flight to freedom into the northern states of Mexico, between the Sierra Madres, where the principal occupation was cattle and sheep raising. This included the hundreds of blacks who immigrated to Coahuila with the Seminole Chief Wild Cat in 1849–1850.[61]

But by far most early black cowboys came from Texas itself. If the cradle of Anglo cowboys is the big diamond south of San Antonio and the cradle of Mexicano cowboys the southern part of that diamond, the Nueces Strip, then the cradle of black cowboys is just eastward of the diamond in the wide coastal prairie of coarse grass and groves of trees and wooded creeks and bayous along the Gulf from the Guadalupe River east below Houston to Louisiana. There Austin's slave-owning colonists first established cattle ranches, and by the time of the Texan Revolution there were large herds on open ranges—for instance, near the Brazos there were herds of over 2,000 cattle—and in the whole colony there were more than a thousand blacks, many of whom were cowboys. These black slaves and some black freedmen, together with hired Anglo cowboys and vaqueros, caught and tamed and moved cattle on horseback without the help of herd dogs, with ropes and with the horned saddles that go with roping. But they managed cattle in many ways differently from the practices of the Brasada or the Great Plains. Frank Dobie describes an instance: "In the coastal brush away east of the Nueces, where Mexican vaqueros give way to Negro cowhands, the ropers [of wild steers] commonly lead out what they rope without help from a neck animal."[62] The cattle ran free on open ranges except for the winter months, when they were driven to graze on the salt grasses of the coast.

When the black crews brought them back in the spring, they assembled them at "cutout" points where they were separated according to brands into herds and the calves branded to return to their respective ranges. The cutout point for ranches in the Houston area was at Sandy Point, where for many years up until at least 1940 there was an annual rodeo sponsored by local black cowboys.[63] Cowboys on those ranches that did not winter cattle on the coast had "cowhunts" and branded cattle in pens. The pre–Civil War senator from Texas, Francis Richard Lubbock, started his cattle ranch in the early 1850s on four hundred acres on the south side of Simms' Bayou, six miles south of Houston on the way to Galveston. He became, as he wrote, the "largest cattle owner between the Brazos and the Trinity" and used Sandy Point as his cutout, where in the spring he sent a pack mule or wagon and two or three horses for each of his cowboys, all of whom, evidently, were slaves. He went cattle hunting at roundup time with all his neighbor ranchers, with his "cowboys at his heels." "Many of our negro boys," he wrote late in the century, "were fine horse-breakers. However [we] preferred saving their 'backs and wrists,'" so he gave all his wild horses to Weed, an itinerant freedman and professional horse breaker from Louisiana.[64]

Much of the work handling cattle on these slave ranches was on foot, in the pens, holding cattle in small pastures in wooded areas, herding along tree-lined trails, even hunting cattle in the brush. Ancient African techniques of herding doubtless were employed. There is good reason to trace the modern rodeo event of bulldogging to early cattle-raising practices by blacks in the South. For example, wrestling wild steers to the ground when the thickness of the brush would make horses and throwing ropes useless. And it is not farfetched to think of rodeo bull riding as reflecting the early practice of slaves without horses, remembering old African practices, riding cattle on the coastal prairies. But horses offer such an obvious advantage to handling cattle that lots of trusted slaves were regularly mounted, although some of those trusted ones ran off.

From Austin's colony before the Texas Revolution, they could just ride east across the Trinity or west across the Guadalupe into free Mexico; afterwards, it was a long and perilous way—although a well-travelled one— along the coastal prairie to the Rio Grande. Some slaves went off with the Mexican army when it retired from Texas after San Jacinto.[65]

Lubbuck speaks about a slave he had bought from a neighbor as his "best cowboy and most expert rider and horsebreaker."[66] Even the unmounted slaves on cattle ranches would learn to ride, willy-nilly, even if their work with cattle and horses was restricted to pens. It is doubtless true that slave-owning cattlemen were slow to move from the coastal prairie to the western plains, less out of fear of Indians than of the relative proximity of the Mexican border, an enticing lure of freedom for blacks, especially those who were expert horsemen.

In fact, many of the newspaper accounts of runaways reported them as mounted and from the prairies of southeast Texas, or up the Colorado on the edge of the plains between San Antonio and Austin, where small cattle ranchers and farmers with their few slaves began to move in the forties and fifties. The Yankee abolitionist Olmsted reported in 1855 that the main increase in blacks in west Texas (west of the Colorado River), where the black population tripled in the first half of the 1850s, was just in those counties bordering the western plains.[67]

The inevitable spread of the cattle business out of the southeast coastal prairie toward the western plains and the Mexican border was fraught with peril for slave-owning cattlemen. In 1837, a group of blacks killed the sheriff of Gonzales County (just east of San Antonio) when he stopped them near Victoria, and escaped to Mexico. In 1845, twenty-five blacks secured some firearms and several of the best horses in Bastrop (just below Austin) and headed for the Rio Grande; only about a quarter of them eluded posses to cross the border.[68] The slaves on the western edge of the cradle of black cowboys were restless and dissatisfied: around Cuero and Victoria less than a year before the war, owners discovered a plot for a slave insurrection and whipped a Yankee abolitionist suspected of organizing it.[69] The fear that Chief Wild Cat's colony of Seminoles and blacks in Coahuila might attract mass flights of Texas blacks doubtless added to the reasons that kept slave ranches from moving west onto the plains and that restricted the number of slaves who were regularly mounted. Before the end of the war, the practice in west Texas was to establish slave ranches not on the prairie but on its edge in wooded areas where the slave quarters were located, around the pens in which cattle were kept at night, and where slaves worked cattle on foot, except for a trusted few who were allowed to trail and hunt cows on the open plains to the west.

Such was the practice of the early cattlemen to the north around Waco and in the Cross Timber frontier west of present-day Fort Worth. Oliver Loving collected herds there with "a few slaves," the most famous of whom was Bose Ikard, first his cowboy, then his bodyguard. Loving's later partner, Charles Goodnight, had his first herd delivered in 1857 "with the help of his negro slaves." After the war, Goodnight "brought [Bose Ikard] out to the wagon," a phrase which suggests that formerly he stayed with the rest of the blacks in the slave quarters.[70] After Emancipation, when black cowboys were no longer inclined to run away to Mexico, they could become part of integrated trail and range outfits.

We can conclude, with the historian of Texas blacks, that "early Texas cattlemen along the Gulf coast employed slaves as cowboys to herd cattle,"[71] and we can add that these ranches using slaves had spread up the Colorado to the northwest and to the north around Waco and to the Cross Timbers—but not onto the plains and not usually employing fully mounted black outfits. In the more northern settlements, what prevented the emergence of slavery onto the plains was not only that slaves would run away but that Indians would massacre them or, less often, take them—like cattle—as booty in raids; also, there was plenty of cheap Mexican labor, which made slaves unprofitable. Thus the halt of slavery on the cattleman's frontier is another indication that slavery had reached its economic-geographic limits *before* the war.

After the war, the new concentration of black cowboys came to be on ranches along the line of Hays and Blanco counties west of Austin in what old Texas cowhands called "the Negro colony." Such old-timers explain that "when the South set their Negroes free" (!), they came with their old masters from south Texas ranches up along the Colorado River and the tributaries of the Brazos and "remained on the different ranches where their bosses located."[72] Such paternalistic views should be received with caution. Some black cowboys in south and east Texas undoubtedly stayed with their former owners as wage laborers in moves to new ranches on the plains, but most just sought employment in the many new squatting ranches and cow-hunting outfits on the open ranges of the new burgeoning industry. Blacks were seeking work for the first time, and there were plenty of jobs for skilled cowboys in west Texas. They were just part of the first wave of black migrants seeking work after the war. Emancipation contributed to making these jobs by allowing cattlemen to move to the plains, the natural location of the cattle industry, without fear of losing their valuable investment in human chattel by flights to Mexico or through theft or destruction by Indians. So black cowboys sought work in the west in the capitalist industry that their freedom had helped create.

Since in the early years there were many small, independent operators without capital hunting and marketing unbranded cattle or selling their hides, some blacks went into this business with nothing but a few horses as investment. But not having capital and the kinds of social connections that facilitate its accumulation, black cowboys soon became wage earners as Anglo cattlemen formed protective associations, passed maverick laws, and settled range boundaries among themselves—that is, took over the industry. A very few black cowboys later became small independent producers. The only one that the powerful Texas and Southwest Cattle Raisers' Association could trot out in bogus demonstration of the equality of opportunity for blacks in Texas, as it often did, was its member of thirty years, "80 John" Wallace, a real single-minded, nose-to-the-grindstone achiever cowboy if ever there was one: born a slave in Victoria County; went up the trail as a boy to west Texas around Abilene; hunted cows and wrangled for a while, then worked with the Clay Mann outfit as a cowboy and banker for his boss on ranges in Texas, New Mexico Territory, and Chihuahua; bought some cattle with most of his accumulated savings from his thirty-dollar-a-month salary and ran them with his boss's cattle for a fee in the eighties, when he bought his first section of land near Loraine, Texas, in Mitchell County, and continued to acquire cattle and land around there while he cowboyed for wages first with cattle barons, then with several corporate ranches, and finally by weathering the Depres-

sion as a stock farmer; ending up with unencumbered possession of fourteen and one-half sections of land, with six hundred acres under cultivation
in cotton and feed and six hundred whiteface cattle.[73]

Of course, all the rest of the black cowboys continued to work for wages.
Many, when their work turned to badly paid jobs on stock farms, to
preserve a bit of their style and their relatively free, roving life, became,
like Nat Love and Matthew "Bones" Hook,[74] Pullman porters, the best
and only such occupation open to them—since rodeo work, Wild West
shows, dude ranching, and Hollywood movie riding were Jim Crow.

The black cowboys of the Great Plains were not, of course, all from
south Texas. They came from the Carolinas, Florida, the Indian Territory,
and Mexico, bringing to the new industry the cowboy skills acquired before
the war. They came to Texas in the second wave of black migration from
all over the South (the first wave is the smaller one from southeastern
Texas west to the plains), this time joined by poor white tenant farmers
and sharecroppers running from economic depression, the crop lien system, and, as we have seen, the new stock and game laws that deprived
them of their customary grazing and hunting rights. Here is the moving
account of this migration by the historian of American populism. Since we
are conditioned by our culture to think only of white cowboys, we should
read this account remembering that half or more of the migrant Southern
farm boys who were coming to Texas in the seventies with dreams of
becoming wild and woolly cowboys were black. A poor black farm boy
had even more reason than his white counterpart to learn the skills to
become a free and stylish roving cowboy, because he was not only fleeing
the tyranny of the furnishing merchant in league with the local bank in the
old South but, after Reconstruction, the degradation of extreme Jim Crow
and the terror of the Ku Klux Klan and the Knights of the White Camellia.

> For simple, geographical reasons, "Going West" for most
> Southerners meant, in the familiar phrase of the time, "Gone to
> Texas." The phrase became so common that often only the
> initials "G.T.T." scrawled across a nailed-shut door were needed
> to convey the message. White and Negro farmers by the thou-
> sands drove down the plank roads and rutted trails of the rural
> South, westward across the Mississippi River to the Sabine and
> into the pine forests of East Texas. The quest for new land and a
> new start drove lengthening caravans of the poor—almost 100,000
> every year of the 1870s—ever deeper into Texas, through and
> beyond the "piney woods" and into the hill country and prairie

Cross Timbers. There the men and women of the South stepped
out into the world of the Great Plains. It was there that the culture
of a new People's politics took form in nineteenth-century America.[75]

On the trail and the range of the new industry blacks could find good
pay equal to whites and integrated outfits and even some camaraderie
with Anglo fellow workers, and in cattle towns a degree of freedom from
Jim Crow. No wonder that the young sons of farm families in the Black
Exodus became cowboys when they got to Texas or Kansas or Nebraska
or Oklahoma. There they would see real cowboy outfits and could begin
a new life if they could get on as a wrangler, a nighthawk, a cook's helper,
or a drag. And this relative freedom and equality lasted as long as the
frontier. As a recent historian of blacks in the West says, "The less stable
a community, particularly if it had no women, the more equality it offered
its black cowboys. The arrival of 'civilization' and white women meant that
the racial bars were about to be erected. Perhaps that is why many a black
cowboy enjoyed a life on the open plains more than city visits, and headed
further west as frontier communities became stabilized."[76] The view seems
to prove Turner's safety-valve theory of the free and democratic frontier,
but we should remember that blacks and whites were both being exploited
by the owning class, East and West, and that terrible racial discrimination
and extreme social hierarchies, although perhaps not quite as bad as in
the East, existed even on the frontier.

The best explanation of why young blacks became cowboys emerges
from Kenneth Wiggins Porter's summary and conclusion to his unique and
definitive account of blacks in the cattle industry after the Civil War:

> Without the services of the eight or nine thousand Negroes—a
> quarter of the total number of trail drivers—who during the gen-
> eration after the Civil War helped to move herds up the cattle
> trails to shipping points, Indian reservations, and fattening grounds
> and who, between drives, worked on the ranches of Texas and
> the Indian Territory, the cattle industry would have been seriously
> handicapped. For apart from their considerable numbers, many
> of them were especially well-qualified top hands, riders, ropers,
> and cooks. Of the comparatively few Negroes on the Northern
> Range, a good many were also men of conspicuous abilities who
> notably contributed to the industry in that region. These cow-
> hands, in their turn, benefitted from their participation in the
> industry, even if not to the extent that they deserved. That a
> degree of discrimination and segregation existed in the cattle

country should not obscure the fact that, during the halcyon days of the cattle range Negroes there frequently enjoyed greater opportunities for a dignified life than anywhere else in the United States. They worked, ate, slept, played, and on occasion fought, side by side with their white comrades, and their ability and courage won respect, even admiration. They were often paid the same wages as white cowboys and, in the case of certain horse-breakers, ropers, and cooks, occupied positions of considerable prestige. In a region and period characterized by violence, their lives were probably safer than they would have been in the Southern cotton regions where between 1,500 and 1,600 Negroes were lynched in two decades after 1882. The skilled and handy Negro probably had a more enjoyable, if a rougher, existence as a cowhand than he would have had as a sharecropper or laborer. . . . Negro cowhands, to be sure, were not treated as "equals," except in the rude quasi-equality of the roundup, stampede, and river-crossing—where they were sometimes tacitly recognized even as superiors—but where else in post–Civil War America, at a time of the Negro's nadir, did so many adult Negroes and whites attain even this degree of fraternity? The cow country was no utopia for Negroes, but it did demonstrate that under some circumstances and for at least brief periods white and black in significant numbers could live and work together on more nearly equal terms than had been possible in the United States for two hundred years or would be possible again for nearly another century.[77]

Appropriately, black rodeo survives only in the cradle of black cowboys, where a revival of the tradition has occurred within the last two decades. There are not now many black working cowboys in south Texas. But in 1947, black rodeo cowboys, virtually excluded from the national rodeo circuit, formed in Houston the Negro Cowboys Rodeo Association, which for a few years organized a circuit of rodeos mainly in south Texas but also in big arenas in San Antonio and Fort Worth, and in Oklahoma and Louisiana. This circuit broke up, but rodeo continues strong south and west of Houston under the auspices of six black cowboy associations, which several years ago provided three to five rodeos every weekend from March to November within a radius of sixty miles. Some of these rodeos go way back and are hoary with tradition, continuing cutout point contests and festivities started during slavery times, like the one at Egypt on June 19, Black Emancipation Day in Texas. But as in Anglo rodeo, almost three-

VOX OUTFIT, NEAR TEXAS-OKLAHOMA PANHANDLE, ABOUT 1890

This chuckwagon scene by photographer A. A. Forbes is unusual in showing a

quarters of the contestants don't win enough prize money to meet the expenses of horses, trailers, travel, and entry fees. Since they must finance their weekend cowboying with higher-paying jobs in and around Houston, this weekend soul-circuit suffers during an economic depression.[78]

3. Women Cowhands

In westerns, the only satisfactory role was to be a woman outlaw: everything else wore thin too quickly: the rancher's daughter, the sheriff's wife, or standing around a smelly saloon in feathers and beads looking like a dyed pigeon in a draft.
—Miriam as a young teenager creating fantasy roles for herself, in Marge Piercy's *Small Changes*

Though women cowhands as a group do not constitute a minority, nor were they wage laborers in trail or range outfits, there is a clear analogy

typically mixed crew. The two seated cowboys in the front center are black and the one on the far right is Mexican. (COURTESY OF THE WESTERN HISTORY COLLECTIONS, UNIVERSITY OF OKLAHOMA LIBRARY.)

between the way patriarchal attitudes and institutions affected women in the cattle industry and the way racist attitudes and institutions affected Mexicans and blacks. Women cowhands shared with vaqueros and black cowboys first their exploitation by a society that treated them as inferiors with unequal rights and, second, their not being represented popularly or by historians as important in the part the cattle industry played in the westward movement. They are presented as aliens on the frontier and as hating every minute of it until churches and schools and picket fences came to give them ordered stability. The frontier woman is celebrated because "she stoically transcends a situation she never would have chosen. . . . her whole posture is in rigid opposition to the wilderness experience."[79] Her glory is that she carried the home and the civilization that supported it inviolate into the wilderness. On big spreads women remain inside baronial ranch houses, directing Mexican servants; in nester cabins they bake apple pies and biscuits and serve men at the kitchen table; in towns they are nagging schoolmarms, like Molly in *The Virginian*, always bewildered by and protesting the aggressive and violent ways of men.

But feminists have recently begun to question this hackneyed image of the unhappy and fearful woman on the frontier by uncovering evidence that women loved the wilderness as much as men did and could survive its dangers and flourish in it just as well as men and without their protection. One such critic cites, for instance, the American writer Agnes Smedley, who as a young woman in the early years of this century rode a horse alone, with a gun slung at her side, through the deserts of the Southwest, safe and unafraid, because, as Smedley says in *Daughter of Earth*, "it was a land where women were strong." Indeed, women longed to be cowhands as much as men did and were only prevented for a time in fulfilling that longing by the patriarchal conventions imposed to keep them in their place.

A young mother on a small ranch in Montana wrote in the eighties: "work on horseback, while dangerous and often very hard, wasn't drudgery. There was freedom to it. *Even we women felt that though the freedom wasn't ours*" (emphasis added).[80] The freedom wasn't hers because of her breeding as a Virginia lady and because of patriarchal attitudes limiting her to domestic and maternal functions. Twenty years later a young New Mexico woman confessed to having similar frustrated longings while growing up on her father's big ranch: "True to aristocratic rearing, I had to lead a ladylike life and should not resemble that of our uncouth neighbors whose women were able to do men's work. I always envied any woman who could ride a bronco, but in my society it was not done. How skillfully they saddled a horse! I often watched them catch a pony out in the pasture, just as men did on our range, but it was never my privilege to have to do it." Every morning her horse was saddled by a vaquero and hitched to a

*In the 1929 version, Molly
Wood (Mary Brian) tries to
prevent The Virginian (Gary
Cooper) from leaving the hotel
room to have a shootout with
Trampus (Walter Huston).*

post ready to be ridden if she chose, but she never did learn to ride an
ordinary cowpony to *work* in a roundup as her plebeian sisters in the
neighborhood did.[81]

If ever there was a contraption designed to keep women inactive, im-
mobile, restricted in range and movement, helpless and demure, it was
the sidesaddle. Not only restrictive but dangerous. Obviously it prevented
clinging to the horse with the knees. The only way to stay on was to hook
the right knee around the horn and press the calf against the inside of the
thigh as tight as possible. The single stirrup was short in order to keep the
legs demurely together, so there was no way to stand in a sidesaddle to
take up shock or to counterbalance. Sometimes there was a second post
just to the left of the horn to brace the left knee against, but this gave little
additional ease or stability. Not only was the woman's perch precarious,

FRONTIER WOMAN DISCOURAGING BANDITS, 1878

Wood engraving from William W. Fowler, Women on the American Frontier
*(1878). The caption: "Mastering Bandits." Surviving was more difficult
sidesaddle than astride.* (COURTESY OF THE DENVER PUBLIC LIBRARY, WESTERN
HISTORY DEPARTMENT.)

but the sidesaddle canted her at an angle to her own natural balance and
the motion of the horse.

Riding costumes were part of that oppressive and risky convention: the
skirts had to extend considerably beyond floor length to cover any glimpse
of ankle when the knee was hiked up to hook around the saddle horn.
She could wear drawers or "pants" or a union suit as undergarments, but
they mustn't show. As a result, the woman was not only awkward and
unbalanced on horseback but, without adequate hoistings, liable to trip
over her own skirt just getting to or from her horse. The convention of
the sidesaddle was particularly galling to Western women who longed for
the freedom that men riders fairly flaunted all around them every day. There
is evidence that lots of women learned to ride astride bareback when they
were girls before the constrictions of womanhood began to close in—or
in secret with ordinary saddles when the menfolk were away. A wonderfully
appropriate story is told by an old cowboy. In the seventies he was driving
some beeves up a long lane in Atoscosa County, just below San Antonio,
when a man and a woman on horseback passed him, the woman riding
"sideways, as was the custom in those days." For some reason the herd
turned and stampeded toward the couple and was gaining on the woman
when "that woman suddenly swung herself astride of the horse she was
riding and pulled off a race that beat anything I ever saw," outdistancing

the herd and riding safely away.[82] This is a bitter story: a woman socialized into compliance momentarily freed by peril.

There was a terrible tyranny to the sidesaddle convention, which was not just restricted to the upper classes but extended to wives of small ranchmen and even to the wives of nesters. This from a wife on a Montana ranch in the mid-1880s: we women, "if we did have to ride a man's saddle, would simply crook a knee over the saddle horn." She says she did this when she occasionally rode out to the chuck wagon after the sidesaddle she had brought from her Virginia home as a bride was destroyed in a fire. But when she had several children, she, with great regret, quit riding altogether.[83] Even an Iowa farm girl turned nester's wife in Johnson County in the early eighties rode sidesaddle and wore a "riding habit." Her son remembers the cabin: "Out in front of the cabin there was a hitch rack for horses. Nearby there was a stile or step for the women who rode side-saddles. Mother would tie her Polly saddle mare to the hitch rack while she changed into her riding habit. The skirt was about two feet too long. There was a jacket made of the same kind of material. After Mother was ready to go she would mount old Polly, reach down and pick me up off the stile. I rode on behind Mother, while Tode [his brother] rode on her lap. This is the way we would go to visit some of our neighbors." This behavior, ironically, was expected of a woman who loved ranching and the outdoors but was married to a man who preferred town: "the folks leased out the ranch and stock against Mother's wishes. Mother was the real rancher. Dad was the town guy. We moved into Buffalo, where Dad got a job as a day cook in the American restaurant."[84]

All classes of men were scandalized to see respectable or married women riding astride. A woman in Deadwood recalls a story told her by Shorty, a bullwhacker, about how Molly, a young woman, deceived his boss in 1877. "She came to the wagon-boss at Bismarck and asked if she could shove through with us. She had her own hoss and would just ride along with our outfit for safety and she said she could help with the cookin'. The wagon-boss thought that would be all right enough. He supposed she had a sidesaddle and would ride like a lady. He forgot all about her, and we were all so busy getting off that nobody noticed her till we were so far out he couldn't send her back. And here she was a-riding à la clothespin." Shorty goes on to explain that all the teamsters "were shocked and hor-rified." The woman who heard Shorty's story muses: "They had been ashamed to come into Deadwood with her—those rough, profane bull-whackers."[85]

Young Molly was not alone. From contemporary sources it is clear that many of the second-generation Western women would have nothing to do with "riding like a lady" and defied tradition, sometimes with their mothers' encouragement, by riding in the natural way. Perhaps they were emboldened by seeing that Indian women rode astride and that there was a Western class of older women, like Calamity Jane, who rode horses and dressed like men. Such women did not even cover their knickerbockers with knee-length skirts, the way farm women on the overland trail partially disguised the pantlike leg coverings they had contrived for their survival. There were many women vagrants and casual workers and drifters, the hobo-type sisters of the road, riding horses and dressed like men, whom young frontier women would see and be tempted to emulate—in their dress and riding style anyway: freighters, stagecoach drivers, herders, pan-handlers, buffalo camp followers, gamblers, cattle thieves. Not only these vagrants and casuals but professional and business women sought the frontier to avoid to some degree the oppressive restrictions of the East. It was easier in the West than in the East to succeed in male-preserve oc-cupations (e.g., in 1870, 14 percent of all women lawyers and 10 percent of all women doctors practiced in the West, which had only 2 percent of the population)[86] and businesses and trades, like baking, fruit marketing, wagon wheel making and repairing. Women came West also because their civil rights were somewhat better established—for instance, Wyoming women could vote and sit on juries after 1870. The motives of Western women riders are analogous to those of black cowboys: women cowpunchers sought some freedom from patriarchal restrictions; black cowboys sought some freedom from Jim Crow.

We can see the generational conflict about riding styles in this Montana ranch woman's reaction to Miss S., a friend of a neighbor's daughter who was "a very bright young woman but very advanced in our day [the mid-1880s]. She scandalized our [cow]boys, who were rather old fashioned, by borrowing their horses and riding astride; when the rest of us, if we did have to ride a man's saddle, would simply crook a knee over the saddle horn. Miss S. was very energetic, too, and always wanted to work with them, hauling poles or helping stretch wire. They admired her intellect, but they were rather non-plussed." This woman's own young daughter a few years later was, to her mother's chagrin, riding bareback like a boy.[87] But the convention was so strong that some Western ranch women who were teenagers in the late eighties, because of class pride and gentility, learned to ride "sideways" and continued in that style until the ridiculous mode went out of fashion with the end of the frontier near the turn of the century. For instance, Agnes Morley grew up on a large family-owned cattle ranch in New Mexico Territory in the eighties and nineties and partially managed it and worked it with her brother. She became such an expert horsewoman that a Buffalo Bill Wild West show scout tried to recruit her; she would ride line alone in outlying camps for several weeks on end; she could tame an outlaw horse; she regularly took part in roundups where she would work herds, turn back runaways, cut out brands, hold cuts; she even went hunting grizzly bears in the mountains on horseback. But all of this was on a sidesaddle. She always wore the long "riding skirt" that was required, with several ordinary skirts beneath it if it were cold. But her cowpunching work was severely limited because, not having a saddle horn to tie or dally to, she could not rope, nor with her long skirt could she even hogtie a calf or a steer roped by someone else.[88]

Most other women riders in America gave up the dangerous and restrictive practice in rapidly increasing numbers near the end of the century. In the Sears, Roebuck catalogue of 1902, twelve models of sidesaddles are offered, compared to twenty-one in the 1897 catalogue; the number of regular saddles offered remained about the same. In 1897 Sears offered one saddle "especially adapted for ladies riding astride"; it looks like an ordinary Western saddle but, significantly, a nonworking one—a bit more petite and with a small horn for holding on to but not for tying to. If women were going to ride astride, especially if they were going to *work* on horseback, why did they need special saddles? They learned quickly that they didn't: by 1902 Sears was no longer offering a special saddle for women riding astride, and by 1908 offered only five sidesaddles. The convention was dead, but there was still no way for women to buy ready-made mail-order pants or trousers or even outside-style full-width drawers or what later were called culottes—although women could get "bicycle suits" with skirts, bloomers, and leggings, a costume which women, for lack of better, probably wore for riding horses. Many just wore men's riding jeans.

What does the coincidence of the end of the frontier and of sideways riding for women signify? Younger Western women had been defying the requirement in increasing numbers; the unconventional fringe in the West had ignored it from the beginning. But why did women riders win their battle to ride horses like men at just the time that the frontier disappeared? The answers seem obvious. Now that civilization, thanks largely to women, had been brought to the West, now that the threats to women were removed, now that the families and the homes had been established in the new land, there was less reason to keep women always close to home. Their job being done and the danger to them removed, they could be let out to ride around some in the settled countryside, to playact and fantasize the Western myth about real men conquering the wilderness.

Just after 1900, when women first began to appear as contestants in rodeos and as mounted performers in outdoor shows, they rode astride in baggy, fringed, split and sewn-together skirts (later called "divided skirts") and were skilled in all the events related to cowboys' work: bronc riding, roping and tying calves and wild steers. The word "cowgirl" is said to have been applied to them at that time, but the word had been current for at least five years (the Montgomery Ward catalogue of 1895 offers lots of Western-style sidesaddles as "cowgirl" models). A daughter of a Wyoming rancher, Prairie Rose Henderson, at the Frontier Days Celebration in Cheyenne in 1901, was the first woman to enter a rodeo contest, in this case bronc riding; she did so against the protests of the judges, who could, however, find no rules excluding her. Her ride was so magnificent that "cowgirls' bronc riding" was soon included in many rodeos. Another daughter of a rancher, this one in Oklahoma, Lucile Mulhall, early on became "the foremost lady steer roper in the world." Mabel Strickland also roped steers, but since there was no woman's event, she was forced, like Mulhall, to do it for exhibition. Fox Wilson, who began her rodeo career as a bronc rider, liked wrestling steers better because the sport went beyond strength and endurance to strategy in timing moves in relation to different characteristics of individual steers. But since there was no woman's event, she had to bulldog steers as an exhibition.

Most women rodeo athletes during the 1920s and 1930s were obliged to compete in the very demanding and dangerous events of ladies' bronc riding, trick riding, and the cowgirls' relay race. As a result of these limited events, the champions never made as much in prize money as their cowboy counterparts, and consequently there were never more than fifteen or twenty women who competed on a regular basis. To make a living, many women champions had to enter related careers. During her long career, bronc rider Prairie Lilly contracted livestock for Western movies, and Mulhall became a rodeo promoter. And they all made their way against the resistance of men who treated rodeo as a male preserve and who feared that women contestants would mar its macho image. One fan, who interviewed hundreds of rodeo cowboys in writing the best book on the subject, testified that "though never particularly welcome as participants in the work [as rodeo athletes], [women] have carved a niche for themselves by sheer audacity, courage, and *female persistence*" (emphasis added—read, "typical female stubbornness").

Women did win a "niche" in a very male sport—for a time, anyway. "Cowgirls" were granted membership in the Cowboy Turtle Association (later the Professional Rodeo Cowboys' Association—PRCA) in 1938. But the cowboys' organization didn't protect its new women members' interests, for during World War II women's contests in rodeo almost disappeared, except for barrel races (running a horse for time in a cloverleaf pattern around three barrels) performed by pretty young women, not by seasoned professional athletes. After a few years of barrel races as the only women's event in rodeo, women athletes formed their own association (Girls Rodeo Association, after 1981 the Women's Professional Rodeo Association—WPRA) to try to win their way back into the position they enjoyed in the sport before the war. But they have not made it. The dozen or so all-women annual WPRA rodeos featuring seven official events don't offer enough prize money to support and therefore to attract professional athletes. As a consequence, three-quarters of the 2,000 WPRA members, on the most expensive horses in rodeo, run barrels, still the only regular woman's contest at PRCA shows, where a champion in this one very specialized event can win almost $50,000. So, in spite of the proven ability of women rodeo athletes, the cowboys have had their way at last—women are relegated mainly to an acceptably decorous and ladylike event in hundreds of cowboy shows and the few all-around athletes to poorly paid, minority status in a mere dozen all-women shows.[89]

Where did these women skilled in the work of cowboys come from at the beginnings of this great Western sport? Where had they already learned these skills? A recent historian is too ready to dismiss the claim of the Miller 101 Wild West show, with its women riders in the early years of the century, that "cowgirls had always assisted with roundups, trail drives, and other aspects of ranch work."[90] The fact is that working women cowpunchers existed, in spite of the tyranny of patriarchal conventions and strict gender roles, since the beginning of the cattle industry and even before. What obscures the existence of all kinds of working women in the West is that all the laundresses, typesetters, dressmakers, midwives, bullwhackers, cowhands, and the rest are subsumed under the mythical figure of the Pioneer Woman, with a sunbonnet, sturdy long-sleeved dress falling full to the ankles, booted, holding one child by the hand and another on her arm. The myth always obscures variety and class. We should look for women cowpunchers by considering the various relations women would have to the cattle industry. There are the single or widowed women who are independent producers or working entrepreneurs themselves (ranchers, road-ranch keepers, cattle thieves); the wives and daughters of owner-managers of corporate herds on the range or the trail; women nesters or the wives and daughters of nesters; and finally a few single women who worked for wages. The last group we would expect to be small because in the West in general there was a lower percentage of women in the paid work force than in the East—13 percent compared to 17 percent (1890). Of the approximately 70,000 women on the Great Plains in 1870, only about 10,000 worked for wages, excluding the uncounted prostitutes, the second largest group of women workers after domestic servants, which was the largest.[91] In the West, most women did not manage to stay single long and thus did family work; as a result, they were not counted as workers by census takers.

There were "cowwomen," that is, unmarried women and widows who owned and managed their own ranches or cow-hunting businesses. The reason there weren't more women ranch owners is that they had to prove up a land claim by being a widow or deserted wife or a woman head of a family, unless you were rich and could buy the land. Single men over twenty-one living alone could file claims for a quarter section under the Homestead Act, but a single woman could not unless she were a family head. But there were some women owners in the cattle industry. For instance, there is the almost legendary Sally Skull, of whom an old-timer says: "For a few years after the [Civil] war there was a woman in that region [south Texas] by the name of Sally Skull, who was quite a character. She traded horses through our country, and operated alone, with a band of Mexican helpers, from Texas into Mexico, and had a record of being the most fearless woman ever known. Nearly all of the old citizens of that section remember Sally Skull."[92] There is "The Pecos Queen," who figures in a cowboy song by that name and seems to be a real person, since her name, Patty Morehouse, appears in the lyrics:

> She is known by every cowboy on the Pecos River wide,
> They know full well that she can shoot, that she can rope and ride.
> She goes to every round-up, every cow work without fail,
> Looking out for her cattle, branded "walking hog on rail."
>
> She made her start in cattle, yes, made it with her rope;
> Can tie down every maverick before it can strike a lope.
> She can rope and tie and brand it as quick as any man;
> She's voted by all cowboys an A-1 top cow hand.[93]

So women also started a spread with a long rope and a hot iron.

Anne Richey, who grew up as a cowhand, even doing roping and branding, on her father's Wyoming ranch, later operated her own ranch and finally was convicted of cattle rustling, the first woman so convicted in Wyoming.[94] Anne Bassett, raised on a horse ranch in Brown's Hole (Brown's Park), Colorado, as a teenager with some friends collected drifted cattle and later championed the nester ranchers in their struggle against the cattle companies. Some say she was the intended of Matt Rash, the former cowboy from Texas and president of the Brown's Park Cattle Association of nester ranchers, and all agree the friend of Isom Dart, the famed black cowboy turned rancher, both men ultimately murdered by Tom Horn, hired assassin for Wyoming cattlemen.[95] The Denver *Post* in 1911 called her a "fearless horsewoman, she can bust a bronc as neatly as any [male] cowpuncher in the Park."[96] She became known as "Queen Anne" or "Queen of the Rustlers." Someone should write a biography of this woman.

There were women who ran road ranches (which if combining prostitution were brutally called "hog ranches" by cowboys) and who collected cattle and horses on the side, sometimes in lieu of payment from customers. Mollie Schwartz ran such an operation in the Nebraska panhandle. Her road ranch catered at first to freighters, later to cowboys: "She had two daughters, tall, full-eyed girls, with ready laughter and kind hearts. But Nell and Rae didn't restrict themselves to freighters long, particularly not Rae, who was slender-waisted, with narrow hands, who danced well and rode wild horses with considerable assurance and grace in a pair of chaps borrowed from her admirers."[97] Such road ranch–saloon–whorehouses were commonly thought to be centers of rustling activities, and many were run by women who tended their own small herds. Calamity Jane, besides raising cattle, for a brief time ran what she called "a wayside inn."[98]

Another example is Ella Watson in the Sweetwater valley of Wyoming, who began as a whore, then moved in with a road-ranch nester and then became a nester herself on a homesteading claim, employing a cowboy or two to build a herd, acquired mainly, it seems, from mavericks customers would give her by way of barter. In 1889, the largest local rancher lynched her as a cattle thief to get her claim, which intruded on the range he didn't own but considered his own; and papers in Cheyenne sympathetic to cattlemen dubbed her a desperado: "The woman was as desperate as the man [she was lynched with], a daredevil in the saddle, handy with a six-shooter and an adept with the lariat and branding iron . . . a holy terror [who] rode straddle, always had a vicious broncho for a mount and seemed never tired of dashing across the range." Later newspaper stories confused her with a real outlaw and called her "Cattle Kate," a name that has stuck.[99] We note in passing how riding astride, as pointedly specified in this news item, is an instant mark of her being dangerous and criminal. Ella Watson was none of these, just a single-woman homesteading rancher and former prostitute. There exists a fine picture of her, often reprinted— a handsome woman in a corral, sitting astride a big horse, in full skirt, button boots, calico apron, blouse, and bonnet.

The last type of single women who worked cattle *not* as part of families or as wage earners was the mounted women outlaws who, along with bank and train robberies, ran some cattle or horses. Belle Starr does not

seem to have been involved actively in running horses, though she associated with men who did. Besides, she rode sidesaddle, which seems strange for an outlaw. In 1878 a posse shot a nameless Colorado horse thief who turned out to be a woman disguised as a man. Flora Quick (alias Tom King), although she rode sidesaddle was also a practicing horse thief. Cattle Annie and Little Britches as teenagers rode with an outlaw gang stealing cattle and horses in the Indian Territory. Etta Place dressed like a man and rode with Butch Cassidy and Sundance and went with them to Argentine, where, between train robberies, they stole livestock.[100] There seems to be a pattern of cross-dressing among Western women outlaws, which deserves a full study.

Finally there were the wives and daughters of the large ranch owners or the ranch managers—what cowboys called "the boss." They would come out to the wagon and help work the herd to get away from domestic confinement and to escape the solitude and loneliness that most Western ranch women complained of. One such woman describes the condition that would cause women to go out to the wagon: "It was this deadly staying at home month in and month out, keeping a place of refuge for the men when they returned from their farings-forth, that called for the greater courage, I think. Men walked in a perpetual adventure, but women waited."[101]

Sally Redus, a very early ranch wife of a south Texas cattleman who drove many herds to Kansas, as an old woman regretted she hadn't worked with her husband more: "I made one trip with Mr. Redus to Kansas, taking along my baby boy, Robert. I have always regretted that I did not go every year, for *I could have gone if I had known it*" (emphasis added).[102] Evidently she discovered that women could go up the trail with a herd in about 1873, just when her husband's trail-driving days were about over after the Panic ruined him. This is a sad story and reveals the restrictions imposed on women contrary to their nature or desire, but many women

---

ISOM DART, RANCHMAN, BROWN'S HOLE, COLORADO

The antler-handled revolver and the chaps look like studio properties, and wearing the chaps over the coat is clearly only to show off the artillery. But Dart was a genuine cowboy turned ranchman and, some would say, cattle rustler. Born a slave in Arkansas in 1849, he went to Texas as a cowboy and later settled in Colorado where he was a friend and associate of Madison Rash and Ann Bassett, the leaders of the small ranchers' local protective organization. In 1900 he and Rash were murdered by Tom Horn, assassin for the Wyoming Stock Growers Association. (COURTESY OF THE DENVER PUBLIC LIBRARY, WESTERN HISTORY DEPARTMENT.)

ELLA WATSON, RANCHWOMAN, NEAR INDEPENDENCE ROCK,
WYOMING, ABOUT 1888

She died at the end of a rope in 1889, lynched by a neighboring cattleman.
Owen Wister supported the lyncher: "the gentleman . . . seemed a good solid
citizen, and I hope he'll get off." Defended by Wyoming Stock Growers
Association attorneys, he did get off because all witnesses to the lynching had
disappeared. (COURTESY OF THE DENVER PUBLIC LIBRARY, WESTERN HISTORY
DEPARTMENT.)

discovered the possibility of an enlarged life before the opportunity for it was fading. Probably Sally Redus went up the trail to Kansas riding side-saddle, her baby son on her lap, brought along, perhaps, because she was still nursing him. Between nursings the cook could have minded him at the wagon and she could have helped turning strays and runaways from the moving herd or holding the herd or the remuda at night. A Texas frontier woman (she grew up near the Hondo, southwest of San Antonio, in the 1850s) would have had no trouble sleeping on a tarp spread on the prairie grass or crossing swollen rivers on horseback. Even a more pampered daughter of Virginia gentility, when she found herself confined to a cabin in Montana in the eighties, sought out the wagon at a roundup of a herd her husband partly owned and managed. "I rode less than a modern girl would do, sleeping late in my tent instead of getting up at dawn and going on the long morning rides with the men, but when they came back with the cattle I would mount and help hold the herd."[103] But her holding the herd was about the minimum work done by women as cowhands although standard for upper-class Eastern greenhorn women riding sidesaddles.

That there were some women who helped out doing the ordinary work of cowboys is made clear by the old folk song "Utah Carl" about a cowboy who dies saving the life of Lenore, the "boss's daughter," fallen in a stampede:

> We were rounding up one morning and our work was almost done
> When on the right the cattle started in a wild and maddened run.
> The boss's little daughter, who was holding on that side,
> Started to turn the cattle, and 'twas there my pardner died.[104]

Which brings us to women tending cattle on family ranches or on their own small ranches. They would be nesters on homestead claims. These nester ranchers grew fodder for their small herds and sheltered and fed them in the winter long before the corporations had the sense to do so. When a cowboy turned rancher, part of his very American dream of having a little spread of his own was to marry and have a family. He could court a Harvey girl if his ranch was near the Santa Fe line. He could be a "heart-in-hander" and for a fee enter into correspondence with a woman who had paid to have her picture and stats listed in one of the many bride catalogues published by Eastern companies making money on the shortage of women in the West. He could attend country dances and enter the stiff competition for the hand of a daughter of a granger family. Many young women refused to marry cowboys "until they acquired ranches of [their] own,"[105] an additional inducement to homesteading. Indeed, women took advantage of the freedom that their scarcity in the West fostered—as wives they were less inclined to put up with brutal or restricting husbands when there were plenty of other men who promised to treat them better, even if you had to take along the children. Some women had several husbands. Divorce was easy and "application for divorces mostly came from the woman's side."[106]

Taking advantage of the Homestead Law, which allowed single women heads of families to file claims, a woman who knew how to farm and handle cattle could become a nester rancher alone with her family or with a woman companion or with a lover. Nester wives refused to stay in their houses or their kitchen gardens or among their chickens but got on horseback and helped their husbands round up their cattle or drive them to the railhead or hold the string of horses. The daughters, raised to the cattle business and riding astride, could even rope calves and wild steers and so could brand and castrate and cut ears. A cowboy gives an account of two young women cowhands, one of whom he later married. The time is 1893, the place the Strip, Oklahoma Territory: "Mr. Goddard ran 700 head of cattle, and his older girls were real cowgirls. I had grown up near them, and rode with them. Both rode 'clothespin style,' as they called it, and threw a rope as well as most cowboys. When the roundup was far from their range, we boys brought their cattle home with the throwback, but if the range work was close at hand, say within fifteen miles of their own ranch, May and Belle would work with the regular roundup, gather their cattle, and cut out their own stock."[107] A widow woman in Montana had to do all the work on her ranch alone with her young daughter Patty because her son was away as a wage-earning cowboy: "most of the man's work was done by Patty, who rode and roped, fixed fences and pitched hay."[108]

Finally, there were doubtless some women cowhands who hired out for wages and keep to small family ranchers successful enough to afford the low wages of a cowhand or two. A poor nester's daughter could hire out for seasonal work to a more prosperous neighbor. Or one of the legion of Western women vagrants who had the skills could punch cows as casual work for a family rancher until moving on. In the course of her varied career, Calamity Jane probably did some cowpunching for wages.

We should expect our national hero to embody what most people valued during his formation. When our hero emerged fully formed in the mid-1890s, he embodied the heroic virtues we thought best possessed by white men. Owen Wister at the time presented the cowboy as "the American

CALAMITY JANE

A commercial picture produced for tourists by the Locke and Peterson Studio, 1876. (COURTESY OF THE ADAMS MEMORIAL MUSEUM, DEADWOOD, SOUTH DAKOTA.)

variety of the Saxon" . . . unified by the "bottom bond of race," "the direct lineal offspring" of knights in the tournament at Camelot, very few "Poles or Huns or Russian Jews" among them, but containing the "fine essence of the Anglo-Saxon . . . through the centuries conqueror, invader, navigator, buccaneer, explorer, colonist, tiger shooter."[109] The blatant racism and swaggering masculinity of Wister's belief in the manifest destiny of Anglo-Saxon men shocks us today but it represented majority sentiment at the time. We expect a racist, patriarchal society to produce an Anglo, male hero. But we should be aware that this popular cowboy hero, although he embodied our values, obscures the real American cowboy.

Cowboys as Entertainers and Athletes

Conversation overheard at a branding table in Texas, mid-1970s:

1ST COWBOY: Every cowboy wants his own cattle.

2ND COWBOY: Every cowboy wants his own land, too. You think they'd learn, since I never seen but one or two who did get it.

3RD COWBOY: It sure is true that there's more cowboys than rich people.[1]

"He had once been a cowboy, but the West was passing and the cattle men were coming into the towns and cities. He was now a mechanic in the copper works of Clifton" (Arizona). The time was about 1912. The ex-cowboy soon afterward went to Mexico "to help in the revolution." Five years before, he was one of twenty other ex-cowboys who worked for the narrator's father in one of the company towns owned by the Rockefeller family in the southeast Colorado coal mine region doing contracted hauling and excavating work with teams of horses and wagons. "They were men who as a rule carried all their worldly possessions with them: a gun or two, a fine belt, a pair of marvelous spurs and boots, perhaps an unusual hat band, a Mexican quirt and gloves. They nearly always owned a horse, a saddle that was far from ordinary, and sometimes a bit and bridle to match. . . . They came from the cattle ranches beyond the Divide. They were silent picturesque men, much mixed with clay. Courageous, kindly, trusting—and foul-mouthed." When the miners fought against strikebreakers in these company towns, her father's crew of ex-cowboy teamsters and earth movers "did not care much one way or the other, because they were not married and did not have a brood of children depending upon them. . . . During strikes, their sympathies seemed whole-heartedly with the miners, but as ex-cowboys they were individualists and did not understand the struggle." In good weather after supper they gathered outside the kitchen door, talking and singing.

> One of the men would sing a song and the others would follow: songs of the West that are long since dead; songs with dozens of verses, all sung in the same tune, low and melancholy, unrolling stories of adventure, of the joys and sorrows of cattle men, of dying cowboys, of disaster, range songs and songs of love.
>
> Sometimes one of the men would take out a "French harp" and begin to play. Another would get up and dance. Once it was a man, young and slender. . . . His blue shirt was open at the throat. He bent over and danced, swaying his body and arms; he stood in one spot on the hard earth and danced until the heels of his boots sounded like pistol shots on the hard, packed earth. He stood tall and straight, his hands on his hips, his face turned upwards to the moon, and the moonlight ran in little shining rivulets up and down the legs of his black boots.
>
> At last the music ceased. There was silence, broken only by the wind rustling gently through the tree tops. The dancer wiped his forehead with a big red handkerchief. He drew his belt in another notch. Big Buck, his boots in the moonlight, his head lost in the shadow of the house, began to tell of another dancer he had seen down in the Texas Panhandle . . . or was it on the Rio Grande? He used to dance around the range fires . . . , "that must 'a' been fifteen years ago . . . no, well-nigh twenty, come to think of it. . . ."[2]

A sad picture this—ex-cowboys turned teamsters and pick-and-shovel men still preserving the culture and pride of craft and life-style of a bygone time with which they nostalgically identify. In the three decades after the cattle boom ended and the change began toward tightly managed, specialized, fenced ranches and feeding pens, cowboys were seeking work.

Homesteading cowboys failed in ranching and returned to earning wages. Cowboys quit working for cattle companies when their work became routine, less diversified, less skilled, and their leisure was restricted by degrading and puritanical company rules.

In an astonishingly short time, cowboys foresaw the end of their craft and way of life and began reminiscing about the old days. Only a dozen years into the cowboy era "Texas Jack," or John Omohundro, wrote an article on "The Cow-Boy" in a national magazine in which he presented him as a dying breed because railroads were taking the place of long cattle drives and because old-time ranch life was being "encroached upon by the modern improvements that will in course of time wipe out the necessity of [the cowboy's] life."[3] When a few years later, in the mid-eighties, cowpunchers felt the effects of corporate management in the Texas Panhandle, they looked back with nostalgia to a period only a single decade removed:

> Having spent several years as a cowboy upon ranches in Western Texas, between the Brazos and Colorado . . . I have thought a brief letter detailing old-time experience in running cattle and the way of the camp and range might prove of interest to your readers and preserve from oblivion the manners and customs of ranchmen and ranch life. . . . No wire fence enclosures then marked out the boundary line of any range. Possession of the range, its grass and water was held simply by occupancy. . . . Here, under employ, were some thirty cowboys as hardy and devil-may-care a set as ever roped a beef, branded a calf or mavericked a yearling. Good ponies, black coffee, light work, and abundance of fun rendered camp life agreeable to most of the hands. Six shooters and Winchester rifles were worn by all, and seldom used except in killing buffalo, deer or turkey, or in an occasional personal difficulty brought about by some incoming outfit locating upon range already claimed. Then there was no market for cattle except by a long drive. Stock could be bought at from $5 to $7. . . . there was no such thing then as either close herding or line-riding. Hands were so numerous that duties were not confining, and more of them could be found at the frontier towns or groceries "bucking at monte," throwing chuck-a-luck, or playing billiards, than about camp. Rounding up and cutting out time, in the spring and fall, were the only times of real hard work in the year. An occasional breeze would stir up the blood of the boys, when a gang of rustlers, Indians or Mexicans made a raid

after ponies or cattle, and a pursuing party took the trail to corral them.[4]

This cowboy's nostalgic picture of old-time Texas range work shows by implication the changes that corporate ownership had introduced: a work speedup resulting from fewer cowboys employed to do the same amount of work; because cattle prices were up, cowboys had to tend cattle more carefully; there were no diversions from working cattle, like pursuing thieves or hunting; with harder work there was less leisure, fewer amusements, and less time in town; cowboys had been disarmed, and their work was more closely supervised. These were some of the changes that encouraged cowboys to begin herds of their own and then to quit wage work and become homesteading ranchers. What became of cowboys and ex-cowboys and their work when the industry underwent its big change to Western financing and new procedures, beginning in the mid-1880s?

Ex-cowboys hung on to their claims as they hung on to the forlorn hope of quitting wage work and running their own herds. Theirs was the later individualist version of the older, deeply ingrained American vision of a nation of independent producers, a dream made dearer as the proceeding industrial revolution eroded its likelihood. During the industrializing period the National Labor Union and the Knights of Labor based their opposition to the privileges of the rich and their companies, to gross material inequality, and to the growing degradation and alienation of work on this ideal of independent producers of equal means receiving equal rewards. Probably such a society has never existed, but there were regional approximations of it, and the popular mind identified it, and still does, with colonial and early federal society before the industrial revolution (beginning about 1840), the ideal of Jeffersonian and Jacksonian agrarian democracy. And the longing became stronger as people increasingly felt the injuries of industrial capitalism to their dignity and spirit and bodies. As more and more people left their farms and family industries and businesses to become wage earners, as work became less skilled, more repetitive and controlled and mechanical, as workers received small return in value from the wealth they produced, and as relations between individuals became less personal, the people longed for what they considered they had lost—the old democratic, community society. They refused to believe that their present situation as wage slaves was permanent and clung to the illusion that they could either return to the dwindling class of independent producers on their own or that their worker or farmer organizations could collectively reform society to recreate the partly mythical old relations, a whole society of equal independent worker-producers. Abraham Lincoln expressed the *individual* solution:

> There is not, of necessity, any such thing as the free hired laborer being fixed to that condition for life. Many independent men everywhere in these States, a few years back in their lives, were hired laborers. The prudent, penniless beginner in the world, labors for wages awhile, saves a surplus with which to buy tools or land for himself; then labors on his own account another while, and at length hires another new beginner to help him. This is the just, and generous, and prosperous system, which opens the way to all—gives hope to all, and consequent energy, and progress, and improvement of condition to all.[5]

On the other hand, the Knights and the reform union movement and Populism later expressed the *collective* solution. According to Uriah Stephens, founder of the Knights, this solution "lay in the abolition of the pernicious wage system and the introduction of a 'Cooperative Commonwealth' " of small producers.[6]

These solutions have not proved possible. Very few people still hope for a reformed society patterned on a vision of preindustrial America. And the individual solution, idealized by Lincoln, becomes increasingly difficult: the proportion of independent producers steadily decreases, and that of wage earners grows. But since these forces were not as apparent then to cowboy homesteaders as they are to us now, we can understand how they clung to their old dream of having a little spread of their own. What were the historical forces in the cattle industry and elsewhere that finally destroyed the dream?

We tend to interpret history to fulfill our wishes. We want to believe that our system works and that personal freedom, independence, and opportunity prevail. So we think that family ranchers took over the cattle industry after the Eastern and foreign corporations failed. Popular Westerns by presenting a preindustrial world of independent producers reinforces this view of the history of the cattle industry. Barbed wire, we believe, doomed the open range that cattle barons depended on. Then two years of drought followed by the blizzards of 1887 forced the barons to turn over the cattle industry to the better management of family ranchers. Nothing could be further from the truth. The industry just changed methods and capitalist hands. The holdings of the cattle corporations were liquidated because profits couldn't be made for Eastern and foreign investors by Western ranch managers of untended and unfed cattle on overstocked open ranges. Many of the old Eastern and Scottish corporations survived for decades by managing their operations differently. The smaller but still large cattle companies, which slowly took over the Plains, many managed by individual owners, borrowed capital from Western banks, owned their own land and leased more public land seasonally, fenced and cross-fenced their ranges into pastures, grew forage by seeding native grasslands and cultivating hay, bought concentrates and supplements for seasonal feeding, developed stock that would provide more meat, and used labor-saving equipment like pickup and horse-trailer trucks, squeeze chutes, calf cradles, propane branding fires, and electrical prods. Most importantly, the industry specialized operations among different types of ranches: breeding, pas- turing calves, pasturing yearlings, grain-feeding late yearlings in pens.

A later development offered incentive plans whereby the ranch manager paid all costs except for new stock and received commissions based on annual weight gain of cattle. A very common system of separation of ownership emerged wherein a land trust owns or leases ranges and receives from another company that owns the cattle an annual rate per head for grazing. The ranch hand that does all the work doesn't, of course, own the ranch or the herd, and only rarely today are both the herd and the land owned by the same company. Old-fashioned cow-calf ranching soon became a nostalgic life-style and a show purchased by the very rich for conspicuous display, usually as a pretense to old wealth. It's a simple matter of economics: the same thirty acres of Texas Panhandle grass required for a cow and her calf for a year can support three yearlings fattening for the feed lot. The cow costs money; the yearlings turn a profit. The amount of acreage varies with the aridity of the range, but the economic logic remains the same—to accumulate capital the modern cowman must ranch in the modern specialized and scientific way, and that takes a very great deal of money. A *small* profit-producing ranch in the Texas Panhandle today requires a million-dollar capital investment.[7] A recent example in the South- west: 11,640 acres; 225 head of cattle; $187,000 capital investment; gross income $16,264; after paying only 4.1 percent on investment, an annual loss of $1,537.[8]

As this new range cattle industry grew, there was less and less room for the ex-cowboy homesteading rancher on his 160-acre claim or in Texas on his small leased range. The end of the open range put the small ranchers out of business—not, as is commonly thought, the big ones. There was no way that a quarter section, no matter how seeded and cultivated, could feed enough cattle, no matter how skilfully tended, to keep a rancher out of the hands of a bank. Very few ex-cowboys owned more land than that. And now his range was restricted to what he owned and fenced. And mavericks were harder to come by now behind fences. Since government grazing lands became increasingly scarce and distant, only the big outfits had the means to lease them and move their large herds to them. There was no way for the small homesteading ranchers to increase their land to profitable size for cattle raising. They had no money to buy it outright. The Desert Land Act of 1877 offered a full section for $800 ($1.25 an acre), but even that price put public land beyond the reach of family ranchers, as is proved by the fact that 95 percent of the titles to land under that act "were acquired fraudulently by or for corporations."[9] Family ranchers couldn't legally take up another quarter section under the old Homestead Act, even if there were still some unclaimed near their ranches; the thousands of fraudulent entrants under that act were almost all expensively bribed individuals or employees acting as dummies for land, timber, and mining companies. In general, the government gave or sold the public domain to speculators and companies, not to grangers and nesters: of the more than 200 million acres given by 1923 to so-called settlers, a large portion went to dummy agents of speculators, and several times as many million acres of public domain went to non-settlers, that is, rich corporations and individuals with the means in Washington to steal and bribe and chisel their ways to even greater fortunes.[10] But the nester had no way to get in on such land grabs. If the ex-cowboy rancher mortgaged his quarter-section ranch to buy more land and cattle, the loan was seldom enough to turn a profit, and sooner or later he had to sell his ranch; or let the bank take it; or turn farmer, if he could find a profitable cash crop; or farm his claim for necessities and cowboy for cash seasonally, if there were neighboring ranches hiring occasional help; or turn dude rancher, if he could bring himself to please rich folks.

There was no way for the ex-cowboy producer to cowboy for himself after the ranges closed and the new Western-financed, specialized industry developed. The cowboy's old dream of having a little spread of his own seemed attainable for a few years; but with dwindling public land for pasturing and fewer motherless calves for branding in a new kind of industry that increasingly excluded all but the rich, the old cowboys had to give up the probability of achieving the dream, even though the dream itself sadly and perversely lingered on. Recently at a branding cradle in the Texas Panhandle an old cowboy said, "Every cowboy wants his own cattle." A fifty-year-old cowboy working with him replied: "Every cowboy wants his own land, too. You think they'd learn, since I never seen but one or two who did get it." And another cowboy agreed: "It sure is true that there's more cowboys than rich people."[11]

While struggling against the economic current to stay in ranching, or

COMMERCIAL PHOTOGRAPH BY C. D. KIRKLAND, CHEYENNE, ABOUT 1885

(COURTESY OF THE DENVER PUBLIC LIBRARY, WESTERN HISTORY DEPARTMENT.)

WOOD ENGRAVING FROM KIRKLAND'S PHOTOGRAPH FOR A BOOK, 1887

From William Makepeace Thayer, Marvels of the New West *(Norwich, Connecticut, 1887). Evidently the author brought home some postcards, but he didn't credit the sources. The fidelity to the original is remarkable. This is an example of how images were quickly made for mass audiences before electronic reproduction.* (COURTESY OF THE DENVER PUBLIC LIBRARY, WESTERN HISTORY DEPARTMENT.)

when seeking a job when they returned to dependency on their wage labor, cowboys had a source of income that others didn't: they could sell their labor to promoters who were marketing their image and myth, and a few could market this image directly for themselves. The popular attractiveness of the cowboy as a type created an early market for accounts and displays of his life and work. This market grew from an immense public curiosity about the West and the frontier: buffalo hunters, Indian fighters and cavalry scouts, gold miners, dance-hall ladies, bartenders, outlaws—and cowboys. Mark Twain, always a keen judge of what would sell, published his first book, *Roughing It*, to profit from this market. Siringo early recognized the value of his experiences and sold them in a series of books. Nate Love, the famous black cowboy, sold his experiences in a paperback hawked by "news butchers" in railroad coaches. Promoters of popular culture and of the growing mass media profited from the interest in cowboys by marketing illustrated articles and stories about cowboys in magazines and newspapers, traveling stage plays about them, exhibitions of cowboys in colorful costumes in itinerant dime museums (arcade or midway shows), stories about them in dime novels, photographs of them on postcards, tourist mementos, graphoscope and stereoscope cards, public contests involving their skills in riding and roping, pageants and exhibitions in Wild West shows, experiences of their lives offered to tourist guests on ranches, performances in vaudeville, and then documentaries and dramas of their lives on the stage and in very early motion pictures.

Cowboys became a hot property, and there was money to be made in their sale and some jobs to be had by workers turned athletes and performers. William Cody turned from army scouting to Buffalo Bill in a traveling stage drama when Ned Buntline told him there was money in it. The small stage troupe in Buntline's play about Indian fighting, *Scouts of the Prairie*, toured in the winter of 1872–73 from Chicago to New York City. It had another army scout, "Texas Jack" (Jack Omohundro), who had briefly been a cowboy and who put on a demonstration of his roping skills, the performance called in the synopsis "Texas Jack and his Lasso."[12] As early as this, Eastern audiences were fascinated with roping and connected it with cowboys—and cowboys with Texas. Perhaps this was the first fancy roping performance onstage, the first stage representation of cowboy skill, a decade before Buffalo Bill made such exhibitions standard in his big Wild West show (and a quarter century before the Oklahoma cowboy Will Rogers became famous with his roping stunts on the vaudeville stage). The point is that from the early years of the cowboy era, cowboys were leaving the range to appear onstage and in tent arenas and in county and town contests and exhibitions to make money for promoters selling the very lucrative cowboy myth.

A few cowboy homesteaders became dude ranchers. Dude ranching is the second stage of the live-in part of the Western tourist industry, that is, the selling of the actual residential Western experience beyond just getting there and observing it through the window of a moving vehicle—a railroad or a horse-drawn coach, which was the earliest form of Western touring. The first resident tourism was the guided hunting trip, which cowboys, using their tracking and outdoor survival skills, organized for Eastern dudes to augment their own income when they were seasonally unemployed or as a full-time job when the liquidating corporations laid them off. Taking dudes out from a hunting camp playing big game hunter of grizzlies, wolves, and bighorns is not all that different from helping dudes on a ranch play cowboy. In the fall of 1887, the "father of dude ranching" in Montana, Dick Randall, with some other unemployed cowboy partners found work by organizing and guiding hunting parties. They continued for fifteen years and established the OTO Ranch near Gardiner to use as a headquarters. "Here his hunters stayed for a few days or weeks in preparation for their trips; they recommended the OTO to friends who wanted a place to visit, and soon Dick Randall had many non-hunting guests, also. He had become a dude wrangler."[13] The Western wilderness outfitter of river runs and pony treks is the modern version of these early cowboy hunter wranglers.

With the decline of free grazing lands, which increasingly eliminated homestead ranching, some family ranchers stayed in business by accepting paying guests, particularly after the Panic of 1893, and some few survived for decades as primarily dude ranches. Dude ranches flourished on tourist routes. The presence of rich hunters in Jackson Hole, Wyoming, led to early dude lodges there, and the first ranch totally dependent on tourists was Holm Lodge near Cody, Wyoming, which catered to wealthy dudes on their way to Yellowstone, the first national park (1872). National parks, by stimulating tourism, opened up possibilities of dude ranching for struggling ranchers and cowboys to preserve their way of life for a time. But rich Eastern dudes generally visited the mountain scenes and lived on ranches before the parks were created: for instance, they came to stay in ranches in the Continental Divide area northwest of Denver before it became Rocky Mountain National Park in 1915. Tourism, and consequently dude ranches, opened up later in the Southwest because it took the rich some time to discover the pleasures of deserts and canyons for winter play and relaxation. Dude ranching didn't get to west Texas until the 1920s, when ranchers there belatedly discovered that "you can run more dudes to the acre than you can cattle."

Dude ranches arose in other ways to provide for the care and amusement of the wealthy. There were ranches that took care of the pampered sons, and later daughters, of the rich on pack trips. When parents arrived to collect their offspring at the end of a summer of dude camping, they needed accommodations. Such is the origin of CM Dude Ranch, which grew from a summer "packing" operation for youths in Wyoming. Before summer dude camps for the young, a ranch could supplement its income by entertaining the scions of wealthy Eastern and European families who because of indolence or stupidity or drunkenness had become embarrassments and were sent out West for extended periods to play cowboy; "remittance men" they were commonly called because of their regular remittance checks from home. Sanders 91 Ranch, west of Laramie, was set up in the mid-eighties to accommodate wealthy young Englishmen, called "learners," who for $500 a year spent time with cowboys to learn riding, roping, and branding.

Most cowboys during the height of the open plains cattle industry were required occasionally to wrangle dudes, because they would have to entertain and care for visitors to corporation ranches—the owners, their friends and families, and likely investors. Cowboy ranch hands would have to take them riding, entertain them around the corral and chuck wagon, guide them on hunting trips, and show off work skills for them in staged rodeos. These visits became so frequent and expensive to the several Dakota Territory ranches of one Pennsylvania cattle corporation that they asked guests to share expenses beginning in 1882 at Custer Trail Ranch, near Medora. Because they were the first to charge guests, the managers are generally called the "founders of the dude ranch industry." But there were doubtless paying guests at ranches before this, particularly at road ranches. Most dude ranches didn't have this kind of corporate beginning but were the result of small ranchers and hunters trying to preserve a way of life by being picturesque for the idle rich.

Not only did ex-cowboy nesters take in guests to keep the banks from foreclosing but some of those increasing numbers who lost their ranches and their work on corporate ranches took jobs as dude wranglers. Some exchanged work on modern ranches—fixing fences, driving tractors, irrigating, spraying insecticides, or work in feed lots—to return to the old-style cowboy in wing chaps, spurs with four-prong rowels and tooled straps, and a throwing rope tied to his saddle, a style among working cowboys that became more and more restricted to Hollywood riders, rodeo athletes, and dude wranglers. If the cowboy was good-looking and could sing to his own guitar, he could get a job on a dude ranch more readily. But most working cowboys would take such jobs only from dire economic necessity, because the full-time job of caring and performing for rich dudes is subservient and degrading, particularly for real cowboys with their independent heritage. Dude ranching reached its peak in the 1920s and 1930s and has since declined—sharply in the last two decades. The rich still play on dude ranches, but they find their Western recreation more often now in less strenuous ways that take advantage of such modern improvements as houseboats and recreational vehicles.

Some cowboys got work in rodeos and in the "Cowboy Fun" part of Wild West, both of which came from the same source. Rodeo is the only major sport in America that grew from the games workers devised during leisure time for their own amusement to show off individual and group work skills. These games are as old as the cattle business. Our system encouraged the marketing of this spontaneous activity from the beginning, even before cowboys developed a popular image. Whenever cowboys found themselves together with some time on their hands, they would bet among themselves on bronc riding, roping, and mainly horse racing. These contests occurred especially when several outfits would find themselves together, with favorite horses and riders whose competition stimulated group spirit and pride. Leisure must be filled up, and cowboys' work, like that of loggers, firefighters, and surf lifesaving crews, involves skills that can be used for spectacle and contest. An old cowboy remembers a time on the trail in the early eighties when, tending stampeding cattle, he couldn't pull off his boots for three days and nights: "We would lay over some place and rest for a few days. We had lots of fun trying to prove who was the best rider."[14] Outfits waiting for a big roundup to begin, trail outfits resting after a week of emergency round-the-clock hard riding, especially when two or three outfits met and had free time together—these occasions spontaneously produced contests and games, going beyond work skills to wrestling matches and footraces.

As soon as these spontaneous games arose, first the cowboys themselves but very soon businessmen and speculators began to create occasions for turning a profit by selling the beauty and excitement of cowboys' work. The earliest record of these cowboy tournaments and exhibitions predates the cowboy era by almost twenty years—a June 1847 branding of calves in Santa Fe: "This round-up is a great time for the cowhands. . . . They contest with each other for the best roping and throwing, and there are horse races and whiskey and wines."[15] These cowboy tournaments spread with the workers of the industry all over the Plains, where they became the main attraction of county and state agricultural fairs and of Fourth of July celebrations. There were local specialties like steer roping contests in Texas and even traveling groups of cowboy performers, the earliest re-

AN EARLY RODEO, 1888

Wood engraving in Frank Leslie's Illustrated Newspaper, *May 5, 1888, "from a photo by C. D. Kirkland, Cheyenne."* (COURTESY OF THE DENVER PUBLIC LIBRARY, WESTERN HISTORY DEPARTMENT.)

corded out of Austin in 1883.[16] Another form of the cowboy tournament troupe went on the road the same year as the Cowboy Fun part of Buffalo Bill's Wild West, the first of its kind—a traveling outdoor show. Wild West sometimes combined with circuses and rodeos, and for sixty years or so flourished with more than a hundred different companies.[17] The first regular annual rodeo was in Prescott, Arizona, in 1888, and what is called the first "commercial rodeo," probably because it charged admission, in Lander, Wyoming, in 1893, and then the giant regular annual roundups, stampedes, frontier days in Cheyenne (1897), Pendleton (1910), and Calgary (1919). (The name "rodeo" only came into common usage after World War I.)

Rodeo became a major professional sport after World War II: million-dollar gates, media contracts, and hundred-thousand-dollar annual prize money for champions. Rodeo also includes the hundreds of small events for local talents ("pun'kin rollers") not on the big-time circuit. All of these cowboy shows leading up to and including modern rodeo were designed to make money for the organizers and owners, even before admission fees to closed arenas were charged. Stock contractors, concessionaires, local merchants—everybody makes money except most of the cowboys, who,

SADDLEBRONC RIDING, 1922

On the back of this photograph in pencil: "Yak riding the horse Cork Screw at Montevista, Colorado, 1922." Yakima Canutt was by the mid-1920s a regular minor actor in Westerns and became the most famous Hollywood Western stuntman and second unit director.

JOSEPH McCOY'S PUBLICITY STUNT, 1868

Wood engraving in McCoy's Historical Sketches of the Cattle Trade *(1874). Six cowboys were employed to rope the buffalo bulls, only about two of which arrived alive in Chicago, where, after being viewed by cattle buyers, they were stuffed for a museum.* (COURTESY OF THE HOUGHTON LIBRARY, HARVARD UNIVERSITY.)

risking and often losing life and limb, put on the show and, unlike any other professional sport, pay out of their own pockets the prize money they contend for. In 1905, to protect contestants' interests, the Industrial Workers of the World formed the Bronco Busters and Range Riders' Union in Denver, but the organization was premature.[18] In 1936 rodeo cowboys succeeded in forming a labor union (Cowboy Turtle Association—after 1945, Professional Rodeo Cowboys' Association) to protect themselves against the U.S. and Canadian owners, who had formed their own organization seven years before (Rodeo Association of America); there were strikes and threats of strikes (Tucson and Prescott in 1937) and within ten years 1,400 rodeo cowboys and cowgirls had joined the PRCA and now have some protection against the corrupt or incompetent judges, timers, and flagmen indifferently allowed by the owners.[19] These athletes thus continue the long tradition of cowboy resistance to owners and bosses.

Businessmen within the industry used cowboys performing on horseback in ways even more directly related to money-making than rodeos and Wild West. They used cowboy shows in public relations, promotion, and advertising. Most obviously, a ranch manager would require his cowboys to put on a show for the entertainment of visiting stockholders, their guests, and investors brought in on promotional excursions. In order to attract buyers to his stockyards in Abilene, the promotional genius Joseph McCoy in 1868 hired four Texas cowboys and two California vaqueros to rope wild buffalo bulls and transport them to Chicago in boxcars, on the sides of which hung giant canvas advertisements "in flaming colors" of McCoy's semimonthly sales of stock and grown cattle; on the way to Chicago by way of St. Louis, the ads and animals, in McCoy's words, "elicited a great deal of attention and newspaper comment."[20] Once in Chicago, the cowboys put on a show at the "Fair Ground," described by one of them later as "rop[ing] them again to show the people how it was done"; after the show, Illinois buyers took a special railroad excursion to the Abilene market.[21] The San Antonio livestock commission magnate George W. Saunders, while building his fortune, hired cowboys to take three hundred Mexican mares to sell in Kansas, Missouri, and Illinois. Typically, in Hannibal, Missouri, he advertised: "Wild Texas Ponies for Sale at William L. Fry's Stable, with an Exhibition of Roping and Riding Wild Horses." At the appointed time and place, Saunders mounted a dry-goods crate and announced that the roping and riding exhibition was scheduled last; in the meantime, as he sold each horse, "two of [his] expert cowboys would lasso it and hold it by the jaws and ears until a hackamore was securely placed on its head" in order to deliver it to the buyer. When the buying slackened, his best cowboy roped "an outlaw horse, saddled him Wild

West fashion," and rode him, "to the great delight and enthusiasm of the crowd."[22] This show to sell Texas ponies occurred during the same spring that the first Wild West took to the road. Thus did cattlemen use cowboys not only to handle cattle and horses but to sell them.

Most important of all, for them and for us, cowboys went to Hollywood, the dream capital of the world. There they helped create the Western, and America's most important national hero, the cowboy.

During the second decade of this century, cowboys went to Hollywood to make Western movies and indeed any kind of movie requiring riders, like medieval knights, Arabs, Cossacks, cavalry soldiers, American Indians. Commonly the work was seasonal—rodeos and Wild West in the spring, ranch work in fall roundups, and movies in the winter months. Tom Mix, Art Acord, Buck Jones, and Hoot Gibson began this way. In fact, Wild West entered the movie industry by training Western actors like Neal Hart; the 101 Ranch in Oklahoma was the location of early movies, and its Wild West wintered near Hollywood and merged with the early production company Bison Life. The migration of cowboys to Hollywood reached major proportions in the twenties because they were out of work and, besides, the fairly standard seven-fifty a day for an extra rider was better than forty dollars a month for up to eighteen hours a day on the range. At the peak of popularity of Western movies in the mid-1920s, there were perhaps five hundred new cowboys a year coming to Hollywood.[23]

There were so many cowboys from the beginning that production companies paid them miserably, submitted them to humiliating and uncertain hiring practices, provided no hospital or unemployment compensation for the many injuries they suffered from their requisite falls and stunt riding, and during the Depression worked them harder than even range cowboys were used to.

Cowboy extras hired on for casual day work with Bronco Billy Anderson in Niles Canyon after 1910 for two dollars a day plus food, reported the daughter of one of them,[24] but according to another source the pay was by stunt, one dollar for a saddle fall and two dollars each for bulldogging another rider (a double saddle fall).[25] Who knows what the bulldogged rider got? There soon developed additional bonuses or "adjustment checks," never standardized and always as small as the supply of unemployed riders allowed, for horse falls (where the rider trips his running horse and goes down with it), "pony express" getaways (mounting a running horse), and jumping a horse over a cliff into a river or lake (often with the aid of a greased tilt chute). By 1920 some companies were paying seven-fifty a day for casual work, but at the bunkhouse on Universal City ranch in San Fernando Valley, the most prolific producer of Westerns, live-in cowboy

HOLLYWOOD COWBOYS PLAY MUMBLE-THE-PEG, EARLY 1920s

Cowboys brought to Hollywood their evening chuckwagon amusements, like poker, fuzzy-guzzy, chuck-a-luck, mumble-the-peg. In this production still, a group of movie riders play while William S. Hart (standing, second from left) and a group of other riders, production people, and visitors look on. The picture proves that early Hollywood cowboys had been real range workers. Hart studied and respected cowboys, and they loved him in return.

extras received thirty dollars a month plus room and board, plus small bonuses for dangerous stunts.[26] In the early 1930s extra riders received three-twenty to five dollars a day with a boxed lunch thrown in, and between two-fifty and five dollars extra for a saddle fall, depending on how many unemployed riders needed work.[27] By the end of the Depression, salaries were up to the seven-fifty level of two decades earlier. The competition offered by the independent studios of Poverty Row, like Mascot and Monogram, always kept wages and bonuses down and irregular by offering jobs at starvation wages to needy cowboys, some with families.

During the Depression the independents tried to keep production costs down by setting up crowded and tumultuous scenes to produce accidental falls for which no bonuses were paid; and even Paramount's Cecil B. De

Mille had a reputation among cowboys for doing this in his medieval and biblical epics: "letting nature take its course in a badly planned melee was a cheap way for a director to pick up some really exciting spills on camera, without having to put out adjustment checks to get them." In 1935 De Mille forced forty mounted cowboys dressed as crusaders to cross a narrow drawbridge four abreast. A delegation of them had earlier warned him that the plan was impossible, but he persisted, and four cowboys and their horses fell thirty feet into a dry moat. The crippled horses were shot. The four cowboys were hospitalized, and De Mille refused to issue any adjustment checks for them for stunt falls, claiming that they had fallen through their own incompetent horsemanship. The unpaid falls appeared in the finished movie. The studios even rejected a plan to let a committee of experienced cowboys regularly inspect the rental horses and equipment at the stock barns, like Fat Jones's near Griffith Park. And bad equipment and horses continued to cause injuries to cowboy extras. Only later, under California workmen's compensation, were studios required to make small settlements for injuries. Even with good equipment cowboy extras were injured, especially before the Running-W trip wires (activated by the rider himself) were banned in the late 1930s (they returned in the 1970s and are still very much with us). In 1935, six hundred cowboys rode as cavalry into enemy fire during the filming of *The Charge of the Light Brigade*. About 125 horses and riders fell by Running-Ws, and dozens of riders took saddle falls to simulate being shot from their horses. In a single day's shooting, twenty-five horses were destroyed and nearly a dozen cowboys were hospitalized. Only the Humane Society observers made a fuss.[28]

Before Central Casting, cowboys coming to Hollywood would just hang around the studios, sometimes no more than rented barns in the early days, waiting for work, or at certain street corners near saloons or drugstores, "the Waterhole" or "Gower Gulch," where assistant directors would round them up as casual labor to take to movie sets or ranches. The growing industry came to depend on a big pool of expert horsemen who were chronically unemployed and "willing to gamble their lives, on a day-to-day basis, for whatever the studio heads decided they could afford to pay." Universal made a "large pen, fenced in wire," outside their gates in which riders could wait to be called. The cowboys called it a "hiring tank."[29] When Universal needed more riders than were in the "tank," they ran a white flag up their studio flagpole.[30] Later, cowboy extras had to "call their names over Central Casting's board before it closed," and wait by a phone, often the pay phone in the Columbia Drugstore at "Gower Gulch," for a summons. An improvement over hiring tanks, perhaps, but also a handy and comprehensive means of blacklisting troublemaking

"INDIANS" EXECUTING RUNNING-Ws

All three riders seem to be going down with their horses. The one in front may be Yakima Canutt. If this is a publicity still for Stagecoach *(1939), the image did not appear in the final cut of the famous running battle on the dry lake.*

cowboys. Also under this system cowboys seldom worked the next day after the end of a job, because by the time they exchanged their vouchers for wages at the cashier's window near the studio gate, the Central Casting board was closed. If time was short, the weary cowboy not called back for tomorrow would enter another race, after eight hours or more of hard riding, but this one on foot: for the nearest pay telephone outside the studio gate to get his name flashed on the board before it closed down. Considering that starting time was five in the morning at the studio gate (no streetcars running at that hour, so the cowboy pays for his own taxi), there was little likelihood of a call that night.

The movie industry did not treat cowboys well, except for a few stars, and cowboy extras knew it and were bitter; but most lingered on because they had bought the dream they were portraying. The daughter of one old stove-up cowboy who, as a horse trainer and wrangler, stuntman, extra rider, and occasionally a minor actor, went from the beginnings in Niles

Canyon to a "last stand at Disneyland" as a stagecoach driver, wrote in her account of his life:

> The Scythians, the Cossacks and the Sioux have been lauded as the most supremely expert horsemen in history, but perhaps that is only because the Hollywood cowboys have lacked a chronicler. They spent their working days riding stirrup to stirrup, or throwing leather at salty teams of two, four and six up; driving army ambulances, buckboards, Roman chariots, stagecoaches, tallyhos, caissons and Conestogas through flood, flames and over cliffs; jumping, falling, swimming, knifing, brawling, killing and being killed a dozen times a day; riding horses as no men have ever ridden them before or since. Proud, fearless, death-defying men, they went on, year in and year out, cheerfully taking falls and breaking bones, all for the princely sum of from three dollars to seven-fifty a day with a sand-dry lunch thrown in.

The author concludes her tribute to her father, who in his middle sixties was still riding as an extra in Westerns, always postponing for one last "big location job," his dream of "buying a little spread up around Sonora, California . . . to run a few head of saddle horses."

> It hurt me to have to admit to myself that good men like Father . . . had been trapped, long ago and unwittingly, in a prefabricated fantasy called Hollywood. It may have been unfenced, and with no fixed admission charge, but in its own way it was every bit as much a set piece as Disneyland itself. Denied those authentic situations where their horsemanship had once counted for something to other men, they had settled for the only place offering an opportunity to live out a shadow-play version of the real thing. But they paid a high price to go on playing cowboy for the rest of their lives, in an alien society that underestimated their values and derided their Code.[31]

The cowboy movie riders tried to protect their interests and resist the studios' exploitation of them. They were very loyal to each other informally and could work together cooperatively on particular occasions, as when a hundred of them as Israelites refused De Mille's murderous orders to race their horses and chariots down a steep bluff in the Mojave Desert for *The Ten Commandments*, or two decades later when seven cowboys dressed as Saracens plotted to murder the hated De Mille by an "unavoidable accident" of runaway horses during the filming of *The Crusades*. They even formed an organization in Hollywood of former working cowboys who had actually trailed a chuck wagon before 1910, to distinguish themselves from the drugstore cowboys. The Chuck Wagon Trailers it was called; at the height of the membership in the mid-1930s, there were only 242 members, almost all of them riding extras. But this organization was fraternal and never involved itself in job actions. During the Depression cowboy extras responded to the example of the Screen Actors' Guild's organizing, to the earlier union actions of cameramen, and to the Humane Society's successful suit against Warner Brothers, by forming their own union, the Riding Actors Association. But their union failed because cowboys thought themselves as a class better than other workers in the industry—the unmounted extras ("streetwalkers"), the carpenters, electricians, hairdressers, makeup people, grips, and the rest. Consequently they would not unite with them in building an industrial union. They couldn't even keep their own separate trade union going because there were disputes over forcing members to refuse unsanctioned jobs and pay scales, like a saddle fall for three rather than five dollars. "With times still as hard as they were, who could afford to hold out for five dollars and then risk that the next man to whom the assistant made his offer would do it for only three?"[32]

So the old elitism and individualism of cowboys, which they had partly and temporarily set aside in the eighties and nineties to make common cause with farmers and industrial workers in resisting the corporations, prevented them from organizing a labor union a half century later in the Great Depression. In that fifty years they had participated in building a popular myth the values of which are incompatible with real, daily life in our present society and which incapacitated them from struggling for survival. The myth they peopled had destroyed them. Now their old worker elitism, the pride in craft and style that set them apart from other workers during the cowboy era, became a nostalgic and romantic conviction that cowboys alone were representatives of a better time, holdouts for a better way of life. The popular Western myth which they helped Hollywood distill and with which they identified, the myth of a Western community of free individuals in a preindustrial frontier society, socialized them into being unable to resist their exploitation by the movie industry in any organized way. Hollywood cowboys were living according to their code of freedom, independence, helpfulness to strangers, protection of the weak, tenderness to horses, the code of the good guys in the frontier communities in popular Westerns. But that code was inappropriate to the dynamics of advanced capitalism, in which workers must organize to survive.

So even with Wild West, rodeos, dude ranching, and movie riding, only a few cowboys managed to get back to their old line of work for themselves and their families. There were a few small ranchers who did make it, in a small way. Bruce Siberts, an Iowa farm boy, became a cowboy and a homesteading rancher in Dakota and ended up parlaying his horse herds into an 8,000-acre ranch in Oklahoma by energetic mustanging and sharp trading. He had the typical contempt of the self-made success for the poor dumb wage earner. He had no use for your ordinary cowboy who didn't become an affluent landholder like him. In the spring of 1895 he worked hard planting potatoes and corn on rented land, mending fences, hunting his cattle. Many years later he recalled that spring from the comfortable gallery of his middle-class Oklahoma ranch house:

> A lot of company came by that spring, mostly riders looking for work. Some stayed for just a meal, others for a day or two. Most of them were burned out bad with whiskey and disease. The ordinary cowhands worked for six or eight months at thirty to forty dollars a month, then went into town and stayed as long as they could. About half of them would then go to some ranch and get a job doing winter chores. The rest were pimps, living off of some cheap prostitute in Pierre. Texas Siftings was one of them. He lived in a shack down in the red-light district and spent most of his time gambling and drinking in the saloons. Most of them had a dose of clap or pox and some had a double dose. All in all, most of the old-time cowhands were a scrubby bunch. Only the few good ones got into the cow business and made good. [33]

Siberts recalls cowboys during the depressions of the nineties, when the free ranges were dwindling, as a "scrubby bunch" of seasonal laborers, managing to find work from half to two-thirds of the time and only a "few good ones" becoming successful independent ranchers. True enough, although we may want to reject Siberts's self-made-man morality, which equates material success with goodness. His highly colored recollection that half of the cowboys, after their earnings ran out, could find winter work on ranches if they wanted to only reflects his own work ethic, because all cattle company account books on ranches in the northern ranges show to the contrary that only a skeleton crew of cowboys stayed on in the winter. And his belief that a full half of cowboys were pimps, gamblers, and drunks merely demonstrates his smug pride in having risen above them. Siberts's middle-class view of cowboys is identical with that of a true representative of the owning class, John Clay, the Chicago cattle commission agent and cattle company consultant who thought that the average cowboy was a natural-born thief who "usually degenerated, drifted, dis-

appeared, or worse still, became a saloon keeper." Clay's Scottish Cal-
vinism reinforced his business values to produce this puritan success ethic.
A modern conservative historian of the cattle industry has the same view
that the average cowboy of the last century, not having any money, could
exert "little influence on the course of American history," and like Siringo
"invariably headed for the Red Lights when he hit town," where he
celebrated all his money away.[34]

This view of cowboys puts them among what Marx called the *lumpenproletariat*, that "indefinite, disintegrated mass" of the "scum, offal, refuse
of all classes,"[35] not just the poorest of the working class but those without
any class or community loyalty or moral principle, those unattached idlers,
drifters, petty criminals, convicts, and con men always found in the combat
zones, skid rows, and hobo camps of cities. But as this study makes clear,
no disproportionate number of cowboys belonged or ended up in the
lumpenproletariat, even during the recurring depressions when there was
terrible unemployment (1873–78, 1884–87, 1893–98).[36] They came from
traditional, preindustrial farm communities, bringing their values and culture with them. Many of them tried to become farmers and ranchers when
they left or were forced out of wage labor; and when they lost their
homesteads, as most of them did, they returned to ranches and farms as
wage earners or hired on as sheepherders or moved on to any of the new
industries selling the cowboy image. As seasonal, migrant, usually unmarried workers on the frontier, cowboys had some of the *lumpen* element
among them, but certainly not more than among lumberjacks and seamen,
say, and certainly less than among buffalo hunters and gangs of laborers
laying railroad track.

There are proportionately fewer working cowboys in relation to cattle
counts today than on the open range because ranching is mechanized and
automated. Even fewer cowboys work year-round for the big outfits, because, except at roundups, cattle can be surveyed from helicopters and
jeeps and reached by a semi carrying the remuda in the trailer and three
or four cowhands in the cab, and fences and windmills can be repaired
from pickups. Roundup crews are composed mainly of casuals hired for
the occasion from migrants or locals who moonlight as cowboys and in
some places by exchanging hands with nearby ranches on staggered schedules. Temporary casual labor for roundups bring their own horses in trailers.
Crews eat from paper plates dispensed from vans.

Just as assembly-line production eliminated specialized crafts, mecha-
nization inevitably has coarsened cowboy skills—less riding and roping
tends toward less skilled riding and roping. But the difference is that modern
cowboys romantically try to keep to the old ways and styles. Their dress

is unchanged; they roll their own; they won't use nylon lariats; and they still think cattle can only be managed by rope. This explains the popularity of old Westerns and of local rodeos and team ropings in ranch country. Even pen riders in feed lots, the least prestigious work of cowboys now because the least like how it was on the open range, try to preserve some of the old pride of craft and style in the new monotony of their jobs by careful attention to sick and injured animals and moving herds smoothly through corrals without having to use ropes or cutting out on horseback. But the only working cowboys who are encouraged by their employers to look and behave like media and open-range cowboys are those working on dude ranches for paying guests and on that other kind of dude ranch maintained like the Ponderosa of *Bonanza* fame—by owners playing cattle king to show off their wealth.

The Cowboy Myth

The Old West is not a certain place in a certain time, it's a state of mind. It's whatever you want it to be.
—*Tom Mix*[1]

Cowboys displaced cavalry scouts as heroes of the West beginning in the mid-eighties. They worked in a relatively small industry. Railroads created, led, determined, and got fat on the cattle industry. But railroads did not produce a national hero. In an age when railroad investments dominated all others, even exceeding investments in all manufacturing industries combined, it was not the railroad engineer or fireman who emerged as our national hero but a cowboy, the worker in the industry probably only a tenth the size of the burgeoning railroads, judging by capital formations in the last two decades of the century.[2] During the boom years, there were fewer than five hundred cattle companies incorporated in the four Rocky Mountain states (New Mexico, Colorado, Wyoming, and Montana).[3] If each company employed about eight cowboys for most of the year, that comes to 4,000. Double the figure for the rest of the Great Plains and we have 8,000. Thus, there were never many regular cowboys, probably, as we have seen from a contemporary labor newspaper, at the most fewer than 10,000 working cowboys on the Great Plains at the height of the cattle empire. Add some for west of the Rockies and the result still comes to there having been one cowboy for every 1,000 agricultural workers or one cowboy for every forty miners or railroad workers nationwide.[4] During their heyday, cowboys constituted only one-tenth of one percent of the nation's agricultural work force! From such a small group of workers grew the giant myth, until in the popular mind cowboys became the principal inhabitants of the West.

What explains the enormous popularity of Westerns, of stories and spectacles and accounts of the frontier? From the beginning of the cowboy era, as we have seen, American people have voraciously consumed shows and stories and pictures of the West and its cowboy hero. There are still tourist trips to reconstructed Western towns and historical museums in national parks, country-western songs about cowboys and outlaws, and amusement-land mock-ups of Western streets. Thirty-five stage plays with "cowboy" in the title were filed for copyright in the first fifteen years of this century.[5] The first plotted movie Western appeared in 1903, and hundreds of one- and two-reelers followed in the next decade. By the mid-twenties, almost a third of all features showing in American movie houses were Westerns.[6] During the twelve months of 1959, when they were at their peak of popularity on television, twenty-eight Western series ran for a total of 570 hours, the equivalent of about four hundred old movies.[7] What accounts for this ongoing appetite for Western subjects, more particularly for Westerns and for the main popular representative of the West, the cowboy?

The only force strong enough to explain such a powerful appetite for the Western is a profound sense of deprivation and loss by the American people and a mass longing for a better world. We continue to feel that we have been robbed of our community, our freedom, and our natural environment; and we long for the world in which we once enjoyed these benefits and rights. The West offered such a world, and the myth of the West offered a later fantasy world after industrial corporate capitalism completed its conquest of the real West. Americans began to sense the loss in the 1870s when the breakup of rural and small-town communities, the overcrowded and polluted cities, and robotized wage labor had developed enough to hurt their bodies and their minds. The Western for a time offered an exciting vision of the lost rural community.

America shares with countries like Australia a history involving the simultaneous conquest of the wilderness and the rise of industrial capitalism, both accompanied by the rise of popular frontier myths (in Australia, notably, stories about the "last outlaw," Ned Kelly, and his populist uprising of bushrangers). In Europe, and in countries like Japan, where no frontier offered stories to satisfy the longings of people deprived of fulfillment by developing industrial capitalism, there emerged popular tales of rural community based on feudal precapitalist worlds (early nineteenth-century European medieval romances and Japanese samurai stories) or on the frontiers of colonial and imperial worlds (some of the fiction of Rudyard Kipling). But the American Western has captured a lost world more compelling and enduring than any of these.

Conceiving of Westerns as offering a world for the one we've lost but still long for best explains their invariable nostalgia. All popular Westerns project something of a those-were-the-good-old-days attitude. By their very nature, origin, and function, Westerns are nostalgic and romantic. Remington's paintings are mostly studio creations of an imaginary world of a he-man, Indian-fighting West gone by before he made his first visit there: the transitory cowboy against the sunset, a stagecoach with its windows warmly glowing in the moonlight. Owen Wister, who never saw from his Pullman window any trail drives or buffalo herds or unconfined Indians, announced to his readers in the introductory note to his famous novel that his story presented a "vanished world." The buffalo, the wild antelope, and "the horseman with his pasturing thousands . . . the cowpuncher, the last romantic figure upon our soil," Wister wrote in 1902, has vanished, and the world that has followed is "a shapeless state, a condition of men and manners unlovely as that bald moment in the year when winter is gone and spring not come, and the face of Nature is ugly."

In seeing Westerns as offering an attractive past as an escape from the contracted present, we should understand the relationship of capitalism and industrialism. This way we can avoid romantic primitivism while recognizing the injuries of progress. Most Americans who acknowledge these injuries blame technology, industry, and the government. But the responsible agent is the system under which minority owners exploit nature and people for their own profit by controlling public opinion and by enlisting the support of government and the favored class of workers. It is obvious that capitalism most quickly and efficiently accomplishes the industrial revolution because owners in their search for profit ruthlessly reject any concern for people. But the recent example of several Third World socialist societies shows that technology and industry can be introduced under auspices other than capitalism, although the process is slower as a result of being more cautious of human consequences. The destroyer is not technological industrialism but the sanctioned use of it for profit by minority ownership. Under a system of democratic collective ownership, technology and industry could have been used to improve the quality of our lives by building a nation of small garden cities located where the land can support them, integrated with small farms and factories, surrounded by countryside and parks and wilderness areas, and all served with public transportation instead of private automobiles.

All popular art forms offer visions of more satisfying lives to postindustrial people caught in daily circumstances that afford little succor and over which they have little control. But Westerns serve to satisfy these yearnings better than other forms, like the urban detective mystery or the gangster story or the Horatio Alger fable, because Westerns present an unspoiled frontier wilderness surrounding the preindustrial community. The world offered is the very world most mourned and yearned for. Industrializing America, owned, directed by, and producing profits for the minority, deprived us of our traditional cultures, our extended families, our organic social relations, our country surroundings, our space, our sense of self-worth, our independence, our skills, our satisfying work, and our healthy and beautiful environment. These deprivations are summed up as loss of community and of nature. Because of the forces of developing industrial capitalism, later nineteenth-century and twentieth-century people in America found themselves increasingly crowded into cities; dependent on mechanical, repetitive, closely supervised wage work; isolated in rootless nuclear families; surrounded by strangers and by strange new cultures; poisoned by chemicals; and in the control of external and impersonal forces. As Raymond Williams said of popular responses to the British industrial revolution, "when we become uncertain in a world of apparent strangers . . . we can retreat, for security, into deep subjectivity, or we can look around us for social pictures, social signs, social messages, to which . . . we try to relate as individuals but so as to discover, in some form, community. Much of the content of modern communications is this kind of substitute for directly discoverable and transitive relations to the world."[8] Westerns in outdoor spectacles, in cheap novels and pulp magazines, in movies, in comic strips, and in radio and television series offered just such pictures, signs, and messages of our lost community and nature.

This view of the Western explains why it took hold as the most popular form of mass culture just as the effects of "progress" and the delayed ravages of the robber barons began to manifest themselves toward the end of the last century. People found solace in Westerns precisely when they began actively to express their social discontent on the streets and in meeting halls and factories. A cowboy hero appeared in a dime novel in the mid-eighties and was followed by dozens more over the next several years. Wister's stories about his first cowboy, Lin McLean, appeared in the mid-nineties, and then came *The Virginian* in 1902, which sold 300,000 copies in two years. The earliest Western movie with a plot, *The Great*

WILLIAM S. HART IN *THE GUN FIGHTER* (1917)

The producer is Ince-Kay Bee. The photographer making this publicity still has asked the cowboys to look where Hart points his gun (two to the right rear ruin the dramatic effect by refusing) and to hook thumbs of idle hands into pockets and belts. The background is the chaparral of the Santa Monica Mountains.

Train Robbery, appeared the year after Wister's novel; an actor in it, G. M. Anderson, became the first movie cowboy hero and directed and acted in almost five hundred Bronco Billy Westerns in seven years following 1910. Tom Mix appeared in his first movie, *The Range Rider*, in 1909, William S. Hart in his first Thomas Ince Western in 1914. B. M. Bower's first Western appeared in 1906. An early comic strip, *Little Jimmy*, began appearing in a regular Southwest locale in about 1910, making it the first of many Western strips.[9] So the period when the public's appetite for the Western became truly voracious and Westerns became by all odds the most popular form of entertainment coincides with people's direct opposition to industrial capitalism—the populist and union movements, the rise of the People's Party and the Socialist Party and the Industrial Workers of the World, the Pullman strike of 1894 and many other big strikes following it, including general strikes that shut down whole cities, like

Seattle in 1919. The seething discontent of these years engendered the most popular drama and narrative in the culture of the people, the Western.

If we see the Western as a response to a pervasive popular longing for lost freedom and rural community, we can explain why a worker rather than an owner became the hero of one of our few popular art forms. The populist myth satisfying the people's longings logically has cowboy heroes. Some elitist historians find it lamentable that the cattlemen in the industry, who, as they say, "were far more important than cowboys in shaping cultural developments, and, incidentally, were far more exciting as well," are not the heroes in Westerns. According to this view, novelists and movie and television directors perversely make heroes of "hired hands on horse-back who compromised with their environment at relatively low levels . . . [and] exerted little influence on the course of American history" but "rel-egate the rancher to a shadow, background role for the main hero of their imagination, the American cowboy," even with such a "magnificent cast of characters" lying "ready at hand for the creative artist" as Conrad Kohrs, George W. Littlefield, Shanghai Pierce—and the list continues with seven more cattlemen.[10] Our most abiding and central popular myth responds to the deep longing of our people, and has nothing to do with cattlemen gaining wealth and exercising their power over workers and industry and government, and everything to do with the hero cowboy's protection of a community of common, free people on the unspoiled prairies and deserts.

There are some exceptions, but they prove the rule. Wister's Virginian is the most important, but Wister did not influence the values of the populist Western. Wister was the beginning of a minority eddy of Westerns on the side of big money, swelling or narrowing according to the times, on the edges of the populist mainstream. There have always been Western nov-elists who look up to monied men and present the rich and powerful as the good guys in need of protection. Andy Adams's love of wealthy cat-tlemen constitutes the only soft part of his realistic art. A. B. Guthrie admires cowmen more than cowboys in *These Thousand Hills*. Even the excellent Elmer Kelton sometimes sides with big old ranchmen, for instance when his cattle detective hero in *Llano River* (1966) finds that the situation in south Texas which he's been paid to investigate is not "the big fish living off of the little ones [but] more like the little ones living off of the big."[11] This formulation, of course, reverses the dramatic situation of most West-erns. In the sixties the elitist eddy almost swamped the populist mainstream with the great television success of what one critic aptly called "property Westerns,"[12] like *Bonanza* and several other series about rich families protecting their big ranches. *Dallas* is a continuation of the property West-ern with variations to suit the Reagan era. But for more than half a century the popular Western tradition of weak communities of common people in need of protection by cowboy heroes continued strong.

Different groups of people want different myths. The aspiring middle class wanted romantic, Horatio Alger cowboy ranch foremen, so the Macmillan Publishing Company of New York and Owen Wister gave them *The Virginian*, and the Kirke La Shelle Company took a five-act play of it on the road and finally a part of the embryo film industry (Lasky/Paramount/C. B. De Mille) gave them a movie version. More people, readers of pulps like the *Police Gazette* and dime novels, wanted adventurous cowboys saving frontier communities, so the Essanay Company of Chicago and Bronco Billy Anderson picked up on the pulp market and gave them that version. In the first fifteen years of the century, when the cowboy was emerging as our national hero, there was a struggle over who he would be among the scores of movie companies, the pulp magazines beginning with Munsey's taking over the dime-novel audience, the theater industry, the book publishers (which now catered to middle-class readers) and the old glossy middle-class magazines (*Harper's, Century,* the *Saturday Evening Post, Colliers*). All of these offered cowboys either as Horatio Alger heroes in the Wister style, who had middle-class cultural and economic pretensions, or as adventurous good-guy heroes to the working-class majority, who most sharply felt the constraints of progress. By the time the movie industry in the twenties and the television industry in the fifties emerged as the dominant media that reflected and shaped popular taste, the community-saving cowboy hero had proved more profitable than the property-saving one, and the popular and populist Western myth dominated.

Hollywood gave people the Western myth they wanted because the independent companies prevented a concentrated unified tendency within the popular culture industry. But after World War II, with growing multinational and conglomerate centralization, the movie and television industries could intrude narrow patriotism, law and order, and patriarchy into the Western and eventually change it completely. Thus, the public got the familiar Westerns they wanted until the media became centralized and powerful enough to emphasize aggressive individualism, the central virtue of capitalism. The change came not, of course, from a decree by some movie or television czar but accrued slowly from the political values of the various producers, and the pressures of advertisers and special-interest organizations. The producers catered to popular taste on the basis of box office and ratings but shaped that taste as far as the overriding consideration of profit would allow. To sum up: the populist Western prevailed so strongly over its elitist rival that it continued as the dominant form for decades.

Only when the film and television industries came to dominate popular culture could they bring the ideology of Westerns more in line with that of advanced capitalism.

We can best understand this early struggle between the populist and elitist myth by looking carefully at the first strong contender for what soon became the losing side, or, more exactly, a minority eddy in the populist mainstream, Wister's *The Virginian*. This was the first high-toned, best-selling novel with a cowboy hero (there had been scores of cheap pulps with cowboy heroes before). Pushing his advantage, in the fall of the year *The Virginian* was published, Wister helped write a stage version of it which opened in Boston, starring Dustin Farnum, went on to New York that winter, toured for a long while, and ended in 1914 as a movie directed by the young Cecil B. De Mille and starring Farnum. The story was popular and influential, but not in essential and important ways as has been claimed. Later Western writers copied two important features of the plot that were to become conventions: (1) a romantic cowboy hero courting a respectable woman, usually a schoolmarm or a rancher's daughter, often an Easterner; and (2) a hero's escalating conflict with a villain, culminating in a triumphant shootout at the end, to which his sweetheart often objects. These two important purely structural contributions aside—and perhaps also his prominent descriptions of the wilderness—Wister's novel has not been much imitated. Subsequent Western writers would have nothing to do with Wister's values; they have rejected his contempt for working cowboys and ex-cowboy nesters, his total identification with the wealthy class, his reactionary politics, and his European culture. Wister was an Eastern snob, a Harvard aristocrat devoted to high society. Before he began summering in Wyoming, he toured the Continent. His literary models were the fiction of that champion of the British raj and Colonel Blimps, Rudyard Kipling, and that Anglophile chronicler of the upper classes, Henry James; two less appropriate guides for the popular Western it is difficult to imagine.[13] His manners are pretentious. The narrator of his novel, after smoking a post-prandial cigar with the gentlemen guests on the ranch, proposes to return to the dining room "to offer our services to the ladies" (Chapter 21). The representatives of religion in the novel, the missionary churchman who stays at the ranch and the bishop of the territory who officiates at the marriage of the hero and Molly, are both Episcopalian, the affiliation of whatever gentry America possesses. Popular non-Mormon Protestant preachers in Western towns dealt out to ordinary folk Presbyterian, Baptist, Methodist, Campbellite services—they didn't sabe Episcopal. When the visiting missionary assumes the Virginian has been on vacation, the narrator is reminded of his ruddy-faced masters at prep school after Christmas holidays (Ch. 18); Wister himself prepared for Harvard at that most stylish and Episcopalian of schools, St. Paul's, in Concord, New Hampshire.

Wister writes clearly for an upper-middle-class audience with social pretentions, mostly Easterners. Discussing the difficulties of being inspected by the relatives of one's intended, his narrator draws the married male reader in with a plural pronoun: "We got through it somehow. We dined with Aunt Jane, and wined with Uncle Joseph, and perhaps had two fingers given to us by old Cousin Horatio, whose enormous fortune was of the greatest importance to everyone" (Ch. 29). This is typical of dozens of passages that could be overheard at a Harvard reunion. Wister worked into his novel as a central theme a dogmatic defense of the Eastern entrepreneurs' armed intervention into populist Johnson County, Wyoming, because all his friends were on that side.

The Virginian appeared just ten years after the nesters of Johnson County defeated the Wyoming Stock Growers Association's invading army of mercenaries and cattlemen. The background of the two elements of the plot, the Virginian's courtship of Molly Wood and his feud with Trampas, is the class war between ex-cowboy ranchmen and the association's corporate cattlemen over mavericks and ranges. Wister valued "accuracy," as he wrote in his journal, "more than any other quality,"[14] but he was concerned only with surface detail of speech and style and conventions (e.g., whether Southwest Indians used sign), not the accuracy of the underlying cultural and economic forces that shape events. Although Wister in his introductory note to the reader claimed his novel presented the historical truth about the "vanished world" of Wyoming between 1874 and 1891, it does no such thing. Wister presents the conflict as one of patrician ranchers trying to protect their cattle against a growing population of "thieves" who "have got hold of the juries in Johnson County" (Ch. 32). Popular Westerns since this most famous early one have also presented ideal worlds of decent citizens struggling against villains, or good guys against bad guys. Thus this novel is quite typical in arcadianizing and antiquing the Great Plains by ignoring corporate hegemony in the West. But it is strikingly unlike most popular Westerns in its identifying completely with the possessing class and their loyal imitators and supporters, that is, the big ranchers and their devoted foremen.

The Virginian is not at all a typical cowboy. He's a top hand bucking for foreman, with a quarter section of his own all "proved upon . . . along a creek that never goes dry" (Ch. 23)—not a ranch on which to run his own cattle in competition with his boss, the way most ex-cowboy nesters did, but "a place where there was coal" (Ch. 36) to sell to the railroad building a branch up his way as a step further into the owning class to which he aspires. The Virginian never speaks of owning his own brand. Wister presents a budding capitalist achiever, not a typical cowboy as hero, because he didn't much admire the cowboys he met. The ordinary cowboys in his novel, like Trampas, Scipio, Shorty, and Steve, are part of the majority class his narrator called complacently "the equality" (Ch. 13) and treats as comic, weak, or dangerous. Lin McLean, the earlier cowboy character in Wister's *Harper's* sketches, is a comic, quaint character, clearly not the equal of the narrator or his aristocratic friends. After all his travel in the West, the only two real cowboys he ever respected and idolized were of the old school, both in Arizona: Skirdan, turned cavalry scout, and Duke, turned ranch foreman for a cattle company. Both of them in these latter days were fighting Indians in the last dying gasp of our Indian wars, the Apache uprisings;[15] and both were what Wister took to be survivors of "those first glorious days" of the cowboys' "prosperity," Texas from 1865 to 1878, when "he fought his way with knife and gun, and any hour of the twenty-four might see him flattened behind rocks among the whizz of bullets and the flight of arrows. . . . Those were the days in which he was long in advance of settlers," fighting "three sorts of inveterate enemies"—cattle and horse thieves, Mexicans, and Indians. Wister presents this cowboy of the golden age as the romantic descendent of the medieval knight battling dragons with his lance. "The knight and the cowboy are nothing but the same Saxon of different environments," descended "from the tournament to the round-up," like "Miles Standish and the

Pathfinder" awaiting their "Hawthorne, Longfellow, and Cooper," but in 1895 "beneath the notice of *polite* writers" (emphasis added).[16] By *polite* Wister means writers from his own class, not vulgar hucksters who write for Beadle's dime novels or for the *Police Gazette*. Wister's view of the cowboy came as much from Sir Walter Scott and Alfred Tennyson as it did from his travels in the West. The cowboy he romanticized had vanished before he went to Wyoming in 1885. Not finding his ideal cowboys in this time of fading glories but wanting to write a novel justifying his friends' side in the class warfare of the early nineties, he created a self-educated aristocratic hero aspiring to Wister's class and achieving it by marriage and sharp business practices.

Indeed Wister makes his hero a Horatio Alger type who proves the American Dream. On his first arrival in Wyoming, "punching cattle at the Bordeaux outfit, north of Cheyenne" (Ch. 31), then only six years later Judge Henry's foreman, and after a few years his partner, he ends up a rich owner of a mine selling coal to the railroad—in short, "an important man, with a strong grip on many various enterprises" (Ch. 36). None of your sad-sack cowboy losers for Wister; he explicitly rejects them in the characters of Shorty and Steve. From rags to riches, from worker to capitalist, according to the ideal if not the reality of American life.

And the whole structure of values that supports this super-achiever Wister presents quite explicitly, sometimes with a curious shrillness. Social Darwinism insures the survival of the fittest, that is, of those most aggressively committed to success. Do all the young men who "have gone away to seek their fortunes in the West" find them? Molly's great-aunt in Vermont asks the Virginian. "Yes, ma'am. All the good ones do," he responds without hesitation (Ch. 36). "Equality is a great big bluff" in a society where the Virginian sees "folks movin' up or movin' down, winners or losers everywhere" (Ch. 12). Competitive struggle sorts out the few exceptional people from the majority of mediocre ones:

> All America is divided into two classes,—the quality and the equality. The latter will always recognize the former when mistaken for it. Both will be with us until our women bear nothing but kings. . . .
>
> We decreed [in the Declaration of Independence] that every man should thenceforth have equal liberty to find his own level. By this very decree we acknowledged and gave freedom to true aristocracy, saying "let the best man win, whoever he is." Let the best man win! That is America's word. That is true democracy. And true democracy and true aristocracy are one and the same

thing. If anybody cannot see this, so much the worse for his eyesight. [Ch. 13.]

The best way to be flung out on top of the scum is to worship success and faithfully serve people in power. When the Virginian is made foreman, we are told that "it meant everything to him: recognition, higher station, better fortune, a separate house of his own." And on that occasion he assures Judge Henry, his "wise commander-in-chief," himself a good "lieutenant": "I'll try to please you" (Ch. 20). And he is so zealous in his resolve that he lynches his oldest friend for stealing what he presumes are his boss's cattle. Wister sees the West as a place of trial where the forces of Social Darwinism become accelerated, more ruthless; where society is particularly red in tooth and claw: "Now back East you can be middling and get along. But if you go to try a thing on in this Western country, you've got to do it *well*" (Ch. 31). You enter this crucible if, like the Virginian, you are "looking for chances" (Ch. 22). Of course, you don't violate laws in keeping your eye peeled for the main chance, unless it's a case of gentlemanly honor: you can have a gunfight "where there is no way out, save only the ancient eternal way between man and man. It is only the great mediocrity that goes to law in these personal matters" (Ch. 35). And gentlemen break the law and lynch people if the latter are their competitors and control the law and violate the most important of all sanctities, private property. Using the old malleable doctrine of government as a resuming contract, Judge Henry tells Molly, who is upset that her sweetheart has just lynched three men: when Wyoming "juries, into whose hands we have put the law, are not dealing the law" (i.e., when they are "letting our cattle-thieves go"), and "when your ordinary citizen [i.e., Judge Henry and his friends] sees this . . . he must take justice back into his own hands" (Ch. 33). What this elaborate doctrine means is that the possessing class takes back democracy if it's not used to support their material interests. This is the thinking that justified the WSGA's mass lynching expedition into Johnson County in April 1892 after their years of terrorist activity directed against nesters, like bushwhackings and hangings, hadn't stopped mavericking. These are the values of the possessing class, which Wister shared with his rich Eastern friends in Wyoming and which, naturally enough, inform his novel.

Wister's classmates at Harvard College, Teschemacher and deBillier, managed and were principal stockholders in a cattle company with five ranch headquarters and about 19,000 head of cattle when Wister came west to visit them in 1885.[17] Wister based himself on the VR ranch, managed by his friend Major Frank Wolcott. All three of these friends were members of the association and were arrested with the invaders a few years later. The model for Judge Henry is both Wolcott and Francis E. Warren, the principal owner and resident manager of the Warren Land and Cattle Company, a founder of the WSGA, a governor of the territory and later the first U.S. senator from Wyoming, in 1890, in which position he helped the invaders escape trial after their capture. At the exclusive Cheyenne Club, between tennis, chess, billiards, bourbon, and Havana cigars, Wister, who called the club "the pearl of the prairies,"[18] met other Eastern investers and rich cattlemen, like Warren's associate Thomas Sturgis, secretary of the association and perhaps the most powerful man in Wyoming, and the tough, reactionary John Clay, Scottish cattle broker, managerial consultant, and lobbyist.

Wister wrote in his journal in 1889, after talking in a railroad smoking car with one of the indicted lynchers of homesteaders Ella Watson and James Averill (one historian called the lynching "the most revolting crime in the entire annals of the West"[19]): "the gentleman . . . seemed a good solid citizen, and I hope he'll get off."[20] Lynching is the work of gentlemen and good solid citizens if it's done for the rich, as the Virginian's lynching was. When Wister passed through Buffalo, the seat of Johnson County, one year before it was invaded by his friends, he wrote his mother that it was "horrible beyond words," full of "motley blackguards." To preserve the dignity of his class, he stayed the night in the officers' quarters in nearby Fort McKinney. During a quick excursion through Buffalo, he saw and admired the association's main hired killer, Frank Canton: "very quiet, very even voice . . . feared by all hands." Later, when Wister's mother objected to the Virginian's lynching party, as did Molly Wood in the novel, and claimed that the "results proved the viciousness of the lynching principle," since the nesters in Johnson County won the war, Wister replied pragmatically that "lynching was perfectly successful in Montana and ended the reign of the Thieves there."[21] Wister was referring to the operation in the early nineties by the Montana Stock Growers Association that resulted in the secret extermination of between twenty and fifty "ringleaders among the cattle thieves . . . in one night," in Wister's own words, by a small army of imported professional assassins. Wister admired this Montana terrorism: "a visit from the Destroying Angel. . . . the stroke was the result of long and elaborate preparation . . . it was a single stroke and a clean one," and when it was accomplished the killers again left Montana, "shut invisible in a freight car on the Northern Pacific Railway."[22] In contrast, Wister disapproved of the Wyoming terrorist operation only because it was bungled.

In the only direct reference to the invasion in the novel, Wister writes

THE INVADERS (1913)

*This populist response to Wister's elitist Western was produced by Kalem,
directed by George Melford, and starred Carlyle Blackwell as John Thorpe, an
Eastern lawyer turned small ranchman, and Nerva Gerber as Helen Sawyer, the
heiress of a neighboring ranch. Here she helps the wounded hero into her
house while the invading army of the big cattle association holds its fire.*

at the very end that Wyoming cattle owners moved their herds to Montana
after the "cattle war" in 1892, when "the thieves prevailed," "putting their
men in office, and coming to own some of the newspapers" (Ch. 36).
When the thieves prevailed, Wister's love affair with Wyoming was over
and he no longer spent his summers there, not only because his friends,
defeated and fearing retaliation, had fled the state, but because his class
had come to be in very bad odor among the people. He wrote his novel
partly as an act of revenge against the nesters of Johnson County. The
world that Wister lamented, the one controlled from the tony Cheyenne
Club, the world of his novel, is not the world that had been slowly shaping
itself in the mind of the American people and the popular Western artists.

There was a growing market for democratic Westerns. In 1913, a year before Lasky (later Paramount) made a movie of Wister's version of the Johnson County War, the early movie company Kalem produced a version of it, *The Invaders*, which openly took the side of the nesters. Directed by George Melford, the movie used the name of the now little-known novel it was based on, *The Invaders: A Story of the Hole-in-the-Wall Country*. Written by the now forgotten John Lloyd (pseudonym for Jacque Lloyd Morgan) and published only eight years after *The Virginian*, it is the people's answer to Wister. John Thorpe, a young New York lawyer, breaks with the past and comes to Wyoming to use the remains of a nearly bankrupt fortune to build a new life as a rancher. Unlike Wister's narrator, Lloyd's hero really dislikes and rejects his snobbish Eastern values and friends and does not try to transport them west. He continues right by the Cheyenne Club on to Casper and thence by stage north to Buffalo, the very stronghold of Wister's "thieves," where he admires the settlers and makes friends with the cowboys and nesters, earns the nickname "New York Kid" by a fistfight with Tom Horn (unhistorically substituting for the real association killer Frank Canton), buys a homesteader's quarter-section ranch, keeps on Nate Champion (the historical martyr and populist hero of the Johnson County War) as a cowboy employee. As a consequence he gets on the "dead list" of the syndicate's hired guns and later of their invading army. He ends up about to marry the Eastern heiress (a school-marm from Boston) to a neighboring large ranch and announces that "the day of the 'big fellow,' and his arrogant and sometimes criminal ways, is over."

Lloyd mystified history to a degree by projecting the temporary populist victory into a permanent one. Almost all Westerns in their fantasy function do this: Americans want to believe that the small producer won, and the media have a vested interest in perpetuating the lie. Lloyd also observes the most fundamental law of Westerns—that social relations must be pre-industrial—by playing down the association and the cattle syndicates' involvement in the fight against nesters. The enemy is clearly the big cattle-men who fight the nesters for the purpose of "the saving of the open ranges." Leader Arapaho Rowan rouses the citizenry of Buffalo to put down the invader with the cry: "Boys, it's a range war. It's the big fellers a doin' this." The big fellows are seen mainly as resident owners or partner managers, basically a *Shane*-like situation; but there are more radical and realistic tendencies than in *Shane*. We hear occasionally about people like the English manager of the "Anglo-American Beef Syndicate's 46 ranch on the Powder River." And the association prepares for the invasion by spreading the false information in the national press that Johnson County is settled up with rustlers who must be exterminated. There is an accurate and wonderful chapter on this association propaganda. Finally, the villain is an Eastern capitalist who schemes to take over his uncle's ranch and whose greed and values make him a leader among the big cattlemen and in the association. It is this Eastern capitalist, indeed, who invents the strategy of the invasion as a cheaper way of exterminating nesters than what it cost to pay Tom Horn to assassinate them, $1,500 a head. But the novel is really without overt politics—it doesn't mention populist politics in Johnson County nor the rival granger and nester protective association, and it doesn't intrude shrill editorials, as Wister does, about the proper way gentlemen should think about things. It's just a good story on the side of the people, as the large majority of Westerns have been, both before and after Wister.

Seeing Westerns as responding to a mass longing explains why consistently from the very beginning they mystify history by settling the Plains with cattle barons, not managers of ranches owned by corporations. We have seen that as the need for capitalization grew, the open-range cattle companies went from ownership by individuals in the beginning to partners in the seventies to joint-stock corporations in the eighties. Why then do we never see the historical reality of corporate ranches or trailing companies in the popular Western? The Virginian's boss, Judge Henry, is a resident cattle king without an association to look out for his interests (and this in the very region of the mighty Wyoming Stock Growers Association and during the height of its power). Ten years later, in Zane Grey's most popular Western, *Riders of the Purple Sage* (1912), the big cattle owner is unincorporated and without a partner—Jane Withersteen, who has inherited her pioneer Mormon father's giant ranch and rules like a queen over "her riders" and the citizens of Cottonwood, the only nearby town. Shane in the movie (1953) and in the novel (1949) fights the old pioneer rancher Ryker (Fletcher, in the novel) who manages his own ranch and menaces the nesters in the valley. The date is clearly about 1890 (judging from styles and technology in the movie; the book explicitly dates it), and the place is Wyoming (you can see the Tetons in the movie; the book says the valley is a day's ride from Sheridan). Almost all the big ranches in Wyoming were then owned by corporations and their interests protected by WSGA's absolute control of the territorial government, but neither the movie nor the novel shows anything but a private fight between a big independent producer and lots of little ones, just as if the time were back before the industrial revolution in an earlier stage of capitalism. The world of *Shane* is truer to that of preindustrial capitalism than to the world of the time it is set in. The Western myth always turns the clock back several decades. When the impact of industrializing capitalism began to hurt, we created from our partially imagined past a world of individual ranchmen with loyal cowboys adventurously combating rustlers, Indians, and Mexicans; an Anglo, agrarian world of free people doing work they enjoyed set fifty years or so before the time it is intended to represent; a world in which individual relations were determined by moral qualities of character, by love and hate or fidelity and betrayal, rather than by money and power alone.

In *Red River* (1948) and in its source, Borden Chase's serialized story "The Chisholm Trail" in the *Saturday Evening Post*, an independent Texas rancher trails north his own and other neighbor ranchers' cattle. Of course, some very early drives were by independent cattlemen, but Howard Hawks, the director-producer, chose to set his Western in this early period and present the drive as typical of them all. In a novel that obviously tries to be historically accurate, Benjamin Capps's *The Trail to Ogallala* (1964), the story concerns a herd owned by a Texas widow rancher and driven by an outfit in her employ, and in the whole odyssey there is not a word of cattle commission companies or trail contractors or corporate ranches. Even the recent anti-Western movies about trail drives, which aim to refute the myth and tell the historical truth, involve independent owner–trail bosses only, not trail bosses employed by trail contractors. The businessman-type trail boss who pays Will Penny (1968) off at the railhead seems to own the herd he manages, and when Will gets a winter job as a line rider, his boss is the independent resident owner-manager of the Flatiron ranch; again there are no cattle companies even in this anticapitalist movie: the bosses who are shown to exploit their brutalized worker cowboys are individual owners, not agents of absentees.

The only other recent anti-Western that obviously wants to challenge the mythic version of cattle drives, *The Culpepper Cattle Co.* (1972), still doesn't show the corporate basis of the industry, although it takes the gilt off cowboys and gunfighting. Frank Culpepper, like Tom Dunsan a quarter century before, in spite of the "Co." in the title, is still a Texas rancher taking his own herd north, and the villain cattleman in Colorado who tries to cheat Culpepper and then to murder his outfit is also an independent rancher, not the historically more realistic employed agent for a cattle company. In perhaps the only movie of all time to show cowboys as exploited workers of absentee corporate owners, *Monte Walsh* (1970), we never see the villainous Eastern capitalists who own the Slash X ranch and who cause all the trouble, and since most of the movie relates to what happens to the cowboys after they lose their jobs, they are not shown in

THE CULPEPPER CATTLE CO. (1972)

A realistic chuckwagon scene created by director Dick Richards. Frank Culpepper (Billy "Green" Bush), the trail boss and owner, sits apart near the wagontongue. The young hero Ben Mockridge (Gary Grimes) on his first drive as a cook's helper, squats in the center. Dixie Brick (Bo Hopkins), one of four recruits replacing cowboys shot in a fight with rustlers, smokes to the left of the fire. The cattle are not longhorns, impossible to get these days in sufficient quantities for movie or video cattle drives.

a world controlled by corporations. In the popular Western we must *see* our villains—absentee exploiters won't do. The need for tangible villains responds to our longing for a precorporate world where evil is personified—a personal force we can understand and deal with.

Thus it is a fundamental law that Western stories be set in preindustrial times in regard to the economic class relations between the characters (a world of independent producers), although by other, more superficial indications of historic period—like railroads and metal cartridges and vanished buffalo and pacified Indians and Sears Roebuck catalogues—they must be set in the three decades after the Civil War, during the very springtime of corporate, industrial capitalism. Even anti-Westerns (debunking, revisionist Westerns) can't break this fundamental tenet: the West is a world of independent producers. Our longing for the flesh-and-blood friends and enemies of the lost preindustrial world and our predicament in a society of impersonal forces, where we never see the owners who control our lives and where our bosses just implement orders to speed up, specialize, and routinize our work and ruin our off-work hours by inadequate wages—this longing and suffering propels us into Western worlds closer to our heart's desire, the world of cattle barons and little ranchers, of small towns on wide prairies and working, resident bosses.

We must enter worlds we long for, not duplicates of the ruined world we feel is inadequate. But we also demand that the mass media make the wish-fulfilling Western world look real and historically accurate. We fool ourselves into believing that Westerns tell the truth; that this is the way it really used to be; that, for instance, the fight on the high plains of northern Wyoming in the late eighties was between little grangers and a few old pioneer Indian fighters become cattle barons. Americans are grossly ignorant of their frontier history during the cowboy era because we accept the media myth as history. Indeed, we want to accept it as a real historical alternative, although now a lost one, to the present unfulfilling world. The few privileged among us can even create this mythic world for themselves by buying ranches and surrounding themselves with cows and horses and cowboys; and thus some few footloose romantic youths can still be working cowboys of the old school on these Disneyesque ranches. The less than very rich can go to dude ranches for a spell of Western fantasy, thereby creating, incidentally, more cowboying jobs for the less affluent dude wranglers. But poor working stiffs must get their fixes at the movies or from the tube or paperbacks. And what we vicariously experience there we take as the way it really was, goldarnit, back when men were men.

The theory that they respond to our longing for a preindustrial world explains another important characteristic of Westerns. Although Westerns are about the coming of civilization to the wilderness, no one is very pleased about its coming. Westerns tend to lament the passing of the wilderness and accept with marked reluctance the advance of civilization. The last old-time outlaw is shot, the sheriff gets married, the town builds a school and a church, and the hero rides off into the western sunset (toward the left of the screen, the same way covered wagon trains always move) to escape the diminished life. The representatives of civilization who bear the torch into the wilderness are not the heroes of Westerns: schoolmarms, indeed all "respectable women," drummers, land developers, ministers, railroad magnates, bankers; in short, all the characters who come from the East trailing the aura of civilization fail to get our particular admiration and approval, although sometimes they get our grudging tolerance. We admire the outlaws more than the good but simpy townspeople trying to wrest their little patch of civilization out of the desert or plains that surround them. The hero identifies more with the outlaws and the Indians of the wilderness who threaten the town, even though he later reluctantly allies himself with the townspeople to resist the threat or kills the outlaws for his own reasons, benefiting the town only unintentionally. The hero is identified more with the wilderness than the town—he rides out of it at the beginning and usually rides back into it at the end.

Critics have long noticed in Westerns this ambivalence toward civilization, but they have not gone beyond the phenomenon to explain it by reference to the history of popular American ideals and feelings. The explanation is not just the very partial one that the American people hate the machines destroying their natural garden. The more inclusive explanation is that, chafing from the injuries and deprivations of industrial society, people relate the civilizing forces in the Western to their own unhappiness. And we subconsciously equate the wilderness that always retreats a bit in every Western with the free, more exciting world that has been lost to us. The progress that encroaches on the wilderness, bringing family life and church services to the cow town, does not look all that good to city workers and farmers who daily suffer from industrial progress. We recognize the inevitability of it, but that doesn't make us like it any better. We sense that this now safe little rural community is just the entering wedge and that this early form of capitalism will progress to the later less benign form we experience daily.

The Western's love of wilderness contradicts its defense of community (women, children, churches, schools, stores, and picket fences). The contradiction is deep in our consciousness and expresses our need for both nature and community, which existed together without contradiction in preindustrial society. Some Westerns (for instance, The Wild Bunch) go beyond the nostalgic rejection of industrial capitalism to a very American and individualistic rejection of society altogether, a total and unambiguous commitment to the wilderness; but most Westerns have it both ways, love of wilderness and love of community, too.

Westerns offer us substitute space and silence in unspoiled deserts, canyons, plains, and rivers. Westerns on their most obvious level satisfy our longings for nature and wilderness, longings that probably arise from instinctive urgings of all human beings. The desire for wilderness became stronger as we were deprived of it in industrializing America. When we are forced to live in huge cities where the jobs are, when city parks are overcrowded, when we can't find nature close by in the suburbs because of sprawl and honky-tonk, when we can't even visit it on vacation because it's been harvested, mined, polluted, or otherwise ruined by the automobile, RV, power boat, and tourist industry, then we seek our lost wilderness from what the mass media offers as a substitute. Westerns provided a substitute wilderness just when Americans were beginning to lament its loss. The rise of the conservation movement coincided with the growing popularity of the Western because they both responded to the spoliation of the wilderness by American industry. Congress passed the first federal law to create national forests as public domain in 1891. In the next two decades, federal laws for the control and administration of forests, minerals, grazing lands, and other resources under the jurisdiction of the federal government "securely laid" the "foundations for the development of national conservation,"[23] even though these foundations have not been proof against rapacious capital.

The spoliation of the plains and deserts of the West began early, and people soon became aware of it. One can't finger the entrepreneurs of the cattle industry as the ones who alone wiped out the buffalo so that their cows could take over the grasslands, grow fat, and multiply. The extinction of the buffalo wiped out the economy of the Plains Indians and speeded up the process of their internment on reservations. This in turn gave rise to a lucrative market in government beef contracts and opened up the Indian lands for development and exploitation. Cattlemen were glad to see the end of the buffalo, but the memoirs of cowboys are full of laments for their passing, usually in the form of nostalgic recollections of the days when herds covered the horizon. The refuse of industrial progress soon surrounded frontier towns. Wister reports that in the mid-eighties there were discarded empty cans of potted sardines, chicken, and deviled ham, "the first of her trophies that Civilization dropped on Wyoming's virgin soil," and less than forty years later, after the cowboy had vanished, "the empty sardine box lies rusting over the face of the Western earth."[24] Even Harvard aristocrats like Wister and Teddy Roosevelt were, in this matter, on the people's side, although their motives are somewhat suspect, given their delight in stalking grizzlies and bighorns with fancy parties of wealthy hunters. Less suspect is the opinion expressed in a little-known saying of the Montana cowboy turned artist, the great Charles Russell. He objected to being called "a pioneer." "In my book a pioneer is a man who comes to a virgin country, traps off all the fur, kills off all the wild

SIXTH EDITION.

BEADLE'S HALF DIME Library

Entered at the Post Office at New York, N. Y., at Second Class Mail Rates.   Copyright, 1887, by BEADLE AND ADAMS.   February 1, 1887.

Vol. XX. $2.50 a Year.   PUBLISHED WEEKLY BY BEADLE AND ADAMS,
No. 98 WILLIAM STREET, NEW YORK.   Price, 5 Cents.   No. 497.

BUCK TAYLOR

OR,
The Raiders AND THE Rangers,

A Story of the Wild and Thrilling
Life of William L. Taylor.*

BY COL. PRENTISS INGRAHAM,
AUTHOR OF "BUFFALO BILL," "WILD BILL,"
"TEXAS JACK," "BUCKSKIN SAM," ETC.

CHAPTER I.
THE VOLUNTEER RANGER.

A CRY of warning rung out from a man
guarding a camp on a Texas prairie.
In a timber motte of several acres, around

* W. L. Taylor, of Texas, and now with Buffalo
Bill's Wild West. Buck Taylor is also known as
"Wild Will, the Dare Devil Rider."—THE AUTHOR.

BUCK TAYLOR.

meat, cuts down all the trees, grazes off all the grass, plows the roots up and strings ten million miles of bob wire. A pioneer destroys things and calls it civilization."[25]

Some Americans in the last century saw what industrial capitalism was doing to our wilderness with remarkable clarity. The penetrating wilderness explorer and art critic John C. Van Dyke, writing during his three years of wandering in the Colorado and Sonora deserts beginning in 1898, reacts to plans to turn the Colorado River into a desert basin for the purposes of land development with this cry of outrage:

> The main affair of life is to get the dollar, and if there is any money in cutting the throat of Beauty, why, by all means, cut her throat. . . . Have we not seen, here in California and Oregon, in our own time, the destruction of the fairest valleys the sun ever shone upon by placer and hydraulic mining? Have we not seen in Minnesota and Wisconsin the mightiest forests that ever raised head to the sky slashed to pieces by the axe and turned into a waste of tree-stumps and fallen timber? Have we not seen the Upper Mississippi, by the destruction of the forests, changed from a broad, majestic river into a shallow, muddy stream; and the beautiful prairies of Dakota turned under by the plough and then allowed to run to weeds? Men must have coal though they ruin the valleys and blacken the streams of Pennsylvania, they must have oil though they disfigure half of Ohio and Indiana, they must have copper if they wreck all the mountains of Montana and Arizona, and they must have gold though they blow Alaska into the Bering Sea. It is more than possible that the "practical men" have gained much practice and many dollars by flaying the fair face of these United States. They have stripped the land of its robes of beauty, and what have they given in its place? Weeds, wire fences, oil-derricks, board shanties and board towns—things

---

EARLY DIME NOVEL COWBOY HERO, 1887

There were earlier completely fictive cowboy heroes in dime novel titles, like P. Ingraham's Cowboy Captain; or, The Mysterious Ranchero, A Romance of Wild Life in Texas, Feb. 7, 1882 *(Half Dime Library, No. 237). The novels like this about Buck Taylor and the publicity for Buffalo Bill's Wild West helped change the old reputation of cowboys as ruffians. The cowboy hero in Beadle novels doesn't punch cattle but fights Mexicans, Indians, and bandits. In this one, the story begins after Buck's cowboy days and relates his adventures as a Texas Ranger. The novel includes a long excerpt from "a New York paper," which refers to Buck's "genial qualities" and characterizes him as "amiable as a child."* (COURTESY OF THE HENRY E. HUNTINGTON LIBRARY.)

that not even a "practical man" can do less than curse at. And
at last they have turned to the desert.[26]

Westerns offered visions of deserts and mountains even before minority
owners flayed the fair face of America. The author of the dime novel *Buck
Taylor, King of the Cowboys* (1887) presents thrilling adventures of the
cowboy turned ranger in the wide-open plains and arroyos of southwest
Texas. The author doesn't seem to know much about the real landscape
and geography there, but he invents lots of conventional natural background for wild rides through regions "infested with Mexican raiders." For
a honeymoon the Virginian took his bride on a camping trip to the mountains, to "another world," where, "the traces of men passing from sight,"
"no hand but nature's had sown these crops of yellow flowers, these willow
thickets and tall cottonwoods." Zane Grey achieved his popularity partly
by including in his stories lengthy descriptions of the mountains and deserts
of the Southwest. In *Riders of the Purple Sage*, Venters takes his wounded
sweetheart to recover in Surprise Valley, where they live like Adam and
Eve in the Garden of Eden; they are the first residents since the departure
of the ancient cliff dwellers: "Around the red perpendicular walls, except
under the great arc of stone, ran a terrace fringed at the cliff-base by silver
spruces; below that first terrace sloped another wider one densely over-
grown with aspens, and the center of the valley was a level circle of oaks
and alders, with the glittering green line of willows and cottonwoods dividing it in half. Venters saw a number and variety of birds flitting among
the trees." Grey devotes a good proportion of his pages to such plodding
descriptions, which evidently please the reader who somehow wades through
them to experience this world vicariously. (Significantly for the relation of
civilization and the wilderness in Westerns, after Venters and Bess leave
Surprise Valley, Lessiter and Jane, the other couple in the story, having
found the outside world too much for them, seal themselves up with rock,
presumably forever, in this secret sylvan paradise.)

Early one- and two-reel Westerns were filmed mainly outside in Niles
Canyon and then in the Santa Monica Mountains, not only because shooting outdoors without sets and artificial lights was cheap but because there
was a market for movie worlds of rocks and canyons and chaparral. Bronco
Billy's movies filmed in California appealed more than the Westerns still
being made in the East on phony-looking painted sets. The people's appetite for images of the wilderness contributed to the movie industry's
migration to the West. The hundreds of posses pursuing hundreds of bandit
gangs through the same dozen or so southern California canyons please
us not only by the excitement of the chase and the skill of the horsemanship

An early Hollywood rider reported that to film a chase the director would run a single posse of cowboys through a canyon shooting toward the front, then the other way over the same course shooting toward the rear, and splice and edit the resulting footage.

but because of the beauty of those dusty landscapes. We delight in the adventures of Red Ryder and Little Beaver, not only because we know Red will trick the bad guys with the last-minute help of his spunky Navajo friend but because we delight in the authentic pictures Harmon draws of rivers and plains and mountains around southwest Colorado. Even on the radio we take pleasure in the sounds of nature, like crickets and running streams, in the adventures of the Lone Ranger.

Popular Westerns take the wilderness for granted as part of the mythic world they project—Westerns set in the twentieth century are not so complacent but comment on its destruction: Edward Abbey in all his fiction blames paved roads and unneccessary machinery and other forms of pollution; Peckinpah attacks land development (*Junior Bonner*) and roadside tourist attractions (*Ballad of Cable Hogue*). He even interjects little lessons on littering. In the moralistic *Ride the High Country*, Steve Judd (Joel McCrea), the old lawman, tells his young companion who has discarded a food wrapper: "Pick it up, son—this mountain doesn't need your trash."

We have been discussing popular Westerns, that is, those whose stories are supposed to have taken place during the cowboy era. Many recent Westerns are about twentieth-century cowboys, or vaguely cowboy-types, after the closing of the frontier: *Lusty Men* (1952), *J. W. Coop* (1972), *Junior Bonner* (1972), and *When Legends Die* (1972)—all rodeo Westerns; *Hud* (1963) and its source, Larry McMurtry's *Horseman, Pass By*

(1961); *Lonely Are the Brave* (1962) and the Edward Abbey novel it was based on, *The Brave Cowboy* (1956); and Abbey's novel *Fire on the Mountain* (1962), also made into a television movie; and Abbey's futurist novel *Good News* (1980); Thomas McGuane's novel *Nobody's Angel* (1981) and his screenplay for *Rancho Deluxe* (1974); *The Misfits* (1960); John Wayne's last movie, *The Shootist* (1976); *Bad Day at Black Rock* (1954), *Tell Them Willie Boy Was Here* (1969), and *Electric Horseman* (1979). This list is by no means complete. Some critics call these modern stories "post Westerns," because they are set in times after the cowboy era. They are not shaped like popular Westerns at all, since they don't have to do with heroes fighting villains who threaten a community. But they all make the same statement: the modern West has been steadily going to hell. They all present a contrast between the implied heroic values of the popular Westerns (the myth of the cowboy era), which the creators of post Westerns assume correctly we all know, and the antiheroic Western life today. The important point is that both types of Westerns reject American society: one by offering an alternative to it, the other by realistic demonstration of its evil and by implied contrast to the better world of the popular myth.

When Hud, lounging behind the wheel of his Cadillac convertible, doesn't help the housekeeper with the groceries, we think instantly of the traditional cowboy's courtesy and solicitude toward women; his Cadillac is instantly recognized as a degenerate latter-day mount. The rustlers in a pickup truck in *Rancho Deluxe* cut up beeves with chain saws and buy dope and motorcycles with their loot. Modern America is indicted on various counts: for destruction of the wilderness (all of Abbey's novels); for lack of individualism and freedom because of intrusive government and technology (again, Abbey's novels and the movies made from them); antisocial selfishness and gross materialism (*Hud*); commercialism fostered by big business (*J. W. Coop* and *Electric Horseman*); and the decay of the old Western values of hard work, honesty, and manliness (Peckinpah's Westerns and McGuane's *Nobody's Angel*).

The very first story, or plotted, Western movie, *The Great Train Robbery*, presents the dynamics of the action that soon were to become standard. The train robbers tie up the stationmaster and rob the railroad passengers, killing one in the process and later flinging a trainman overboard during their flight; after the little girl discovers the crime at the station and the cowboys dancing and bullying a greenhorn at the saloon hear of it, the mood suddenly becomes serious; the cowboys form a posse and chase the outlaws, who have left the train up the line to flee on horseback; the ending is a shootout between the holed-up robbers and the besieging

HUD (1963)

Alma (Patricia Neal) and Hud Bannon (Paul Newman). Neal received an Oscar for her performance in this film. The on-location set in the background is the town of Claude, Texas, thirty miles southeast of Amarillo.

cowboys in which the heroes save the threatened community by killing the villains. For fifty years this remained the basic structure of the popular Western plot.

Bronco Billy Anderson did more than anyone else to establish the popular form with the almost five hundred one- and two-reelers he made in Niles Canyon. Since almost all of these very early movies are lost, we must study them from detailed synopses of the stories which appeared in a movie magazine. These show that there was a great deal of variety, many with other than cowboy heroes (like the Eastern tenderfoot making good), some with comic situations, and some, almost without plots, about rodeos and horse races. But most presented a cowboy hero who saved a threatened young woman or child. (The family had to symbolize the whole community because there was not yet the standard street set with its hitching posts, shops, and boardwalks.) The threat to the family can merely

THE GREAT TRAIN ROBBERY (1903): THE ALARM

This frame enlargement shows the telegraph operator seeking help from cowboys at the dancehall. Earlier he had been tied up by the bandits and then released by his little daughter.

THE GREAT TRAIN ROBBERY (1903): THE CHASE

A frame enlargement of the cowboys chasing the bandits through the New Jersey woods, the least convincing part of the one-reel movie because of bad riding and falls. The young industry had not yet learned to hire real cowboys as riders and stuntmen, but within five years all riders were cowboys.

be sickness, but most often a villain assaults a nester woman or seizes a nester family's holding. And the crime is always personally motivated and unrelated to social conflict. The hero who saves the woman or family is a good outlaw who reforms for the occasion, or an ordinary citizen cowboy who rises to it, or a sheriff or his deputy who does his duty. The hero's motive is usually love for the woman or the single mother of the child he saves, and he is often rewarded with marriage or at least prospects. What emerges from the wild rides of posses and individuals, already a staple ingredient, is a good guy saving a threatened representative of the community.[27] The form develops in subsequent silents and B Westerns and post–World War II feature and television Westerns: the hero becomes more chary of matrimony, the threatened community becomes larger, saloon shots become standard, a concluding duel-like throwdown becomes mandatory, at times (William S. Hart) the redemption of outlaws predominates, at others (Tom Mix) action scenes of chases and fights and escapes exclude psychological conflicts; but the basic structure remains remarkably the same—cowboy heroes on the side of threatened rural communities.

We can see the community-saving function of the hero by examining the standard Western plots. A well-known historian of Western movies conveniently presents ten standard plots based on the types of villainy the hero combats:

1.   The hero defeats an owner of a gambling/dance hall who tries to extend his influence over a frontier hell town by stage coach robberies, cattle rustling, or other illegal activities.

2.   He defeats a heavy who ruthlessly builds a vast business empire, usually cattle, at the expense of small settlers and townspeople.

3.   He defeats a villain who is sabotaging progress for his own purposes, like cutting telegraph lines to preserve his own stagecoach business or preserving lucrative lawlessness by dissuading citizens from voting for statehood.

4.   He defeats an outlaw gang by posing as a badman and joining them.

5.   He fights carpetbaggers and marauding guerrillas during Reconstruction in Texas.

6.   He exposes and brings to justice white traders and crooked agents who are selling liquor and guns to Indians or otherwise stirring them up.

7.   He escapes or returns from jail to prove his innocence by capturing the real perpetrator of the crime for which he was sent up.

8.   He ends a bloody family feud by capturing the villain who is encouraging it to his own advantage.

A SCENE FROM A BRONCO BILLY ANDERSON TWO-REELER, ABOUT 1912

This publicity still is of a scene from one of about five hundred short Westerns Anderson produced and directed in Niles Canyon, California (about thirty miles from Oakland), between 1910 and 1916. None of them is known to have survived. Anderson himself starred in most of them as Bronco Billy, thus establishing the Western star system, the Western series, and the Western as a genre or type. Here Bronco Billy (right) comes too late to the rescue of the woman (Josie Collins) supported by the sheriff (Arthur Mackley?). Her husband or brother lies dead on the floor. A pencilled note claims she is saying, "It was a couple of Chicago racketeers." Vic Potel, Harry Todd, and Fred Church are the cowboys in the rear.

9. He helps a group of good businessmen who are attempting to run a stagecoach or freight line or to get a contract to supply horses to the Army by defeating the purposes of a rival group of baddies using violence and illegal tricks to do the same thing.

10. He searches out and kills the man who killed his father, inevitably a villain who is a threat to a community.[28]

All the plots share in common heroes saving frontier communities from villains who are threatening them. Our cowboy hero champions the rural community we long for but can no longer find. This is the constant mythic center of the popular Western.

The hero may start off bad, but he always turns good to save the community. William S. Hart took this good/badman plot over from Bronco Billy Anderson and worked it so hard that his audience finally tired of it. In *Toll Gate* (1920), Hart as the good outlaw Black Deering flees toward Mexico after his gang is ambushed in what had been planned as their last mail-train robbery. During his flight, he stops in the tough town of Rincon, where he burns down the cantina of villain Jordan, who was the Judas who set the gang up and who now leads an evil pack of his Mexican followers in pursuit of Black Deering. (Deering's burning of the cantina is greeted—in subtitles—by townspeople as "helping us all," because wiping out Mexicans is "doing this country a big favor.") A sheriff's posse also is in pursuit. Just as Deering is about to ride to safety across the border, his horse breaks a leg; at the risk of exposing his location to the posse by the report, he mercifully shoots the injured animal. On foot, he again shows his goodness by interrupting his flight to rescue a child from drowning. The child's mother, who Deering later learns is the deserted wife of his enemy Jordan, reforms Deering completely by the example of her innocent domesticity; Deering goes to the rescue of the sheriff's posse, now besieged by Jordan's gang, and after being deputized to make it legal, kills Jordan. At the end we see Deering ride off to a lonely life in Mexico with the sheriff's blessings, after realizing that he must pay the price of his past at the toll gate of life by forfeiting the widow's proffered love and companionship. Besides the typical Hart sentimentality and shocking Western racism against Mexicans, we see the basic structure of the popular Western: a cowboy hero saves the community (the deserted mother and her child, the sheriff's posse, and the citizens of Rincon) from the menace of the villain and his gang, not through an act of personal revenge but for love and social responsibility.

In *Hell's Hinges* (1916), Hart as Blaze Tracey is a professional gunman in the employ of the villain Silk Miller, leader of the lawless cowboy element of the town named Hell's Hinges. The decent part of town has called a weak Eastern minister to preach in their new church, but Miller, his hired gun Blaze, and the saloon cowboys set their faces against this religious threat. The minister's pretty sister Faith instantly converts Blaze through her beauty and purity, and for the rest of the movie he resolutely defends the religious citizens against the villain and his antisocial crew, who nevertheless first humiliate the minister and then shoot him as they burn down the new church. Tracey, like an avenging angel, after averting an ambush, shoots Silk, sets fire to his saloon, and as the conflagration envelops the entire town, he and Faith move off toward the mountains, "whatever the future, theirs to share together." Although we may feel that our hero has been a bit carried away in his defense of the churchgoers in destroying, along with the iniquitous saloon, the whole town, he is nevertheless clearly converted to the side of the settled, decent community. So again for motives other than personal revenge or profit, the hero defends a threatened community.

Even in plots that are mere vehicles for the typical Western action, the community-saving myth provides the basic structure. Tom Mix, who took over from Hart as the most popular and productive Western hero and director in the twenties, made five-reel feature Westerns for Fox in which plotting is secondary to the stunting, fighting, coming to the rescue in surprising ways, trick riding, and lassoing. Mix chose his plots to facilitate his action-packed entertainment—he regularly wrote stunts into working scripts he thought deficient in that regard—but below the dust there is the popular Western structure of the strong hero saving a weak community from villainy. Mix himself described his favorite stories: "I ride into a place owning my own horse, saddle, and bridle. It isn't my quarrel, but I get into trouble doing the right thing for somebody else. When it's all ironed out, I never get any money reward. I may be made foreman of the ranch and I get the girl, but there is never a fervid love scene."[29] There is never any doubt whose side Mix is on, for he never drinks or swears or uses unnecessary violence and in fact becomes the precursor of the boring All American Boy singing Western hero of the thirties, typified by Gene Autry and Roy Rogers in their fancy cowboy uniforms. And since nature was spectacularly beautiful in Mix's Westerns because of his love of on-location shooting in national parks and the fine work of his cameraman, Daniel Clark, the audience satisfied its hunger for wilderness as well.

A systematic structural analysis of the most popular Western sound movies confirms the view of Westerns as fulfilling our longing for the lost community of preindustrial America. Will Wright, a perceptive sociologist, applied his "cognitive theory of myth structures" (mainly derived from

Claude Lévi-Strauss) to an analysis of the Western to determine "how its social meanings are communicated by its symbolism." Of the thirty-three highest-grossing Western movies from 1930 through 1955, almost all have what Wright calls "classical" plots or a modified form he calls "vengeance variation." This is "the prototype of all Westerns, the one people think of when they say, 'All Westerns are alike.' It is the story of the lone stranger who rides into a troubled town and cleans it up, winning the respect of the townsfolk and the love of the schoolmarm." *Shane* is, as Wright says, "the classic of the classic Westerns." With all its variations, the popular Western is, again in Wright's words, "the story of a hero who is somehow estranged from his society but on whose ability rests the fate of that society. The villain threatens the society until the hero acts to protect and save it." The movie almost always begins with "the hero coming into a social group, a fledgling society consisting of families and elderly people with a settled, domestic life." Looking for its social meaning, Wright sees in the standard plot of the popular Western a resolution of the underlying contradiction of the free-market, competitive society: the ideals of family and community (love, cooperation, support) on the one hand and the ideal of aggressive individualism (self-interest and self-sufficiency) on the other.[30] Wright sees the myth as a means by which we resolve the contradictions of our society, whereas the theory offered here claims that the myth offers the gratifications and benefits that the society we daily experience doesn't provide.

Before the mid-fifties, heroes bent on revenge were made to convert their personal mission to a community one before they kill the villain. This is a striking indication that Western heroes act for social, not personal, motives; that they serve threatened rural communities, not their own passions. Ringo (John Wayne) in *Stagecoach* gives up his purpose of avenging his father's death by killing the Plumber brothers in return for Dallas's promise to marry him. When he does in fact finally kill them, the shootout is presented as sanctioned by law, self-defense, and public service. Sometimes the avenging hero corners the murderer he seeks but, unable to shoot him in cold blood, leaves him to be killed by others; an example is Jimmy Stewart as Will Lockhard in Anthony Mann's *The Man from Laramie*. Stewart plays another of Anthony Mann's obsessed heroes in *The Naked Spur*, where he gives up his lust for revenge when a woman gives him her love. An avenger is lawless and thus outside the community. The common agent for bringing him back is a woman, appropriate since, beside her stereotyped role of the gentle tamer, she most fully represents and speaks for the settled family in a community. Jimmy Stewart in this case punishes himself by bounty hunting to get money to buy back a ranch his intended bride treacherously sold in his absence. He gives up this purpose in the end. Before the sixties it would have been shocking to see the hero as a bounty hunter. Such completely material and personal motives were inappropriate to a Western hero. Bounty hunters are out for personal gain and thus always villains and outside the community. Heroes always ended up pursuing social ends and using violence to benefit the community.

In the early days of television, Western heroes were also fighters for justice and the protectors of the weak. The series included *Roy Rogers* (with Trigger, his horse), *Gene Autry* (with Champion), *The Lone Ranger* (Clayton Moore as the hero; Jay Silverheels as Tonto, his sidekick; and Silver, his horse), *Hopalong Cassidy* (William Boyd as the hero and Topper, his horse), *The Cisco Kid* (Pancho, his sidekick, and Diablo, his horse). All of these popular television series, largely skewed to juvenile audiences, came from movie and radio series and had their comic strip and comic book versions and often a breakfast cereal tie-in; they featured the hero's horse as a principal actor; the heroes all had sidekicks, several of whom were racist stereotypes; and, more to the point, all the heroes fought bad guys threatening communities. They often lived outside the formal law, especially Cisco and Pancho, but they always implemented an unwritten code of justice that served an imperiled community of ordinary people. A husband-wife team of television Western critics, who themselves were adolescent fans of these series, write:

> The early TV Western hero has a mission to perform—to right whatever wrongs he may come across. *The Lone Ranger* is perhaps the most explicit about this vision. The Ranger is not only a knight errant, he is the cutting edge of civilization, for by setting things right he encourages the conditions that bring more settlers and towns. One of the early shows contains the description of the Ranger as "a man whose presence brought fear to the lawless and hope to those who wanted to make this frontier land their home." In a 1953 episode entitled "Hidden Fortune" the Ranger says, "Unsolved crimes are a double threat to order and progress in the West. It encourages other men to break the law."[31]

The Westerns we have been considering may be what Wright calls "classic" but to most fans they seem old-fashioned. They flourished for more than half a century, but in the last two decades or so popular Westerns have changed fundamentally. By the late fifties they began emphasizing older, occasional tendencies that soon led to a basically new kind of Western. The change was not, of course, sudden. It slowly gathered together specimens and subtypes recurrent over decades to blend into an entirely different Western. The old outlaw doesn't reform but ends up as he began, outside society. The avenger doesn't give up his purpose. The corrupt town doesn't have a decent faction worth saving. The hero of the New Western is out for himself or for others like himself in an isolated or elite group. He performs with style and skill because of the pleasure he derives from the performance itself, because his professional duty requires it, because of private motives of self-fulfillment or satisfaction, or because of commitment to a primitive community of peasants, most decidedly not the mainstream frontier town, the now alien element in which the hero moves. Usually his allegiance is only to himself. Sometimes his loyalty extends to an elite group of other professionals who come together briefly to protect an isolated community or family of foreigners or outcasts. Most commonly his motive is, simply, money. For the first time heroes are often bounty hunters (for instance, Clint Eastwood in Leone's *Dollar* movies, 1966), the trade which was always the very mark of villainy in traditional Westerns. The frontier community is either unimportant (*The Professionals*, 1966) or childishly bickering, shading into corrupt and malevolent, and not worth saving (*High Noon*, 1952) or allied with the villains and thus the object of the hero's hatred and scorn (*High Plains Drifter*, 1973).

The beginning of the change could be seen in a group of movies of the early fifties—*Broken Arrow* (1950), *High Noon* (1952), *Johnny Guitar* (1954)—where the heroes fight villains for reasons of personal ideals, not to save communities, which are shown as not worth the effort. The sociologist Will Wright, who first noted this departure and tendency, called this a "transition" plot to indicate its relation to the New Western, which emerged more fully developed a few years later.[32] There also developed a tendency in vengeance-type Westerns for the avenging hero to remain forever outside the community by reason of his unreformed lust for revenge (for instance, the audience is clearly intended to admire John Wayne in *The Searchers* (1956) for his monomaniacal and unrelenting vendetta against Comanches; *Nevada Smith* (1966) is another example, where the hero's single humane impulse is not to kill his third victim after he has permanently maimed him).

In television, the change to the New Western occurred strikingly with the rapid development of so-called adult series. Most had lawmen heroes, beginning with *Wyatt Earp* in 1955 and followed by *Lawman, Have Gun, Will Travel, Bat Masterson*, and several dozen more. In these the hero kills the villains out of professional, not social, duty. In another type, the society that is protected is the mobile group, not the settled frontier community. In *Wagon Train* (beginning in 1957), Ward Bond sees that his group of pioneers survives in a hostile world by iron control and authoritarian leadership. In *Rawhide* (beginning in 1959), Favor, the trail boss, with his ramrod, Clint Eastwood, moves his herd on the trail by ruling his outfit absolutely. John Wayne had played this role of the trail boss over twenty years before in *Red River*, but, significantly, in those days his brutal authoritarianism transformed him into a villain and a threat to the outfit— whereas now Favor repeatedly is its salvation. In still another type of New Western we have what has been called "property Westerns," that is, those series popular in the sixties about rich families protecting their giant ranches from all kinds of threats and persuading the nearby community to settle down and accept the leadership of the big ranch owners. *Bonanza* was the first in 1959 (about the Ponderosa ranch in Nevada), and then came *The Big Valley* (Barbara Stanwyck's ranch in California), *The Virginian* (Wyoming), and *High Chaparral* (Arizona). *The Virginian* (later called *The Men from Shiloh*) we can hope was the last gasp of Wister's novel; in one episode the hero, still the ranch foreman, conquers a nester for his boss, not by lynching him as he did in the original, but by convincing him to become an organization man and join the association![33] Again, heroes in property Westerns do not save threatened frontier communities but their own property and family interests. Some Western series—*Gunsmoke* (1955), *Laramie* (1959)—had aspects of all three of these varieties of TV New Westerns (lawman, trail group, property), as well as aspects of the traditional Western.

Of the thirty-one top-grossing Western movies from 1956 to 1972, Will Wright classified two-thirds of them as "professional," a classification he did not need for earlier movies, and which he formulated to account for the New Western. Some better-known examples of these are *Rio Bravo* (1959), *Four for Texas* (1964), *The Professionals* (1966), *El Dorado* (1967), *True Grit* (1969), *Chisum* (1970), and *Rio Lobo* (1971)—all but the second and third are, of course, John Wayne movies. Wright here describes the main features of the plot of this new type of movie Western, which predominates after the mid-fifties:

> The heroes are now professional fighters, men willing to defend society only as a job they accept for pay or for love of fighting, not from commitment to ideas of law and justice. As in the classical plot, society is portrayed as weak, but it is no longer seen as particularly good or desirable. The members of society are not unfair and cruel . . . they are simply irrelevant. The social values of love, marriage, family, peace, and business are things to be avoided, not goals to be won. As a result, the relations of the heroes, or of the villains, with society are minimal. Society exists as a ground for the conflict, an excuse for fighting, rather than as

a serious option as a way of life. . . . How the fight is fought is now the crucial issue, since the fight itself generates the values that replace the values of the society in the myth. . . . The social values of justice, order, and peaceful domesticity have been replaced by a clear commitment to strength, skill, enjoyment of the battle, and masculine companionship. . . . At the end of these films, when the fight is over, there is no sense of the heroes having won a new, peaceful way of life. Instead of marrying and settling down, they stay together as a group in order to maintain the relationships created by the fight. In some sense their victory has made a new and meaningful life possible, but this new way of life involves a special masculine society separate from, independent of, and a little better than the ordinary society of families and businesses.[34]

It follows that, in the plot of the New Western, women no longer represent civilization nor quarrel with their heroes about violence. Since the community is not important, neither are women in the New Western; occasional exceptions are members of the fighting group, who share the values of the heroes.

The New Western movies of John Wayne, although all "professional," according to Wright's classification, constitute a special subtype which it seems appropriate to call fascist Westerns: all involve an elite group of male mercenaries under the military discipline of an authoritarian leader whose purpose is to kill an army of villains for personal, not social, reasons. Besides the four New Western top-grossers just mentioned, there are *The Alamo* (1960), *The Comancheros* (1961), *Sons of Katie Elder* (1965), *The War Wagon* (1967), *Big Jake* (1971), *The Cowboys* (1972), *The Train Robbers* (1973), and *Cahill, United States Marshal* (1973). In almost all of his New Westerns, Wayne plays the role he inaugurated in his first Howard Hawks movie, *Red River*—the dictatorial leader of a male group of warriors—a role he expanded in the three later Hawks-Wayne movies (*Rio Bravo*, *Rio Lobo*, *El Dorado*) about male bonding and reforming drunks. A student of popular culture writes that these John Wayne Westerns show "the return of the rugged individual" and deal with an aging hero whose "day seems over but who embarks upon one more heroic quest or battle." The quest has a seeming moral purpose (in *True Grit* a marshal is employed by a woman to bring in the murderer of her father; in *Big Jake* the hero seeks to recover his grandchild kidnapped by outlaws; in *Chisum* an old cattle baron combats thieves bent on stealing his empire). But "the air of morality seems more like a ritual than a reality, a cloak for

naked aggression, rather than the reluctant violence of the heroes" of the
traditional Westerns. The more peaceful and less aggressive young members of Wayne's posses seem inadequate to overcome alone the evil they
confront, and at the end society is no better or any less threatened.

> Society is usually represented as weak and corrupt; its agencies,
> like posses and armed forces, are given to impulsive and ineffi-
> cient violence which is more likely to bring on further innocent
> suffering than to establish true justice. Because society is violent
> and corrupt, the only solution lies in the private action of a good
> leader who is able to overcome the outlaw's evil aggression and
> society's own endemic violence and corruption by superior ruth-
> lessness and power of his own. . . . The fantasied solution is to
> fall back on the Godfather—or, in the case of the western, on
> the grandfather, Big Jake—and to create under his absolute au-
> thority a close-knit small group, like a family, which in return for
> absolute loyalty will protect its members.[35]

In *The Shootist* (1976) Wayne left his fascist Western behind and went
out gloriously for the last time as the hero of a traditional Western story:
the community is not much threatened by the antisocial villains in the
saloon, but Wayne, an old gunfighter dying of cancer, chooses to go out
with style by wiping them out.

We are invited in the fascist Westerns of John Wayne to seek our survival
in small groups of disciplined warriors led by authoritarians. In the Italian
Westerns of Sergio Leone, those that became popular in America—*A
Fistful of Dollars* (made in 1964, released in 1966), *For a Few Dollars
More* (1966), *The Good, the Bad, and the Ugly* (1967), and *My Name Is
Nobody* (Leone produced, Henry Fonda starred, 1973)—and in the American imitations of them—*Hang 'Em High* (1967) and *High Plains Drifter*
(1973)—we are invited to go it absolutely alone in a dark and treacherous
world. The critic of popular culture who characterized the New Westerns
of John Wayne has this to say of the Leone-Eastwood Italian type:

> Their ostensible heroes are marked not by moral purpose and
> righteous courage, but by superior stratagems, unscrupulousness,
> and skill in violence. Their style . . . is one of supreme detachment
> and coolness. Eastwood as "the man with no name"—an ano-
> nymity which underlines his lack of human feeling and motive—
> performs his most violent deeds without a quiver of his charac-
> teristic cigarillo or a ripple of his serape. His role in a number of
> the films is that of bounty hunter, the man who kills with no

personal interest but the monetary reward—a despicable occupation in the moral universe of the traditional western. If the hero
has any motive beyond money, it is usually to perform some
terrible revenge for a long-past deed, a revenge which commonly
seems more like a dehumanizing obsession than a justifiable moral
purpose.

These movies show us "a world that seems to deserve whatever violence
can be wreaked upon it. Because the world is violent, treacherous, and
corrupt, the moral man is the one who can use violence, treachery, and
corruption most effectively. The chief thing that differentiates hero from
villain is the hero's coolness and lack of violent emotion."[36] It is significant
that when Leone made a Western to celebrate, and perhaps lovingly to
parody, the spirit of the whole tradition, *Once Upon a Time in the West*
(1969), for this once, while preserving his baroque camera and art work,
he returned to the traditional story of (1) the weak but desirable frontier
community (the McBain family ranch and then the widow's new railroad
town) threatened by (2) a consummate villain (the outlaw Frank, played
by Henry Fonda) and (3) defended by good heroes, one out for justifiable
revenge, the other for love (The Man, Charles Bronson; Cheyenne, Jason
Robards), together saving the community.

If we see the essentials of the New Western as a nonsocial concern for
individual and small-group survival in a hostile environment, we can see
that there are, of course, other mass media stories and dramas that show
and foster this tendency of mass consciousness. The cop movies and TV
shows, where elite groups of alienated males combat the mob and Black
and Latino gangs for professional pride, and where the community and
government offer more opposition to their work than do the criminals—
civil rights bleeding hearts, hysterical neighborhood mothers, interfering
feds and internal security forces, and corrupt supervisors and city coun-
cilmen. Urban Dirty Harry–type vigilantes, usually Clint Eastwood or Charles
Bronson, who do the job of killing thugs that the police can't or won't.
Mafia families under the ruthless leadership of the godfather or the mob
boss presented in movies and television shows in admiring and attractive
ways. Green Beret and soldier-of-fortune movies and novels. Galactic
adventures where spacecraft crews survive attacks by evil aliens through
skill and teamwork under strong leadership.

The New Western is just one among all these new mass media stories
and dramas reflecting and fostering a striking and important change in
American mass consciousness. It differs from them only in that, unlike,
say, cop and space shows, it alone emerges from an old popular tradition,

venerable with age, which continues to survive in the occasional appearance of fairly pure specimens (*The Shootist, Comes a Horseman*) and with
traces of the old structure in the new form and which may in the future
arise once again to displace in modified form what will then prove to have
been an aberrant type. It is instructive to speculate about the social causes
of changes that occurred in this oldest and most important of American
popular myths.

The transformation from the half-century-old traditional cowboy hero
as protector of the community to the new cowboy hero out just for himself
or his elite group occurred as the pulp Western magazines and such slick
outlets as *Colliers* folded. With them went the Western short story. But at
about the same time, first-publication paperback Western novels appeared
and flourished and the enormous popularity of television Westerns grew.
So the shift affected and reflected the interests and values of, if anything,
a proportionately larger audience for Westerns than at any time before.

Economically the changeover coincided with the prosperous boom years
stimulated for a time by arms and space production. Yet this prosperity
was accompanied by a growing sense of powerlessness. Since the gigantic
corporations, the government, and the media increasingly seemed to take
charge, people developed a deep and helpless resentment to whatever
was organized, big, and sanctioned. This hostility would explain the individualist, antisocial features of the New Western. Ideologically, the
changeover coincided with a time of fear caused by the Cold War—fear
of internal enemies during the McCarthy witch hunts and of nuclear holo-
caust after the Berlin Wall and Cuban missile crises. This Cold War and
nuclear dread explains the New Western's emphasis on individual and
small group survival in a dangerous world of enemies. This attitude was
manifested later in the go-it-alone groups within the youth and antiwar
movements, the greening-of-America communalists in Vermont, and the
Weatherman invasion of Chicago. There was also pressure from inside
the movie and TV industry, now that it had the power radically to alter
the old form. The pressure came, not from any master plan, but from
politically conservative producers who used Westerns to embody their own
views. Now that the two giants of the mass culture industry were in control,
producers had the power to change the myth completely, eliminating the
cooperative and supportive social virtues and glorifying the aggressive,
individualist ones.

But the reactions of a growing mass audience against giant institutions
and to the Cold War and the emergence of media giants only partially
account for the New Western. After half a century, the old dream of
community and nature as a fantasy substitute for an unfulfilling and in-

jurious society no longer seemed to satisfy or have much reality. We are not, after all, going to get back to that vital community of flesh and blood friends and enemies on the edge of the wilderness. After a long while the dream wears thin. In fact, our social surroundings are worse, more antagonistic to human life, and take us farther away from that lost ideal for which we long. It becomes increasingly difficult to fool ourselves. As the discrepancy between the mythic and the real world widens, and as time goes on to prove their permanent separation, we lose our faith in the possibilities of attaining the ideal and look about for new ways of surviving. In the first half of this century we fulfilled our needs in our fantasies of living in a preindustrial Western community set on the edge of the wilderness. But we have lost our hope of attaining that populist world of independent producers in traditional communities among desert mountains and plains. And we have substituted fantasies of survival in hostile worlds closer to those of the present and the probable future. We now identify with lone heroes surviving in contemporary and futurist settings by the skillful and ruthless and often lawless pursuit of self-interest and with heroes in elite professional groups surviving by teamwork and strong leadership among enemies in inner-city melees or Third World or intergalactic wars.

We still long for community and nature—and we always will. But for the past two decades or so we have not had a living myth of the frontier. The old settings and conventions, used to project new hopes and fears in the New Western, seem on the way out. Despite many attempts, there hasn't been a financially successful Western movie for twenty years, and the recent attempts to bring back television Western series (*Maverick* and *Best of the West*) have not lasted long. Louis L'Amour and a few others continue to produce and sell paperbacks, but their audience is relatively small and probably composed mostly of those Americans who mainly supported the successful comic Western TV series of the mid-sixties (*Petticoat Junction*) and who continue to cling to the old myth by subscribing to nostalgic magazines of Western historical trivia like *True West*. The New Western arose because the moving forces in the culture industry saw that we no longer could persuade ourselves that the experience of community on the frontier was an alternative to our real lives. It is dying because the values and dynamics that replaced the old ones in the myth seem more real and attainable in contemporary and future dramatic settings. Where is the popular story that can allow us to experience community and nature? Perhaps the traditional Western will make a return to serve that function, but there are no signs on the horizon. Well, maybe a small glow. The Lone Ranger returns as Kemosabe to make a most gratifying nighttime rescue of a fine anarchist in a glorious Western novel, Edward Abbey's *The*

Monkey Wrench Gang (1975), which is about a dedicated squad of en-
vironmental Luddites out to stop big business and the government from
further destroying the deserts of the Southwest.

The cowboy still lives in America, but he has lost his connection with a
storied, living myth. Without a popular story or mythic function, he becomes just fashion, life-style, or public relations image—a commodity.
Cowboys in an earlier time used their moral stature to sell cereal to kids;
now they use their style to sell jeans or tobacco or pickup trucks or beer
to adults. Since Willie Nelson's return to Texas, he has been creating for
himself an outlaw image. He plays an avenging outlaw in southwest Texas
in the recent movie *Barbarosa* (1983). Even when he doesn't play an
outlaw, he uses the image of himself as one to good effect, as when he
plays a driven wanderer in the story of a country-western singer in *Hon-
eysuckle Rose* (1981). He created a one-shot myth for a narrative sequence
of songs about a preacher turned outlaw, the "Red-Headed Stranger"
(1975), "wild in his sorrow," who shoots his wife and her lover in a saloon,
then shoots another woman who tries to steal his dead wife's bay, which
he trails behind him as a memento, and drifts around for eternity in his
dangerous, lonely misogyny, "ridin' and hidin' his pain." Such bizarre
creations result from image-building without the restraints of the popular
myth of cowboys, now dead or moribund these twenty years.

Without the guidance of storied myth and as a variant of the outlaw
ideal, cowboys now embody male fantasies and self-justifications, like the
lonely wanderer without family responsibilities, the doomed loser in romantic flight from some hidden hurt or in endless quest of identity and a
dream. This image serves some of the open-road male longings that the
Beats exemplified and also reflects something of Zane Grey's restless, solitary
heroes popularized in comic book versions. Waylon Jennings's song "My
Heroes Have Always Been Cowboys" (1976) best portrays these "mod-
ern-day drifters" with "no place to stay," loving then leaving "the ladies,"
miserable with their "worn-out saddles and memories" and "sadly in
search of, and one step in back of, / Themselves and their slow-moving
dream." Released the same year, Ed Bruce's song "Mamas, Don't Let
Your Babies Grow Up to be Cowboys" presents essentially the same image
of the misunderstood wandering loner, also a powerful male fantasy, although the song ostensibly counsels more conventional careers. Why do
so many modern American males, even when we're not morosely drunk,
so eagerly identify with this sad cowboy? In flight from an unfulfilling society
that serves only minority needs, and lacking the traditional popular hero
who protects the weak, we find even the wanderings of this loser, antisocial
cowboy an attractive fantasy alternative to our real lives.

Politicians also use the cowboy image to sell themselves, especially that old version of it, the reactionary, no-nonsense superpatriot, always anti-intellectual, anti-bleeding-heart, racist, imperialist. Teddy Roosevelt was the first to use this image, with his warmongering recruiting of Rough Riders and in his mounted and costumed campaign appearances and reunions. Any resident of the West, particularly Texas and southern California, knows how politicians wear hats and boots and string ties to get votes. Right-wing cowboy entertainers, John Wayne being the most obvious example, campaign for reactionary cowboy politicians. There is a whole tradition of superpatriotic cowboy songs from before, during, and after World War II, beginning with Gene Autry's disgusting warning to immigrant radicals, "Don't Bite the Hand That's Feeding You"; followed by Elton Britt's "There's a Star Spangled Banner Waving Somewhere," which sold a million and a half copies during the year after the U.S. entry into the war; then, a year after that, Zeke Clements's and Earl Nunn's "Smoke on the Water," updated in the sixties by Cowboy Copas to attack the Soviet Union and Cuba; and finally Montana Slim's prowar "A Mother's Son in Vietnam."[37] There must be a less warlike and more tolerant image that populist and left-Democratic cowboy politicians, particularly in Texas, cultivate (son of the earth and the working class, a friend of women and the poor, including Chicanos and blacks), but the political image of the cowboy most of us know is reactionary. As this book has shown, the reactionary cowboy does not reflect most working cowboys in the last century, nor most media cowboys in this one.

United States Representative Clint Roberts of South Dakota best illustrates the politician who cultivates the superpatriotic cowboy image. He went to a professional image maker in Denver, the president of I. F. Images, to help him. Since he looks like the Marlboro Man, he tried out for that role (but he didn't beat out the regular star, Darrell Winfield). He appeared as a cowboy in a 1974 television beer commercial (with Telly Savalas), has had small roles in television and regular Western movies, and is a director of the South Dakota Cowboy and Western Hall of Fame. Helped by his cowboy image, he went to Congress in 1981 wearing a large belt buckle, snakeskin boots, and a pin-striped Western-cut suit, and in a personal visit presented Ronald Reagan with a Stetson (white, for good guy) embossed in gold with the President's name inside the brim. He doesn't make the old cowboy-cowman distinction and thinks of himself as the former in spite of his 4,000-acre ranch. In an interview he said: "Being a cowboy is not something I get up and put on in the morning. A cowboy is what I am, and I'm confident with my image, because cowboys are great people. . . . The basic philosophy of the cowboy is what built America. A day's work for a day's pay. Integrity. Caring for the land and all that God created. Freedom and opportunity. A clean life." He serves on the Advisory Board of Directors of Young Americans for Freedom. Clint Roberts puts the superpatriotic aspects of Tom Mix, Gene Autry, and John Wayne to the service of his radical-right politics. He said soon after his arrival in Washington that "America is returning to the fundamentals on which it was founded and entering a new Era of the Cowboy."[38]

But our Western myth cannot effectively serve simple reaction, although its complexity encourages public-relations people to select from it for short-term and limited purposes. Its most important hero, the cowboy, dispossessed for a quarter century and turned into a commodity, will have to return to his source to survive as a social force in our collective consciousness. That source, the full Western myth, embodies, with changing emphases, all our contradictions, our fears and conflicting wishes: longings for wilderness, fears of progress and civilization; longings for personal control, fears of inexorable forces and faceless relations; individualism pulling one way, community the other; aggressive personal power against social compassion for the weak; macho violence against systematic, democratic justice; control of women and people of color against equality; personal against cooperative survival. This popular consciousness and the culture it expresses cannot for long be made to serve minority interests.

NOTES

Chapter 1: Cowboys and Cowmen

1. First used as an epigraph by Harry E. Chrisman, *The Ladder of Rivers: The Story of I. P. (Print) Olive* (1962).

2. For the history of this Southern, Anglo cattle business, see Terry G. Jordan, *Trails to Texas: Southern Roots of Western Cattle Ranching* (1981).

3. Dana Coolidge, *Old California Cowboys* (1939), pp. 148–50.

4. Charles Siringo, *Riata and Spurs* (1927), p. 132.

5. E. C. Abbott and Helena Huntington Smith, *We Pointed Them North* (1939, reference here to 1955 ed.), p. 112.

6. John Clay, *My Life on the Range* (1924, references here to Antiquarian Press, 1961), p. 304.

7. Abbott and Smith, *We Pointed Them North*, pp. 7–8.

8. Siringo, *Riata and Spurs*, p. 25.

9. John A. Lomax, *Cowboy Songs and Other Frontier Ballads* (1910, references here to 1936 reprint), p. 247.

10. Ibid., p. 18.

11. Ibid., p. 230.

12. Abbott and Smith, *We Pointed Them North*, pp. 211, 101, 102.

13. Siringo, *Riata and Spurs*, p. 36.

14. Diana S. Cary, *Hollywood Posse* (1975), p. 166.

15. Siringo, *Riata and Spurs*, p. 118.

16. Abbott and Smith, *We Pointed Them North*, pp. 7, 40.

17. J. Frank Dobie, *A Vaquero of the Brush Country* (1929, references here to 1957 ed.), p. 91; and J. Marvin Hunter, ed., *The Trail Drivers of Texas* (vol. 1, 1920; vol. 2, 1923; reference here to rev. ed. in one volume, 1925, Antiquarian Press, 1963), p. 438.

18. Charles Siringo, *A Texas Cowboy* (1885, reference here to 1966 ed.), p. 78.

19. J. Frank Dobie, *Cow People* (1964), p. 222.

20. Hunter, *Trail Drivers of Texas*, p. 378.

21. Ibid., pp. 230–31, 568.

22. John M. Hendrix, *The Cattleman* (February 1936), p. 24.

23. A. S. Gillespie, *The Cattleman* (June 1936), p. 32.

24. Ike Fridge, *History of the Chisum War, or Life of Ike Fridge* (Electra, Texas, n.d.).

25. Andy Adams, *The Outlet* (1905), p. 87.

26. Ike Blasingame, *Dakota Cowboy: My Life in the Old Days* (1964), p. 180.

27. Frederick Law Olmsted, *A Journey Through Texas* (1857), p. 163.

28. Dobie, *Vaquero*, pp. 59–62.

29. Andy Adams, *The Log of the Cowboy* (1903), ch. 12.

30. Adams, *The Outlet*, p. 168.

31. Hunter, *Trail Drivers of Texas*, p. 187.

32. Charles Siringo, *Cowboy Detective* (1912), p. 133.

33. Abbott and Smith, *We Pointed Them North*, pp. 150, 102.

34. Olmsted, *Journey Through Texas*, p. 163.

35. Unpublished typescript of the diary of Michael Erskine in Witte Memorial Museum, San Antonio, p. 11.

36. Abbott and Smith, *We Pointed Them North*, p. 109.

37. "The Trail to Mexico," "Wild Rovers," "The Range Riders," in Lomax, *Cowboy Songs*, pp. 134, 383, 269.

38. Abbott and Smith, *We Pointed Them North*, p. 106.

39. Hunter, *Trail Drivers of Texas*, p. 334.

40. Adams, *Log*, ch. 10.

41. Abbott and Smith, *We Pointed Them North*, p. 23.

42. Adams, *Log*, ch. 21.

43. Abbott and Smith, *We Pointed Them North*, p. 24.

44. Hunter, *Trail Drivers of Texas*, p. 573.

45. All three excerpts from Clifford P. Westermeier, "The Cowboy in His Home State," *Southwestern Historical Quarterly* 58 (October 1954), pp. 218–34.

46. Siringo, *Cowboy Detective*, p. 319.

47. Siringo, *Riata and Spurs*, p. 59.

48. Westermeier, "Cowboy in His Home State," p. 222.

49. Nannie Tiffany Alderson and Helena Huntington Smith, *A Bride Goes West* (1942, references here to 1969 ed.), pp. 72–73.

50. Dobie, *Vaquero*, p. 99.

51. Abbott and Smith, *We Pointed Them North*, pp. 212–13, 8.

52. J. Frank Dobie, *Prefaces* (1975), p. 11.

53. Cary, *Hollywood Posse*, pp. 207–10.

54. Abbott and Smith, *We Pointed Them North*, pp. 212, 87.

55. Eugene Manlove Rhodes, "The Cowboy: His Cause and Cure," in *The Sunny Slopes of Long Ago*, Wilson M. Hudson and Allen Maxwell, eds. (1966), pp. 27–32.

56. Larry McMurtry, *In a Narrow Grave* (1968), p. 168.

57. Coolidge, *Old California Cowboys*, p. 73.

58. Theodore Roosevelt, *Ranch Life and the Hunting-Trail* (1915, references here to Bonanza 1978 ed.), p. 109.

59. Clifford P. Westermeier, *Who Rush to Glory: The Cowboy Volunteers of 1898* (1958), p. 34.

60. Theodore Roosevelt, *Cowboys and Kings: Three Great Letters* (1954), p. 14.

61. Roosevelt, *Ranch Life*, pp. 108–9.

62. *Ibid.*, pp. 55–56.

Chapter 2: Cowboys as Workers

1. By cowboy Kid White, reprinted in *Folklore of the Great West*, John Greenway, ed. (1969), pp. 200–201.

2. J. Marvin Hunter, ed., *The Trail Drivers of Texas* (vol. 1, 1920; vol. 2, 1923; reference here to rev. ed. in one volume, 1925, Antiquarian Press, 1963), p. 120.

3. Hunter, *Trail Drivers of Texas*, p. 121.

4. J. Frank Dobie, *A Vaquero of the Brush Country* (1929, references here to 1957 ed.), pp. 194–95.

5. Article by Andy Adams (1905) reprinted in *The Sunny Slopes of Long Ago*, Wilson M. Hudson and Allen Maxwell, eds. (1966), p. 38.

6. E. C. Abbott and Helena Huntington Smith, *We Pointed Them North* (1939, references here to 1955 ed.), pp. 137–38.

7. William W. Savage, ed., *Cowboy Life: Reconstructing an American Myth* (1975), p. 148; Joseph McCoy, *Historic Sketches of the Cattle Trade* (1874), p. 137.

8. Charles Siringo, *Riata and Spurs* (1927), p. 53.

9. Andy Adams in article reprinted in Hudson and Maxwell, *Sunny Slopes*, pp. 35–36.

10. Abbott and Smith, *We Pointed Them North*, p. 63.

11. Andy Adams, *The Outlet* (1905), p. 31.

12. Abbott and Smith, *We Pointed Them North*, pp. 64–66.

13. Wallace Stegner, *Wolf Willow* (1966), p. 152.

14. Dobie, *Vaquero*, p. 99.

15. Hunter, *Trail Drivers of Texas*, p. 70.

16. Siringo, *Riata and Spurs*, pp. 68, 24.

17. Lewis Nordyke, *Great Roundups: The Story of Texas and Southwestern Cowmen* (1955), pp. 179–80.

18. Adams, in Hudson and Maxwell, *Sunny Slopes*, p. 35.

19. James Emmit McCauley, *A Stove-Up Cowboy's Story* (1965), p. 72.

20. Ibid., pp. 17–18.

21. Clifford P. Westermeier, *Trailing the Cowboy: His Life and Love as Told by Frontier Journalists* (1955, reference here to 1978 ed.), pp. 94–106.

22. Gene M. Gressley, *Bankers and Cattlemen* (1966, references here to Bison 1971 ed.), p. 107.

23. Jimmy M. Skaggs, *The Cattle-Trailing Industry* (1973), p. 10.

24. Andy Adams, *The Log of a Cowboy* (1903), ch. 4.

25. McCoy, *Historic Sketches*, p. 268.

26. Siringo, *Riata and Spurs*, p. 29.

27. Skaggs, *Cattle-Trailing Industry*, p. 96.

28. Gressley, *Bankers and Cattlemen*, pp. 39–61.

29. McCoy, *Historic Sketches*, p. 238.

30. Harold L. Oppenheimer, *Cowboy Arithmetic: Cattle as an Investment* (1961), pp. 59–60.

31. Skaggs, *Cattle-Trailing Industry*, p. 75.

32. John Lomax, "Cowboy Lingo," in Hudson and Maxwell, *Sunny Slopes*, p.18.

33. Charles Siringo, *A Texas Cowboy* (1885, references here to University of Nebraska Press ed., 1966), p. 45.

34. Theodore Roosevelt, *Ranch Life and The Hunting-Trail* (1915, references here to Bonanza 1978 ed.), pp. 8, 47.

35. Louis Pelzer, *The Cattleman's Frontier, 1850–1890* (1936), p. 73.

36. Gressley, *Bankers and Cattlemen*, p. 42.

37. Oppenheimer, *Cowboy Arithmetic*, p. 71.

38. Dobie, *Vaquero*, p. 106.

39. John L. McCarty, *Maverick Town: The Story of Old Tascosa* (1946), p. 83.

40. Ibid.

41. Gressley, *Bankers and Cattlemen*, pp. 222–23.

42. Ibid., pp. 233ff, 259.

43. Harvey Braverman, *Labor and Monopoly Capital* (1974), p. 65.

44. Kenneth Wiggins Porter, *The Negro on the American Frontier* (1970), p. 496.

45. Gressley, *Bankers and Cattlemen*, p. 151.

46. Stanley Lebergott, *Manpower in Economic Growth: The American Record Since 1800* (1964), p. 539.

47. McCoy, *Historic Sketches*, p. 11.

48. Pelzer, *Cattleman's Frontier*, p. 157.

49. Oscar (Jack) Flagg, "A Review of the Cattle Business in Johnson County," serialized in Buffalo (Wyo.) *Bulletin*, May 5–July 14, 1892, reference here to reprint, Arno Press, 1969), p. 15.

50. Pelzer, *Cattleman's Frontier*, p. 166.

51. Porter, *Negro on the American Frontier*, pp. 495, 511.

52. Lebergott, *Manpower*, pp. 530, 535.

53. Philip Foner, *History of the Labor Movement in the United States*, vol. 2 (1955), p. 20.

54. Clarence D. Long, *Wages and Earnings in the United States: 1860–1890* (1960), p. 51.

55. United States Bureau of the Census, *Historical Statistics of the United States, Colonial Times to 1957* (1960), pp. 68, 282, 72.

56. Foner, pp. 20, 248.

57. Flagg, "Review of the Cattle Business," p. 14.

58. Clifford P. Westermeier, "The Cowboy in His Own State," *Southwestern Historical Quarterly* 58 (October 1954), pp. 225–26.

59. The Rules are reproduced in full by J. Evetts Haley, *The XIT Ranch of Texas* (1929, references here to Oklahoma University Press ed., 1953), pp. 241–45.

60. *Texas Live Stock Journal* (organ of the Panhandle Livestock Association), October 21, 1882, and April 28, 1883, as quoted in Westermeier, *Trailing*, pp. 42–43, 129.

61. John Clay, *My Life on the Range* (1924, references here to Antiquarian Press ed., 1961), pp. 82, 83–84, 268–69, 307, 234, 123.

Chapter 3: Cowboys Fight Back

1. From "Freighting from Wilcox to Globe," in John Lomax, *Cowboy Songs* (1910, references here to 1936 reprint), p. 210.

2. *Atlantic Monthly* (January 1903), reprinted in *Frontier and Section, Selected Essays of Frederick Jackson Turner*, ed. R. A. Billington (1961), pp. 90–91.

3. C. Van Woodward, *Origins of the New South* (1972), pp. 108–9.

4. Lawrence Goodwyn, *The Populist Moment* (1978), p. 33.

5. Steven Hahn, "Hunting, Fishing, and Foraging: Common Rights and Class Relations in the Postbellum South," *Radical History Review* 26 (October 1982), pp. 55–57.

6. Bob Beverly, *The Cattleman* (May 1954), p. 60.

7. Lomax, *Cowboy Songs*, pp. 231, 60–61, 22, 92, 210.

8. Austin E. Fife and Alta S. Fife, *Cowboy and Western Songs* (1969), p. 90.

9. Lomax, *Cowboy Songs*, pp. 233, 237, 115.

10. Ibid., pp. 27, 149–50, 195, 96–97.

11. E. C. Abbott and Helena Huntington Smith, *We Pointed Them North* (1939, references here to 1955 ed.), pp. 28–29.

12. Charles Siringo, *A Texas Cowboy* (1885, reference here to University of Nebraska Press ed., 1966), p. 46.

13. J. Frank Dobie, *A Vaquero of the Brush Country* (1929, reference here to 1957 ed.), p. 108.

14. Will S. James, *Cowboy Life in Texas; or 27 Years a Maverick* (1893), pp. 63–66, 127.

15. Dobie, *Vaquero*, p. 108.

16. J. Marvin Hunter, ed., *The Trail Drivers of Texas* (vol. 1, 1920; vol. 2, 1923; reference here to rev. ed. in one volume, 1925, Antiquarian Press, 1963), p. 471.

17. Ibid., p. 784.

18. Chris Emmett, *Shanghai Pierce: A Fair Likeness* (1953), p. 74.

19. J. Evetts Haley, *The XIT Ranch of Texas* (1953), pp. 233–34.

20. Dobie, *Vaquero*, pp. 157–58.

21. Louis Pelzer, *The Cattleman's Frontier 1850–1890* (1936), p. 75.

22. B. A. Borroum interview by J. Evetts Haley, October 7, 1926, p. 3, in Panhandle-Plains Museum, Canyon, Texas.

23. Tom Lea, *The King Ranch* (1957), vol. 1, p. 328.

24. Siringo, *A Texas Cowboy*, pp. 113–14.

25. Bob Kennon, as told to Ramon F. Adams, *From the Pecos to the Powder: A Cowboy's Autobiography* (1965), p. 38.

26. David Montgomery, *Radical America*, vol. 12, no. 6 (1979), p. 9.

27. Siringo, *A Texas Cowboy*, p. 61.

28. James E. McCauley, *A Stove-Up Cowboy's Story* (1965), pp. 19–20.

29. Quoted in Don Walker, *Clio's Cowboys: Studies in the Historiography of the Cattle Trade* (1981), p. 101.

30. Gene M. Gressley, *Bankers and Cattlemen* (1966, references here to Bison ed. 1971), pp. 121–22.

31. Helena H. Smith, *The War on Powder River* (1966), p. 101.

32. Gressley, *Bankers and Cattlemen*, pp. 122–23.

33. Ibid., pp. 125–26 and note.

34. John Clay, *My Life on the Range* (1924, references here to Antiquarian Press edition, 1961), pp. 124–27.

35. Frederick R. Beckdolt, *Tales of the Old-Timers* (1924), p. 114.

36. Emmett, *Shanghai Pierce*, p. 56.

37. Charles Siringo, *Two Evil Isms: Pinkertonism and Anarchism* (1915), p. 100.

38. Hunter, *Trail Drivers of Texas*, p. 260.

39. Abbott and Smith, *We Pointed Them North*, p. 86.

40. Gressley, *Bankers and Cattlemen*, p. 123.

41. Charles Siringo, *Riata and Spurs* (1927), p. 200.

42. W. Henry Ingerton interview (April 3, 1927), p. 48, in Panhandle-Plains Museum, Canyon, Texas.

43. Smith, *War on Powder River*, p. 32.

44. Ibid.

45. Ruth Alice Allen, "A Cowboy Strike," p. 2, in volume on "Cowboys" of manuscript "History of Grazing in Texas," W.P.A. Project, 1935, Archives of the University of Texas.

46. *The Labor Enquirer* (Denver), December 6, 1884, December 26, 1885, and January 8, 1887.

47. Ibid., May 24, 1884, p. 3.

48. Ibid., May 1, 1886, p. 1, 3rd column.

49. Edward and Eleanor Marx Aveling, *The Working-Class Movement in America* (1891, reference here to Arno reprint, 1969), pp. 154–65; and Edward Aveling, *An American Journey* (1887), pp. 154–55.

50. *Labor Enquirer*, May 7, 1887, Supplement, p. 3, 2nd column.

51. Ibid., October 27, 1883.

52. John R. Commons, *History of Labour in the United States* (1918, reference here to 1966 reprint), vol. 2, p. 224 note.

53. Norman Ware, *The Labor Movement in the United States, 1860–1895: A Study in Democracy* (1929), p. 362.

54. Joseph R. Buchanan, *The Story of a Labor Agitator* (1903), p. 269.

55. Rosalyn Baxandall, L. Gordon, and S. Reverby, eds., *America's Working Women* (1976), pp. 82–84.

56. Ruth Alice Allen, *Chapters in the History of Organized Labor in Texas* (1942), p. 41.

57. Ruth Alice Allen, *The Great Southwest Strike* (1942), p. 23.

58. Allen, "A Cowboy Strike," p. 1.

59. Clay, *My Life on the Range*, p. 123.

60. Ibid., pp. 124–26.

61. Oscar (Jack) Flagg, "A Review of the Cattle Business in Johnson County," serialized in Buffalo (Wyo.) *Bulletin*, May 5–July 14, 1892, reference here to reprint edition, Arno Press, 1969, p. 15.

62. Smith, *War on Powder River*, pp. 32–33.

63. Fort Collins *Express*, in Clifford Westermeier, *Trailing the Cowboy* (1955, reference here to 1978 reprint), p. 130.

64. Smith, *War on Powder River*, p. 33.

65. John McCarty, *Maverick Town, The Story of Old Tascosa* (1946), pp. 107–15.

66. Lewis Nordyke, *Great Roundup: The Story of Texas and Southwestern Cowmen* (1955), pp. 110–11.

67. Robert Zeigler, "The Cowboy Strike of 1883: Its Causes and Meaning," *West Texas Historical Association Year Book*, vol. 47 (1971), pp. 37–38.

68. Allen, "A Cowboy Strike," p. 3.

69. Ingerton interview, p. 48, and Allen, *Chapters*, p. 36.

70. William H. Forbis, *The Cowboys* (Time-Life Books, The Old West Series, 1973), p. 128.

71. Allen, *Chapters*, p. 38.

72. Jack Potter, *The Lead Steer and Other Tales* (1939), pp. 31–33.

73. Ibid., p. 30.

74. McCarty, *Maverick Town*, pp. 123–24.

75. Allen, *Chapters*, pp. 38, 40.

76. Elmer Kelton, *The Day the Cowboys Quit* (1971), p. 102.

77. Elmer Kelton, "Converting History into Fiction," *West Texas Historical Association Year Book*, vol. 48 (1972), pp. 93–94.

78. Dulcie Sullivan, *The LS Brand: The Story of a Panhandle Ranch* (1968), pp. 69–70.

79. Zeigler, "Cowboy Strike," pp. 32–46.

Chapter 4: Cowboys as Homesteaders

1. E. C. Abbott and Helena Huntington Smith, *We Pointed Them North* (1939, reference here to 1955 ed.), p. 106.

2. Helena H. Smith, *The War on Powder River* (1966), pp. 112–13.

3. Floyd C. Bard, as told to Agnes Wright Spring, *Horse Wrangler: Sixty Years in the Saddle in Wyoming and Montana* (1960), p. 14.

4. A. H. Webster interview in Amarillo, April 9, 1927, conducted by J. Evetts Haley, manuscript in Panhandle-Plains Museum, Canyon, Texas.

5. Smith, *War on Powder River*, p. 115.

6. See, e.g., Bob Kennon, as told to Ramon F. Adams, *From the Pecos to the Powder: A Cowboy's Autobiography* (1965).

7. *Rocky Mountain News* (Denver), April 17, 1892.

8. Denver *Labor Enquirer*, January 8, 1887, p. 2.

9. *Cattlemen's Advertiser*, April 1, 1886, in Clifford P. Westermeier, *Trailing the Cowboy: His Life and Lore as Told by Frontier Journalists* (1955, references here to 1978 reprint), pp. 133–34.

10. Fort Morgan *Times*, April 16, 1886 in Westermeier, *Trailing*, p. 150.

11. James O'Connor's review of Douglas Dowd's *The Twisted Dream* in *Monthly Review* (March 1975), pp. 41–63.

12. Douglas Dowd, *The Twisted Dream* (1975), p. 163.

13. Lawrence Goodwyn, *Democratic Promises: The Populist Moment in America* (1976), p. 569.

14. Jim Herron and Harry E. Chrisman, *Fifty Years on the Owl Hoot Trail* (1969), pp. 18–22, 71.

15. Denver *Daily News*, April 24, 1892.

16. Lee Moore in Bart McDowell, *The American Cowboy in Life and Legend* (1972), p. 113.

17. A. P. (Ott) Black, *The End of the Long Horn Trail* (1936), p. 33.

18. J. Evetts Haley, *The XIT Ranch of Texas* (1929, reference here to 1953 ed.), p. 122.

19. John McCarty, *Maverick Town* (1946), pp. 125–26.

20. Will S. James, *Cowboy Life in Texas, or 27 Years a Maverick* (1893), pp. 122–26.

21. Smith, *War on Powder River*, p. 151.

22. Robert B. David, *Malcolm Campbell, Sheriff* (1932), as quoted in ibid., p. 154.

23. Oscar (Jack) Flagg, "A Review of the Cattle Business in Johnson County," serialized in Buffalo (Wyo.) *Bulletin*, May 5–July 14, 1892, reference here to reprint ed., Arno Press, 1969), p. 28.

24. Bard, *Horse Wrangler*, p. 19.

25. McCarty, *Maverick Town*, pp. 123–24.

26. Westermeier, *Trailing*, pp. 131–32, 134–35.

27. Louis Pelzer, *The Cattleman's Frontier 1850–1890* (1936), pp. 87, 97.

28. Lewis Nordyke, *Great Roundup: The Story of Texas and Southwestern Cowmen* (1955), p. 175.

29. Goodwyn, *Democratic Promises*, p. 98.

30. Lawrence Goodwyn, *The Populist Moment* (1978), p. 89.

31. Flagg, "Review of the Cattle Business," pp. 58–59.

32. David, *Malcolm Campbell*, p. 331.

33. Smith, *War on Powder River*, p. 266.

34. Herron and Chrisman, *Owl Hoot Trail*, p. 19.

35. Goodwyn, *Democratic Promises*, p. 173.

36. Goodwyn, *The Populist Moment*, pp. 25–26.

37. Thomas Arthur Krueger, "Populism in Wyoming" (M.A. thesis, University of Wyoming, 1960), p. 11.

38. Robert W. Larson, *New Mexico Populism* (1974), pp. 56, 10–16.

39. All information on Wyoming populism from Krueger, "Populism," pp. 8–62, augmented for Tidball by *Progressive Men of Wyoming* (1903), pp. 297–99.

40. Goodwyn, *Democratic Promises*, pp. 319–20.

41. Robert J. Rosenbaum, *Mexicano Resistance in the Southwest* (1981), pp. 90–96.

42. James P. Jones interview by J. Evetts Haley, January 12–14, 1927, in Panhandle-Plains Museum, Canyon, Texas.

43. Dean F. Krakel, *The Saga of Tom Horn: The Story of a Cattleman's War* (1954), pp. 5–6.

44. McCarty, *Maverick Town*, pp. 129–55.

45. Larson, *New Mexico Populism*, pp. 35–58.

46. Buford Elijah Farris, "An Institutional Approach to the Texas Cattle Ranch" (M.A. thesis, University of Texas, 1949), p. 66.
47. Eric J. Hobsbawm, *Bandits* (rev. ed., 1981), p. 142.
48. Ibid., p. 154.
49. John Lomax, *Cowboy Songs* (1910, reference here to 1936 reprint), p. 27.
50. Austin E. Fife and Alta S. Fife, eds., *Cowboy and Western Songs* (1969), p. 256.
51. Kent Steckmesser, reprinted in John Greenway, ed., *Folklore of the Great West* (1970), p. 339.
52. Lomax, *Cowboy Songs*, pp. 149–50.
53. Charles Siringo, *Riata and Spurs* (1927), p. 101.
54. Abbott and Smith, *We Pointed Them North*, p. 47.
55. Charles Siringo, *A Texas Cowboy* (1885, reference here to 1966 ed.), p. 172.
56. Siringo, *Riata and Spurs*, pp. 106, 89.

Chapter 5: Minority Cowboys and Women Cowhands

1. *Harper's New Monthly Magazine* (September 1895), p. 617.
2. J. Marvin Hunter, ed., *The Trail Drivers of Texas* (vol. 1, 1920. vol. 2, 1923; reference here to rev. ed. in one volume, 1925, Antiquarian Press, 1963), p. 453.
3. Kenneth Wiggins Porter, *The Negro on the American Frontier* (1970), p. 495.
4. Américo Paredes, *A Texas-Mexican Cancionero* (1976), p. 55.
5. George M. McBride, *Land Systems of Mexico* (1923), p. 38.
6. François Chevalier, *Land and Society in Colonial Mexico: The Great Hacienda*, Lesley Byrd Simpson, ed. (1963), p. 294.
7. Philip Russell, *Mexico in Transition* (1977), p. 23.
8. William H. Dusenberry, *The Mexican Mesta: The Administration of Ranching in Colonial Mexico* (1963), p. 185.
9. Dana Coolidge, *Old California Cowboys* (1939), pp. 62, 88–90.
10. Manuel A. Machado, Jr., *The North Mexican Cattle Industry, 1910–1975* (1981), pp. 123–24.
11. Walter Prescott Webb, *The Great Plains* (1931, reference here to Grosset's Universal Library ed.), p. 208.
12. Juan Gómez-Quiñones, *Development of the Mexican Working Class North of the Rio Grande* (1982), p. 47.
13. Joseph M. Nance, *After San Jacinto: The Texas-Mexican Frontier, 1836–1841* (1963), pp. 46–48.
14. Ibid., p. 45.
15. Terry G. Jordan, *Trails to Texas: Southern Roots of Western Cattle Ranching* (1981), p. 151.
16. Webb, *The Great Plains*, p. 210.
17. Gómez-Quiñones, *Mexican Working Class*, p. 47.
18. Robert J. Rosenbaum, *Mexicano Resistance in the Southwest, "The Sacred Right of*

Self-Preservation" (1981), p. 43, and Frederick Law Olmsted, *A Journey through Texas* (1857), p. 427.

19. Oscar J. Martinez, "On the Size of the Chicano Population, 1850–1900," *Aztlán* 6 (Spring 1975), p. 55.

20. Florence Johnson Scott, *Historical Heritage of the Lower Rio Grande* (1937), pp. 179–84.

21. Ibid., pp. 38–39, 77, 42, 58.

22. Ibid., pp. 41–42.

23. Ibid., pp. 100–101.

24. Frank C. Pierce, *A Brief History of the Lower Rio Grande Valley* (1917), p. 129, and Tom Lea, *The King Ranch* (1957), vol. 1, p. 120.

25. Jordan, *Trails to Texas*, pp. 80, 130–33.

26. Scott, *Lower Rio Grande*, p. 128.

27. Américo Paredes, *"With His Pistol in His Hand": A Border Ballad and Its Hero* (1958), pp. 9–10.

28. Ibid., pp. 10–11.

29. Gómez-Quiñones, *Mexican Working Class*, p. 47.

30. Oscar J. Martinez, "A Precise and Tentative Bibliography on Chicano History," *Aztlán* 1 (Spring 1970), p. 136; and Rosenbaum, *Mexicano Resistance*, p. 43.

31. Ronnie C. Tyler, "Fugitive Slaves in Mexico," *Journal of Negro History* 57 (January 1972), pp. 11, 6.

32. Joseph G. McCoy, *Historic Sketches of the Cattle Trade of the West and Southwest* (1874), p. 154.

33. Andy Adams, *The Outlet* (1905), p. 168.

34. Hunter, *Trail Drivers of Texas*, p. 265.

35. McCoy, *Cattle Trade*, p. 180.

36. Hunter, *Trail Drivers of Texas*, p. 574.

37. Gómez-Quiñones, *Mexican Working Class*, p. 23.

38. Lea, *King Ranch*, vol. 1, p. 114.

39. Ibid., pp. 123, 131, 437.

40. Rosenbaum, *Mexicano Resistance*, pp. 41–43.

41. Paredes, *Pistol*, p. 12.

42. Andy Adams, *The Log of the Cowboy* (1903), ch. 12.

43. Robert W. Larson, *New Mexico Populism* (1974), p. 51.

44. Fabiola Cabeza de Baca, *We Fed Them Cactus* (1954), pp. 17, 75, 68, 48.

45. Larson, *New Mexico Populism*, p. 12.

46. Ibid., p. 56.

47. Paredes, *Pistol*, pp. 72–74.

48. Porter, *Negro on the American Frontier*, p. 508.

49. Ralph Brauer and Donna Brauer, *The Horse, the Gun and the Piece of Property: Changing Images of the TV Western* (1975), p. 90.

50. Bailey C. Hanes, *Bill Pickett, Bulldogger* (1977), p. 40.

51. Ibid., pp. 184–86.

52. All quotations from Sidney Kaplan, "The Black Soldier of the Civil War in Literature and Art," *The Chancellor's Lecture Series: 1979–1980* (Amherst: University of Massachusetts, 1981), pp. 3, 20, 2.

53. William Sherman Savage, *Blacks in the West* (1976), pp. 86–95, and William Loren Katz, *The Black West* (1971), pp. 143–66.

54. Philip Durham and Everett Jones, *The Negro Cowboys* (1965).

55. Kenneth Wiggins Porter, "Negro Labor in the Western Cattle Industry, 1866–1900," in *The Negro on the American Frontier* (1970), pp. 494–523.

56. John H. Harmon, "Black Cowboys Are Real," *The Crisis* (September 1940), pp. 280–81, 301–2.

57. Jordan, *Trails to Texas*, p. 143.

58. William W. Savage, ed., *Cowboy Life: Reconstructing an American Myth* (1975), p. 163.

59. William W. Savage, *The Cowboy Hero: His Image in American History and Culture* (1979), pp. 7–10.

60. Jordan, *Trails to Texas*, pp. 25–51.

61. Tyler, "Fugitive Slaves," p. 4; this paragraph is greatly indebted to several pages of the late Kenneth Wiggins Porter's unpublished "Black Riders."

62. J. Frank Dobie, *The Longhorns* (1941), p. 309.

63. Harmon, "Black Cowboys," p. 281.

64. Francis Richard Lubbock, *Six Decades in Texas*, ed. C. W. Raines (1900), pp. 120–40.

65. Nance, *After San Jacinto*, pp. 232–33 note.

66. Lubbock, *Six Decades*, p. 136.

67. Olmsted, *Journey through Texas*, p. 441 note.

68. Alwyn Barr, *Black Texans: A History of Negroes in Texas, 1528–1971* (1973), p. 29.

69. Tyler, "Fugitive Slaves," p. 4.

70. J. Evetts Haley, *Charles Goodnight, Cowman and Plainsman* (1936), pp. 13, 20, 242.

71. Barr, *Black Texans*, p. 20.

72. Bob Beverly, *The Cattleman* (May 1954), pp. 56–57.

73. John M. Hendrix, *The Cattleman* (February 1936), pp. 25–26, and Hettye Wallace Branch, *The Story of "80 John"* (1960).

74. William Sherman Savage, *Blacks in the West*, p. 92.

75. Lawrence Goodwyn, *The Populist Moment* (1978), p. 25.

76. William Loren Katz, *The Black West* (rev. ed., 1974), p. 147.

77. Porter, *Negro on the American Frontier*, pp. 521–22.

78. Wendy Watriss, "The Soul Circuit," *GEO* magazine (December 1980), pp. 134–50.

79. Dawn Lander, "Eve Among the Indians," *The Authority of Experience: Essays in Feminist Criticism*, Arlyn Diamond and Lee R. Edwards, eds. (1977), pp. 196–97; Lander also notices Smedley's example, as cited below.

80. Nannie Tiffany Alderson and Helena H. Smith, *A Bride Goes West* (1942, reference here to University of Nebraska Press ed., 1969), p. 55.

81. Fabiola Cabeza de Baca, *We Fed Them Cactus* (1954), pp. 129, 132.

82. Hunter, *Trail Drivers of Texas*, p. 204.

83. Alderson and Smith, *Bride Goes West*, pp. 125, 169.

84. Floyd C. Bard, as told to Agnes W. Spring, *Horse Wrangler: Sixty Years in the Saddle in Wyoming and Montana* (1960), pp. 11, 17.

85. Estelline Bennett, *Old Deadwood Days* (1928), p. 96.

86. Barbara M. Wertheimer, *We Were There: The Story of Working Women in America* (1977), pp. 255–56.

87. Alderson and Smith, *Bride Goes West*, pp. 125, 168.

88. Agnes Morley Cleaveland, *No Life for a Lady* (1941), especially pp. 106, 119, 127, 130, 140, 173, 208, 341.

89. Clifford Westermeier, *Man, Beast, Dust: The Story of Rodeo* (1947), pp. 82–85, 48, 119, and Teresa Jordan, "Cowgirls: How the Fairer Sex Succeeded in the Rough World of Rodeo," *True West* 30 (July 1983), pp. 19–23.

90. Lonn Taylor and Ingrid Maar, *The American Cowboy, An Exhibition at the Library of Congress* (1983), p. 68.

91. Wertheimer, *We Were There*, p. 255.

92. Hunter, *Trail Drivers of Texas*, p. 438.

93. John Lomax, *Cowboy Songs* (1910, reference here to 1936 reprint), p. 369.

94. Grace Ernestine Ray, *Wily Women of the West* (1972), pp. 33–34.

95. Will Henry, *I, Tom Horn* (1975), pp. 210–11.

96. Ray, *Wily Women*, pp. 39–50.

97. Mari Sandoz, *Old Jules* (1935), p. 174.

98. Ray, *Wily Women*, p. 87.

99. Helena H. Smith, *The War on Powder River* (1966), pp. 122–34.

100. Ray, *Wily Women*, Plate 1, pp. 1–15, 30–33.

101. Cleaveland, *No Life*, p. 156.

102. Hunter, *Trail Drivers of Texas*, p. 813.

103. Alderson and Smith, *Bride Goes West*, p. 62.

104. Austin Fife and Alta Fife, *Songs of the Cowboys* (1969), p. 218.

105. Robert B. David, *Malcolm Campbell, Sheriff* (1932), pp. 97–99.

106. Dee Brown, *The Gentle Tamers: Women of the Old Wild West* (1958, reference here to Bantam ed., 1974), pp. 202, 232.

107. Jim Herron and Harry E. Chrisman, *Fifty Years on the Owl Hoot Trail* (1969), p. 146.

108. Alderson and Smith, *Bride Goes West*, p. 271.

109. Wister, *Harper's Monthly*, pp. 606, 610, 604.

Chapter 6: Cowboys as Entertainers and Athletes

1. Jane Kramer, *The Last Cowboy* (1977), pp. 60–61.

2. Agnes Smedley, *Daughter of Earth* (1929, reference here to Feminist Press ed., 1973), pp. 169, 186, 119–20, 107, 121–22.

3. John Omohundro, "The Cow-Boy," in *Wilkes' Spirit of the Times*, March 24, 1877.

4. *Texas Live Stock Journal*, May 17, 1885, in Clifford P. Westermeier, *Trailing the Cowboy* (1955, reference here to reprint ed., 1978), pp. 70–71.

5. Quoted in Gerald N. Grob, *Workers and Utopia* (1961), p. 189.

6. Ibid., p. 40.

7. Kramer, *Last Cowboy*, pp. 68–69.

8. Harry E. Chrisman, *1001 Most-Asked Questions about the American West* (1982), p. 73.

9. Frederick Merk, *History of the Western Movement* (1978), p. 464.

10. Charles Beard and Mary Beard, *A Basic History of the United States* (1944), p. 295.

11. Kramer, *Last Cowboy*, pp. 60–61.

12. Don Russell, *The Lives and Legends of Buffalo Bill* (1960), pp. 192, 194.

13. Lawrence R. Borne, "The Cowboy and Dude Ranching," *Red River Historical Review* 2 (Spring 1975), p. 119; most of the data in this and the following four paragraphs comes from this article, pp. 115–35.

14. J. Marvin Hunter, ed., *The Trail Drivers of Texas* (vol. 1, 1920, vol. 2, 1923; reference here to rev. ed. in one volume, 1925, Antiquarian Press, 1963), p. 145.

15. Westermeier, *Trailing*, pp. 343–44.

16. Clifford P. Westermeier, "The Cowboy in His Home State," *Southwestern Historical Quarterly* 48 (October 1984), pp. 230–31.

17. Don Russell, *The Wild West: Or, A History of the Wild West Shows* (1970), pp. 121–27.

18. Bill Haywood, *The Autobiography of Big Bill Haywood* (1929), p. 190.

19. Clifford P. Westermeier, *Man, Beast, Dust: The Story of Rodeo* (1947), pp. 100–126.

20. Joseph G. McCoy, *Historic Sketches of the Cattle Trade of the West and Southwest* (1874), p. 181.

21. Hunter, *Trail Drivers of Texas*, pp. 99–101.

22. Ibid., pp. 440–41.

23. Kevin Brownlow, *The War, the West, and the Wilderness* (1978), pp. 256, 290–99.

24. Diana Cary, *The Hollywood Posse* (1975), p. 19.

25. Mody Boatright, "The Cowboy Enters the Movies," *The Sunny Slopes of Long Ago*, eds. William M. Hudson and Allen Maxwell (1966), p. 52.

26. Brownlow, *War*, p. 290.

27. Cary, *Hollywood Posse*, pp. 144, 202, 208.

28. Ibid., pp. 217–25, 154.

29. Ibid., pp. 45, 46.

30. Brownlow, *War*, p. 290.

31. Cary, *Hollywood Posse*, pp. 144, 257–58.

32. Ibid., pp. 98–100, 230–32, 136, 208.

33. Walker D. Wyman, ed., *Nothing but Prairie and Sky: Life on the Dakota Range in the Early Days* (1954), pp. 100–101.

34. Lewis Atherton, *The Cattle Kings* (1961), pp. xi, 49.

35. Karl Marx, *The Eighteenth Brumaire of Louis Bonaparte* (1852), ch. 5.

36. Beard and Beard, *Basic History*, p. 320.

Chapter 7: The Cowboy Myth

1. Reported by Tom Mix's last wife as being said to William Fox, Darryl Ponicsan, *Tom Mix Died for Your Sins* (1979), p. 143.

2. Paul A. Baran and Paul M. Sweezy, *Monopoly Capital* (1966), pp. 220–21.

3. Gene M. Gressley, *Bankers and Cattlemen* (1966, reference here to Bison ed., 1971), p. 109.

4. Stanley Lebergott, *Manpower in Economic Growth: The American Record Since 1800* (1964), pp. 510–11.

5. Lonn Taylor and Ingrid Marr, *The American Cowboy* (Catalogue of Library of Congress Exhibition, 1983), p. 120.

6. Kalton C. Lahue, *Winners of the West: The Sagebrush Heroes of the Silent Screen* (1970), p. 33.

7. Ralph Brauer and Donna Brauer, *The Horse, the Gun and the Piece of Property: Changing Images of the TV Western* (1975), p. 54.

8. Raymond Williams, *The Country and the City* (1973), p. 295.

9. Maurice Horn, *Comics of the American West* (1977), p. 19.

10. Lewis Atherton, *The Cattle Kings* (1961), pp. xi, 241.

11. Elmer Kelton, *Llano River* (1966), p. 22.

12. Brauer and Brauer, *Horse*, pp. 126–27.

13. Owen Wister, *Owen Wister Out West, His Journals and Letters*, ed. Fanny Kemble Wister (1958), p. 221.

14. Ibid., p. 223.

15. Ibid., p. 256.

16. Owen Wister, "The Evolution of the Cowpuncher," *Harper's Monthly* (September 1895), pp. 608, 606.

17. Gressley, *Bankers and Cattlemen*, p. 250.

18. Ibid., p. 69.

19. Helena H. Smith, *The War on Powder River* (1966), p. 123.

20. Wister, *Journals and Letters*, p. 91.

21. Ibid., pp. 18, 115–16.

22. Wister quoted in Paul Trachtman, *The Gunfighters* (1974), p. 206.

23. Charles A. Beard and Mary R. Beard, *A Basic History of the United States* (1944), pp. 329, 409.

24. Owen Wister, *The Virginian* (1902), ch. 4.

25. J. Frank Dobie, *Prefaces* (1975), p. 70.

26. John C. Van Dyke, *The Desert* (1901), pp. 60–61.

27. Mody Boatright, "The Cowboy Enters the Movies," *The Sunny Slopes of Long Ago*, eds. William M. Hudson and Allen Maxwell (1966), pp. 51–69.

28. William K. Everson, *A Pictorial History of the Western Film* (1969), pp. 5–9.

29. George N. Fenin and William E. Everson, *The Western from Silents to the Seventies* (rev. ed., 1973, reference here to Penguin ed., 1977), p. 116.

30. Will Wright, *Six Guns and Society: A Structural Study of the Western* (1975), pp. 15, 32, 40, 135–37.

31. Brauer and Brauer, *Horse*, p. 48.

32. Wright, *Six Guns*, pp. 74–90.

33. Brauer and Brauer, *Horse*, pp. 126–27.

34. Wright, *Six Guns*, pp. 85–86.

35. John G. Cawelti, "Reflections on the New Western Films," *Focus on the Western*, ed. Jack Nachbar (1974), pp. 116–17.

36. Ibid., p. 114.

37. William W. Savage, *The Cowboy Hero: His Image in American History and Culture* (1979), p. 87.

38. Boston *Globe*, March 11, 1981, p. 2.